MW01502710

Picture the Scripture

365 Devotionals That Visualize God's Word

By Jan Kent

Picture the Scripture: 365 Devotionals That Visualize God's Word

Copyright © 2021 Jan Kent
All rights reserved.
Independently published.

ISBN paperback: 979-8-4514-5901-0

All rights reserved. No portion of this book may be reproduced, stored in a retrieval system or transmitted in any form or by any means - electronic, mechanical, photocopy, recording, scanning or other - without the prior written permission of the publisher, except for brief quotes in printed reviews.

Scripture taken from the HOLY BIBLE, NEW INTERNATIONAL VERSION ®. Copyright © 1973, 1978, 1984 by International Bible Society. Used by permission of Zondervan Publishing House. All rights reserved.

Praise for

Picture the Scripture

A quick read, tethered to the Word, always with a thoughtful encouraging application. You'll get hooked on your daily reading, and you'll face the temptation to 'read ahead.' Don't do it. Let that day's text sink in, meditate on it, and live out its life-principles.

Dr. Daniel B. Wallace, Senior Research Professor, New Testament Studies, Dallas Theological Seminary

Riveting! That is how Picture the Scripture reads. Jan, with her more than 30 years of missionary service in France, is well qualified to write such a devotional!

Dr. John Glass, missionary with Grace Ministries International, Founder of Calvin Tours Geneva

Like Jesus who pulled profound truth from everyday examples, Jan insightfully connects everyday pictures to biblical truth.

Dr. Ric Rodeheaver, Senior Staff Elder, Christ Community Church, Laguna Hills, CA

Jan offers pearls of wisdom, nuggets of gold and rare pennies in this collection of God-warranted treasures that daily nourish one's soul.

Dr. Richard Kronk, Associate Professor of Global Ministries, Toccoa Falls College

I love it! Jan's insights, application and prayer for each day are matched with a whimsical photo and a verse that truly prompt you to, "Picture the Scripture."

Stan Jantz, Author and President of Evangelical Christian Publishers Association

To my husband, Randy

Thank you for your suggestion that I write this book!
You believed in me, encouraged me, prayed for me and continually built me up!

And may the LORD receive the glory due Him.

Psalm 32:8–9

I will instruct you and teach you in the way you should go; I will counsel you with my loving eye on you. Do not be like the horse or the mule . . .

Barn Sour

If the path to the left leads back to the barn, these horses may show signs of being "barn sour." Once a barn-sour horse is turned back toward home, he will pick up speed. If left unchecked, he will gallop back to the barn like a madman! Becoming barn sour could be the result of fears and insecurities from being away from his comfort zone, or just plain stubbornness.

Today's verse tells us not to be like a horse or a mule. They have no understanding and need the control of the bit and bridle. We, on the other hand, have God's promise to instruct and teach us in the way we should go. The Lord promises to instruct those who fear Him in the ways they should choose (Psalm 25:12). He promises to guide the humble (Psalm 25:9). His loving eye is on us, seeing every choice we need to make. He knows about every decision we face. His counsel is always available if we are humble enough to seek it.

Quite frankly, I sometimes prefer being "barn sour." That way, I know I am returning to the comfortable and familiar. But He doesn't always lead that way. He is more interested in growing my faith and dependence on Him. The path that He chooses may be more challenging, but it is a path with adventures that will bring me closer to Him! His guidance and counsel is given with love. And I can trust that He knows what He is doing even if it is far from my "comfort zone."

Lord, thank You for Your loving guidance.

Titus 2:12

It [grace] teaches us to say "No" to ungodliness and worldly passions, and to live self-controlled, upright and godly lives in this present age . . .

Rosa Carte Blanche

This beautiful rose did not grace our earth until its creation in 1982. The rose begins as a dark pink bud, opening as a pale pink bloom and then fading to near white. Its name, "Carte Blanche," meaning blank page, is an idiom attributed to King Charles II of France. He gave his workers a blank page with his signature, allowing them freedom as to how a task was completed.

Some may believe that grace gives us "carte blanche" to do what we please. But today's verse gives insight into the role grace plays in the life of a believer. At the start, grace, or God's unmerited favor, is how we are saved (Ephesians 2:8–9). But it does not stop there. Grace continues to impact our lives, teaching us to say no to what is ungodly and worldly. Grace, rather than giving us carte blanche to do whatever we like, teaches us to be self-controlled. Grace motivates believers to lead godly, upright lives. It is God's favor that provides a way out of temptation (1 Corinthians 10:13).

His grace is greater than all my sin. There is not a single sin that He is not willing to forgive! But rather than presume on His grace, I want to live up to it. I do not want His grace for me to be in vain. He knows I blew it yesterday. He knows I will blow it today. His grace means that my relationship with Him continues. I want to grow in God's grace (2 Peter 3:18) and understand God's grace (Colossians 1:6) but I know it will be a lifelong process.

Thank You, Lord, that You show grace to me.

Psalm 84:2

My soul yearns, even faints, for the courts of the Lord; my heart and my flesh cry out for the living God.

Gorilla Prayers

If this gorilla is really praying, I wonder what his request might be. Perhaps he is praying for a mate! Could he be praying for freedom from his zoo habitat? Maybe he is praying for something special for his next meal. It seems ludicrous that any animal would pray. Their needs are simple both physically and emotionally, and there doesn't seem to be any awareness of a spiritual realm.

Today's verse puts a finger on exactly what separates us from animals. An animal, even if one argued that he had a soul, does not yearn for the Lord. His heart and flesh do not cry out to the living God. The longing for a relationship with the God of the universe is something beyond their capacity. But for man, it is exactly why we were created. God Himself put the idea and longing for eternity in the human heart (Ecclesiastes 3:11). We are made to cry out for Him in our innermost being. Even just one day in His presence is better than one thousand days elsewhere (verse 10).

The Lord fills and completes me. It is my communion with Him that enriches my very existence. When my relationship with Him is interrupted by my own wandering or indifference, it does not take long to sense that something is missing. Feeling that lack, I cry out to Him for reassurance that He is there and that He still loves me. He always answers. And somehow, I am more human when I am connected to my Creator. The yearning is satisfied and it is "well with my soul."

Thank You, Lord, for completing me.

John 4:13–14

Jesus answered, "Everyone who drinks this water will be thirsty again, but whoever drinks the water I give them will never thirst. Indeed, the water I give them will become in them a spring of water welling up to eternal life."

Pink Water

I never knew water could be pink! Lake Grassmere, a seaside lake in New Zealand, can be anywhere from pink to purple in the summer months. This is a result of natural salt production there. The color appears in the crystallization ponds, caused by microscopic green algae in this high salt concentration. As colorful as this water is, drinking it would only increase one's thirst!

Today's verse describes a water that is unique, not for its color but because it will quench thirst for all time. Jesus offers this water to the Samaritan woman at the well. The gift of the Holy Spirit is this unique living water (verse 10). God's presence in us quenches a thirst for a deep and satisfying relationship. When filled up with Him, we no longer dip into wells of water that only leave us wanting more. Not only is thirst quenched here on earth, but for all eternity.

I am so attracted to other kinds of water. But somehow, worldly pleasures never really satisfy. There is a deep-seated thirst inside me that can only be quenched by my Creator. He made me that way. If I am discontented and looking elsewhere, I start to feel thirsty. For a time I can ignore it, but eventually my lack of spiritual water becomes too difficult to dismiss. He is so gracious to always welcome me and fill me to capacity! Every day His invitation stands to come to the water (Isaiah 55:1).

Lord, thank You for quenching my thirst!

Ephesians 4:32

Be kind and compassionate to one another, forgiving each other, just as in Christ God forgave you.

Thick-skinned?

When I think of thick-skinned animals, I think of the pachyderms: the rhinoceros, the hippopotamus, and the elephant. But the giraffe has thick skin too—up to seven inches! They need that thick, tight skin on their lower extremities to maintain high extravascular pressure on their weight-bearing blood vessels. The pressure of that thick skin works just like a pilot's "g" suit!

Today's verse commands us to be compassionate or tenderhearted. This seems like the exact opposite of being thick-skinned! If we are tender towards others, then we can be kind and we can be compassionate. But having tender hearts towards others means we could be hurt, or vulnerable to attack, which is why the next words are about forgiveness. Whether or not we are hurt, it is a tender heart that can offer forgiveness.

When I have a tender heart towards others, I feel their hurts. But then I feel my own as well. It would be so much more comfortable to be thick-skinned and avoid emotional hurts. Those insults, name calling, and gossip don't feel so good. But the wonderful part about having a tender heart is that I can more deeply appreciate Christ's forgiveness for me! Not only can my tender heart experience His complete pardon, but I can extend that forgiveness to others. When I close my heart against the one who hurt me, developing "thick skin," I am less able to feel God's unconditional love for me. Having a tender heart has a price, but not as high as the cost of thick skin!

Lord, keep me tenderhearted!

Mark 7:15

Nothing outside a person can defile them by going into them. Rather, it is what comes out of a person that defiles them.

Inside-out Flower

If one were to take a walk in the coastal forests of the Pacific Northwest right now, this delicate wildflower might be seen. It is a wildflower with petal-like sepals that, being swept back, make it look as if the flower were inside out! Its official name is, "Vancouveria hexandra." But I prefer the more creative name of "Inside Out."

Today's verse has an inside and an outside. The Lord is speaking to the Pharisees who challenged Him about following their ceremonial laws. Jesus pointed out that laws and policies do not have the power to change what is on the inside. What sullies and makes one dirty is not anything on the outside of man. It is the evil that comes from inside (verse 23). One can change laws, leaders, or levels of education and privilege, but none of this will change the core problem: an unclean heart.

In a troubled world where social injustice is on everyone's mind, I do not want to be "inside out." The core problem is not on the outside but on the inside of all of us. Lasting change is only possible when Christ makes me a "new creation" in Him (2 Corinthians 5:17). My most loving unselfish response is to point others to the One who can change a heart for all eternity. What an incredible shame if in addressing the outside of man I miss the inside!

Thank You, Lord, for the change You bring to the inside.

John 3:16

For God so loved the world that he gave his one and only Son, that whoever believes in him shall not perish but have eternal life.

Colorless

D o you remember when toilet paper came in a variety of colors? One could choose just the right shade to coordinate with one's bathroom decor! Our white-only choices today seem boring by comparison. There was a time in North America when talking about toilet paper shortages was replaced by heated discussions regarding skin color. As important as this dialogue is, there is one even more important: what color is our soul?

Today's well-known verse declares that God loves His creation. He loves the world, and His offer of salvation is inclusive to "whoever believes." As divided as mankind is, the need for forgiveness through God's Son is a need that we all share. The value He places on each of us individually is so high that He was willing to sacrifice Jesus so we could be with Him for all eternity. Deep down in every human is a soul that is colorless in that we have the exact same need for salvation. The ground before the cross is level. No one is more deserving than another, despite race, economic advantage, or educational background.

This is a truth that changes how I view myself and others. Because of God's undeserved grace toward me, I can extend this same grace to others. There is no sin too grievous for Him to forgive. When violating even one of God's laws I am guilty of all (James 2:10). This is the way we are all the same, needing His forgiveness and grace. I do not want to focus on what separates us, but rather on what unites us all in our shared need for Him!

Lord, thank You for Your all-inclusive love.

Psalm 54:7

You have delivered me from all my troubles, and my eyes have looked in triumph on my foes.

The Peacock Butterfly

The peacock is not the only creation that can boast about its "eyes." The peacock butterfly is recognizable for its four large eyespots, similar to the peacock bird. But for the butterfly, these eyes are not just for looks. They serve to confuse and startle its predators. Their predators sense that the spots may belong to a potential enemy. That moment of hesitation is often all that is needed to save the life of this butterfly.

Today's verse is from a psalm that cries out to God for help. David was being pursued by Saul with the help of the Ziphites. (1 Samuel 23:19–29) The situation was serious, as they were intent on killing him. David found reassurance in proclaiming God as his help (verse 4). Instead of allowing his predicament to overwhelm him, David remembered that God had delivered him in the past, and his eyes had looked in triumph on his enemies. And that is exactly what happened again! Just as Saul and his men were closing in, a messenger arrived to bring Saul back to deal with the invading Philistines!

My eyes will one day look in triumph over my enemies as well. The Lord is for me, and though I encounter plenty of trouble, Christ has already overcome the world (John 16:33). This is my encouragement. My enemies are sometimes visible, but many times are not, as the battle is spiritual in nature (Ephesians 6:12). Regardless, He has given me spiritual eyes to see His presence and protection! And His eyes are on me! He is El Roi, the God who sees, and I can count on Him.

Thank You, Lord, for getting me out of what can appear hopeless!

1 Corinthians 2:4–5

My message and my preaching were not with wise and persuasive words, but with a demonstration of the Spirit's power, so that your faith might not rest on human wisdom but on God's power.

Colorful Iris

This burgundy is a surprising color for an iris! But in fact, the iris comes in an array of different colors, including a deep purple that looks black. It makes sense, then, that the word "iris" originally meant "rainbow" in Greek. In the language of flowers, iris symbolizes eloquence. And its three petal segments are said to represent faith, wisdom, and valor.

There is faith and wisdom in today's verse as well as courage to speak the truth. There is not, however, any eloquence. Wise-sounding words can be empty. Persuasive words can be negated by hypocrisy. But Paul explains that his message did not need either, as his words were a demonstration of the power of the Spirit. Paul never claimed to be eloquent in his speech. Because he spoke simply, God's power was evident. And he resisted the temptation to speak only what "itchy ears" wanted to hear (2 Timothy 4:3).

My faith does not rest on a fancy discourse or the latest fad or book. Human wisdom can never replace the power of God's words. It is not what exact words are used, but God's Spirit who helps me understand (verse 12). He is the One who explains spiritual realities to me (verse 13). And His Spirit uses my words of testimony even when I am not eloquent. I may not feel strong or confident in sharing. But thankfully, His power does not depend on my word choice!

Thank You, Lord, that my faith rests on Your power.

Psalm 38:4

My guilt has overwhelmed me like a burden too heavy to bear.

Albatross Around the Neck

The albatross looks nice enough, but I would not want to wear him around my neck! The old expression comes from a nineteenth-century poem, "The Rime of the Ancient Mariner." The narrator flippantly shoots the albatross, a bird thought to be a sign of good luck. The sailors are so incensed that they oblige him to wear the dead bird around his neck as penance. The expression today means having a heavy burden one cannot escape, and being kept from doing what one wants to do.

Today's verse describes the guilt David felt as being a burden too heavy to bear. He describes it as a searing pain in his back, making him feeble and crushing him (verses 7–8). He recognizes his sin and that he is experiencing the rebuke and discipline of the Lord. He groans in "anguish of heart" and confesses his sin (verse 18). Not only does David experience God's wonderful forgiveness but even the guilt is lifted from him. It was because David acknowledged his wrongdoing that God forgave even the guilt of his sin (Psalm 32:5).

The guilt of sin is never something I have to feel around my neck, weighing me down. When I agree with God about my sin in repentance, He is there to lift that burden from me. His forgiveness means that sin is removed as far as the east is from the west (Psalm 103:12). Memories of past failures do not have to influence me, and any reminder of them does not come from Him! His forgiveness is liberating and freeing. He never brings up the matter again and He gives me a light heart, reassuring me of His constant, unconditional love.

What a gift! Thank You, Lord.

James 4:6

But he gives us more grace. That is why Scripture says: 'God opposes the proud but shows favor to the humble.'

Humble Pie

This pie looks good enough to eat! But the word "humble" in the expression "humble pie" actually came from a different word. In the early 1400's "numble" was the word for chopped organ meat from venison, often baked in a pastry. The "n" was eventually dropped and the "h" added. Numbles were for the huntsmen, his family and his companions whereas the choice deer meat was sold to the upper class. Today, eating "humble pie" means to act apologetically and admit one's error.

Today's verse talks about more grace that is given to the humble. As undeserving as we are, those who can come clean with the Lord about their failures experience His favor. But there is something in all of us that bristles at the thought of admitting our errors. Sometimes, the only way it can happen is if we can point to extenuating circumstances! Or we can maybe admit we were wrong if someone can share our chagrin. Eating humble pie is never a very comfortable experience.

As difficult as it is to humble myself, His grace makes it worth it! I would much rather live in His undeserved favor than have Him be opposed to me. But each time I allow pride, stubbornness and determined independence from Him to creep into my day, I am foregoing His desire to bless me. Half the time I do not even realize it is happening as I am so full of myself! How good of Him to bring me to my knees in humility!

Forgive me my pride, Lord. Oh how I need your grace today!

2 Corinthians 1:3

Praise be to the God and Father of our Lord Jesus Christ, the Father of compassion and the God of all comfort.

Bleeding Heart Flower

One can immediately see how this flower got its name! The larger petals resemble a heart, and the smaller petals look like drops of blood. These perennial flowers have been growing wild for centuries in Asia. But it has only been since the 1800s that the bleeding heart has been cultivated in the Western world. This flower has not only been used as a symbol for love, but also for the compassion we are to feel for those who suffer.

Today's verse describes our God as one of comfort, and a Father of compassion. He understands and feels with us our sadness and pain. His heart bleeds for the brokenness of our world. But He did not stop there. He did something about it by paying for the sin that allowed this brokenness to enter our lives. He knows when our souls are "downcast within us" even when no one else is aware. His comfort is a balm to the sorrow that our suffering brings.

He sees when I am overwhelmed with fear and worry. He cares when I am feeling too sad to get up from bed. Better than physical comfort, He gives me the amazing comfort of His love and goodness. He knows better than anyone else how to lift my head and my spirits. He brings to mind a song lyric. He uses a long-forgotten verse. And so often, He gives comfort through the encouragement of other believers. His heart bleeds for me and He asks me to have that same heart for the suffering of others.

Thank You, Lord, for Your precious comfort, and help me share it with others.

Psalm 27:4

One thing I ask from the Lord, this only do I seek: That I may dwell in the house of the Lord all the days of my life, to gaze on the beauty of the Lord and to seek him in his temple.

Essential Oils

Why are essential oils called "essential"? For some, it is because they are concentrated to the essence of the odor, characteristics, and taste of the plant. Others believe they are essential oils being essential to life. In either case, to become essential is to be reduced to a highly concentrated form. An example is one ounce of peppermint oil, which takes sixteen pounds of fresh peppermint leaves to produce.

Today's verse reduces all of life down to one concentrated desire on David's part. He views his relationship to the Lord as the most essential component to his well-being. All of David's attention is on the Lord. Above all else he wants to enjoy His presence. David asks of the Lord only one thing. Nothing is quite as important than spending time in His presence and enjoying His beauty. All else pales in comparison to the importance of his relationship to the lover of his soul.

There is lots of talk today regarding what services in our world are "essential services." Some are obvious and some seem to be up for interpretation. But one thing is essential to life here and to life eternally. I can regain my health, my finances, and my social connections, but what good is any of it if I forfeit my soul (Mark 8:36)? I need Him. The Lord is essential. When everything else is stripped away, HE is still there. His presence and beauty are essential to my life. If I learn nothing else in life, may it be this!

Lord, You are my life.

Colossians 3:12–13

Therefore, as God's chosen people, holy and dearly loved, clothe yourselves with compassion, kindness, humility, gentleness and patience. Bear with each other and forgive one another, if any of you has a grievance against someone. Forgive as the Lord forgave you.

The Hedgehog

We had hedgehogs living under our one-hundred-year-old home in France. They were quite harmless when left alone. Coming out at night, they would mosey around the yard. These hedgehogs were certainly slow creatures and very timid. When we approached them, they would roll up into a spiky ball and stay immobile. Our cat pretty much ignored the hedgehogs. Perhaps there was an "incident" that convinced him to leave them alone! They can look cute and cuddly but the up-to-sixty spines that clothe their bodies are a strong incentive to keep one's distance.

Today's verse describes a clothing that is beautiful and approachable. We are to clothe ourselves with mercy, kindness, humility, gentleness, and patience. We are to be forgiving because we ourselves have been forgiven. These adjectives bring to mind the character of Jesus, who is "gentle and humble in heart." This list also brings to mind the fruit of the Spirit. And as one having a new nature, they are also to characterize me.

But I am not always so soft and approachable. Quite frankly, before that first morning cup of coffee, I can be quite prickly. There are times when being a hedgehog is just easier. But because God has chosen me and I am dearly loved, I can respond to others with these beautiful qualities He is slowly developing in me. This clothing is not only more comfortable for others, but for me as well!

Lord, help me to resemble You today.

Matthew 16:25

For whoever wants to save their life will lose it, but whoever loses their life for me will find it.

Pelican Flower

This pelican flower on the streets of Ocean Beach, California, looked so unusual with its brown color and huge size. These heart-shaped flowers only live TWO days! On day one, they attract bees and flies by their stench to enter the tunnel shape in the middle. The little hairlike growths inside guide them along until they are stuck with no way out! On day two, the insect is covered in pollen, and they are released as the flower slowly withers and dies.

Today's verse presents a true paradox. Jesus is saying that those who are intent on saving their lives at any cost will end up paying in other ways. Lives that are selfishly lived will in the end be lost. Even if a person should gain the world—riches, honor, health, and ease—they can still lose their soul (verse 26), whereas those who pour out and sacrifice their lives for others as a service to the Lord will have meaning and purpose. They will, in fact, find their lives, and the soul will not be lost for eternity.

Losing my life for the One I love is the best way I know to demonstrate that love. I lose my life each time I choose to obey God's way rather than my own. I lose my life every time I put His agenda of good works ahead of my own selfish plan. When I desire Christ's love above and beyond any human love, then my life is spent serving Him. In losing my life to Him, He fills it and makes it meaningful!

Thank You, Lord, that in You I have found my life!

Matthew 8:20

Jesus replied, "Foxes have dens and birds have nests, but the Son of Man has no place to lay his head."

Creature Comforts

This cat is not letting a little thing like missing a bed, pillow, or comfy blanket stop him from his nap! He doesn't seem to mind that the concrete is hard or that the wood chips may poke at him. Me, on the other hand, I enjoy my creature comforts. My poor children did not have any camping experiences until they were adults. If I have a choice, I choose the comfortable bed and pillow.

This is why today's verse is so shocking. Jesus describes Himself as having no place to lay His head. He gave up the comforts of hearth and home to be on the road, sharing the good news of salvation and meeting people's needs. Jesus was speaking to a teacher of the law who declared he would follow Jesus anywhere. But perhaps this teacher was being overly optimistic or unrealistic. Jesus knew that His itinerant ministry would pose a problem for this man.

The cost of following God's individual plan for me may mean I will have to relinquish some creature comforts. How inconsequential they seem when compared to what He gave up for me! Thankfully, as my Creator, He knows my limits. He will not call me to do something that He would not empower me to do (Philippians 2:13). But am I willing to follow Him, regardless of what He asks me to give up? I hope I can say "yes" to whatever He asks of me. He is trustworthy. But there is one creature comfort I could never do without, and that is the reassuring comfort of His presence and blessing.

Lord, thank You for what You gave up for me!

John 17:15

My prayer is not that you take them out of the world but that You protect them from the evil one.

Seashells

This shell collection of my father's was a surprise. He was always an avid rock collector but I did not realize he was collecting shells as well. He kept them in a large tin canister, each one meticulously wrapped. The myriad of colors and shapes gave beauty to each seashell. The variety and detail of God's creation is amazing! Of course, the seashell is about more than beauty. The shell is there to protect that living creature inside.

Today's verse is a prayer of Jesus specifically for the protection of His disciples. There would be persecution ahead as each one would take a stand for Him. This prayer is equally applicable to believers today (verse 20) as Jesus includes all who will believe the message of His disciples. It may seem as if God did not answer this prayer of Jesus. Most of the original twelve disciples died a martyr's death. Were they not protected? Today, we see horrible scenes of Christians being killed for their faith in Christ. Is this prayer invalid?

In His grace, He protects me repeatedly from bodily harm. So often, I am not even aware of His protective hand. But this prayer of protection concerns the evil one. My soul is protected. Though the body is destroyed, no evil can touch the soul and its sure destination (Matthew 10:28–29). As the world becomes increasingly hostile to true Christ followers, I can live without fear. My soul belongs to Christ (2 Timothy 1:12), and I am persuaded that He will keep what I have committed to Him.

Thank You, Lord, for Your beautiful protection.

Romans 15:13

May the God of hope fill you with all joy and peace as you trust in him, so that you may overflow with hope by the power of the Holy Spirit.

Laughing Hyena

Hearing the spotted hyena laugh never fails to at least elicit a smile from me if not a laugh of my own. Their maniacal "laugh" can be heard when hyenas are agitated or showing aggression. One can especially hear it when there is a feeding frenzy. As the hyena is not certain when they will eat next, they gorge themselves whenever they can. No joy or happiness here. This is no laughing matter!

Today's verse speaks of a deep-seated joy that is accompanied with peace. Unlike happiness which depends on happenings, this joy comes from God through His Spirit (Galatians 5:22). Because of its divine source, the result of being filled with this joy is an overflowing hope. However, it is through the conduit of trusting Him that believers experience this joy with peace. As we trust Him, we are filled with a joy and peace that has little to do with our circumstances.

Our world is daily changing, and with it, our plans as well. When things abruptly fall apart, so does my sense of well-being. Tears, disappointment, and even anger are my immediate reactions. But when I stop to consider God's sovereignty in everything, I am reassured. I continue to be disappointed but at the same time I can take heart. The more I can manage to trust Him and His plan, the more I can experience this unexplainable joy. When my heart trusts Him, then my heart can "leap for joy" (Psalm 28:7). Circumstances do not need to defeat or define me.

Thank You, Lord, that YOU are my hope. YOU are my peace. YOU are my joy.

Deuteronomy 10:18

He defends the cause of the fatherless and the widow, and loves the foreigner residing among you, giving them food and clothing.

The Foreigner

It is not a comfortable experience being a foreigner. In fact for many, the thought of being classed as a foreigner in another culture keeps people happily and comfortably cocooned in their own worlds. I completely understand this preference. It is not easy to stand out from the crowd. Living almost thirty years in France, I learned how to blend in to the culture and lifestyle. However, early in our marriage we spent a summer in Taiwan. There was no chance of blending in there. I was constantly regarded as the foreigner and I had to deal with it.

Today's verse reveals the loving heart of the Lord. He is especially attentive to the needs of the orphans and widows. But in addition to that care, He has a special place in His heart reserved for the foreigner and his hapless predicament. I wonder if it was because His Son would one day descend from heaven and Himself be a foreigner on earth! The Lord shows special love to the lost, lonely, and displaced person.

The foreigner is often in a humbled position of having to depend on the kindness of others in his host country. Not only does God offer His love and help, but these verses urge me to do the same (verse 19). Having been a foreigner myself, I can feel a special empathy, as I've experienced this turmoil. It is a privilege to reach out with God's love to the foreigner residing among us.

Help me Lord, to have the same heart for him as You do.

1 Corinthians 10:12

So, if you think you are standing firm, be careful that you don't fall!

Sunk!

It never occurred to us that this would be our last view of the Pilgrim in all its grandeur. After forty years at the Dana Point Harbor, it sank. What a heartache! This tall-masted ship was a full-sized replica of the merchantman brig from the novel Two Years Before the Mast by Richard Henry Dana. The Ocean Institute there had been battling a slow leak but thought it was under control with regular maintenance of the hull (recently postponed) and with a pump.

Today's verse is part of a warning against the mistakes of the Israelites in the wilderness. Their blunders are to be an example of what not to do! The Israelites failed the multiple opportunities God put them through to strengthen their faith. Paul lovingly warns that no one is exempt from falling. The problem comes when we pridefully think we are standing firm, when in reality we are being slowly weakened by our failure to obey. Like the small leaks in the hull of a ship, our compromises can slowly erode our faith, leaving us vulnerable. It is not that one wakes up in the morning and decides to give in to temptation. Being drawn away from Him is usually a slow, unseen process.

Thankfully, standing firm does not depend entirely on me. The Lord is faithful to always provide a way out of temptation (verse 13). But I need to be humble enough to realize that I cannot handle it on my own and look for that escape route! Like David, I want to regularly ask the Lord to examine my heart and my mind (Psalm26:2). This is an uncomfortable prayer but I can pray this with confidence, being convinced of His unfailing love and faithfulness (verse 3). There are times when I feel overwhelmed. But because of His love, His strength, and His faithfulness, I will not sink!

Thank You, Lord, that You are my confidence.

Psalm 34:8–9

Taste and see that the Lord is good; blessed is the one who takes refuge in him. Fear the Lord, you his holy people, for those who fear him lack nothing.

Roseate Spoonbill

This wading bird lives in the mangroves, or tropical swamps of the southeastern United States. His pink plumage, red eyes, and partly bald head make him recognizable, but what really distinguishes him is that giant spoon-shaped bill! With it he may look a bit comical, but this bill allows him to sweep underwater from side to side and scoop up fish and crustaceans.

Today's verse has no spoon but is an invitation to "taste and see." There are those who say they have tried God or tried religion. And perhaps they have in some manner. But to "taste and see" means coming to the Lord in humble fear, recognizing who He is. We realize just how good He is when we throw ourselves on His mercy and take refuge in His love and power. When He opens the "eyes of our hearts" (Ephesians 1:18), we are ready to fully engage and scoop up every spiritual blessing He offers (Ephesians 1:3).

I have tasted and I have seen His goodness. And unlike the temporary good feeling of eating something tasty, His goodness and blessing keep me satisfied in the deepest part of me. He knows exactly what I am craving, as He created me to hunger for Him. When I fear and respect Him, I will lack nothing. He is that good! He satisfies my deepest desires for love, peace, beauty, and significance. How amazing He is! I am blessed when I make Him my refuge. And what is so amazing is that His goodness never fails to satisfy!

Lord, thank You for blessing me.

Philippians 4:6–7

Do not be anxious about anything, but in every situation, by prayer and petition, with thanksgiving, present your requests to God. And the peace of God, which transcends all understanding, will guard your hearts and minds in Christ Jesus.

Lavender Fields

Driving through Provence in the south of France is best done with the windows open! The wonderful aroma of growing lavender is not to be missed. Fields and fields of this beautiful flower delight the eye and its fragrance is calming. Lavender is said to have many health benefits. The oil is an anti-inflammatory and helps with headaches, burns, and insect bites. It is also a good insect repellent and smells so much better than most! But what intrigues me is its relaxing and soothing properties, easing stress and aiding sleep.

Today's verse tells us not to be anxious. Rather than suggesting lavender to ease stress, a much more effective remedy is ours! Prayer. When overcome with anxiety, God offers His amazing peace. And that peace envelops both heart and mind, feelings and thoughts. Tension in the body can be replaced with an amazing sense of calm when we are able to give over to God every worry and every "what if?"

My first inclination is to worry and tense up about things over which I have no control. Not only is my sleep disturbed, but I can work myself up to the point of tension headaches! But when I give over my concerns to the Lord in prayer, I am acknowledging that total control is in His loving and powerful hands. In relinquishing to Him any flimsy control I think I may have, I can relax. Because He is love He will always do what is good for me. Because He is just, He will always do the right thing.

Thank you Lord, that talking with You calms me down.

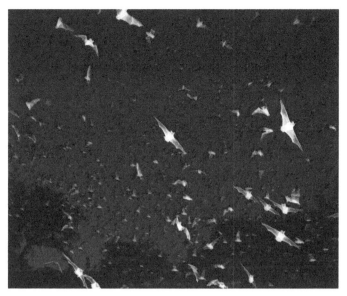

2 Corinthians 5:7

For we live by faith, not by sight.

Blind as a Bat

It certainly does not seem as if these Mexican free-tailed bats are blind. Although it is pitch dark, they seem to know exactly where they are going. They are not bumping in to each other or the walls of Bracken Cave, their summer home in Mexico. Theirs is the world's largest bat colony, housing more than 15 million. It is actually a myth that bats are blind, although some species prefer relying on echolocation rather than their sight.

Today's verse states that a believer will not rely only on his sight to navigate this life. The one who places their confidence in the Creator has the advantage of faith or "spiritual sight" to guide him. It may sometimes seem like a blind faith as we cannot understand the work of God completely (Ecclesiastes 11:5). We do not see the path of the wind or how the body is formed in the mother's womb. There is so much we do not understand. But we trust our Heavenly Father without knowing all the details.

What is reassuring about our faith is that it is not really blind at all. We know the One in whom we place our trust, and that makes all the difference! When I cannot understand what He is doing, I can still trust that He will be true to His character; loving, good, faithful, and true. I can trust that He will be true to His Word. He is never random or capricious. My faith is not blind, as it is placed in the One who sees all. As Corrie ten Boom said in The Hiding Place, "Never be afraid to trust an unknown future to a known God."

Thank You, Lord, that my faith in You is never blind.

Habakkuk 2:1

I will stand at my watch and station myself on the ramparts: I will look to see what he will say to me, and what answer I am to give to this complaint.

Ramparts

The view from the ramparts of Haut-Koenigsbourg seems to go on forever on a clear day! This castle was about an hour from our house in France and we often took visitors there. Half the fun is walking these ramparts and identifying the villages in the distance. Today it is all about tourism, but when this castle was inhabited, these ramparts were important for security. Its elevated position gave those on watch ample time to see approaching danger and prepare to meet it.

In today's verse, Habakkuk is standing on the ramparts. He is watching, but not for the enemy. This prophet of God is wondering when God will deliver them from the evil and violent Chaldeans. He is watching and waiting expectantly for God to answer. I can just see him, shielding his eyes and squinting into the distance, thinking, "How long?" He expects the Lord to reprove him for all his questions and his doubts. But God does not. Instead, he is promised that a vision is coming describing the destruction of their enemy. "Though it tarries, wait for it; it will certainly come" (verse 3). So Habakkuk still had to wait, but with a promise.

God asks me to wait too. He allows those delays to test my faith. Having to wait develops in me patience, serenity, and strength. I am to watch and to wait on those ramparts, looking for His answers. But I wait with His precious promises in my heart, and that makes all the difference!

Lord, help me keep watch with faith!

My heart, O God, is steadfast; I will sing and make music with all my soul.

Cordon Bleu Finch

I normally think of Cordon Bleu as a dish of crumb-enrobed rolled chicken filled with Swiss cheese and ham. But this name is also given to these sweet finches. The red-cheeked variety is among the most popular exotic finches. They are native to Africa, and our friends living in the Ivory Coast enjoy seeing them in their yard. A pair will sing to each other and it is thought that this helps with "pair bonding," developing a strong affinity and a lifelong bond.

Today's verse talks about singing and making music. This is a love song and it comes from a heart that is steadfast. It is music that involves all of the soul. And like the song of the finch, it strengthens a bond, our bond with our Creator. He is the only One who can discern when music is made with all of our soul. Because He loves us, He listens intently to our impromptu concert, and we feel His pleasure. With the singing, our heart becomes even more steadfast as the bond of love grows stronger.

If I do not feel much like singing or making music for this audience of One, it may be that my heart is far from steadfast. When I am discontented, focused on the negative, or unstable from worry and fear, there is no incentive to praise Him. Thankfully, my heart becomes steadfast again after spending time in His Word. He reminds me of His love and strengthens my faith. His Word, full of reassurance and promise, is His love song to me. It is only then that music returns to my soul and can be directed back to Him!

Lord, keep me singing today!

John 15:1–2

I am the true vine, and my Father is the gardener. He cuts off every branch in me that bears no fruit, while every branch that does bear fruit he prunes so that it will be even more fruitful.

Bleeding Grapevine

Did you know that grapevines bleed? At the very site of a pruning cut in the wood, the sap will gently seep, sometimes up to two weeks. After being dormant all winter, it is the first sign of a vineyard reawakening. It is no cause for concern and can even help the vine. The process can push out trapped air bubbles, avoiding interrupted water flow later in the season. Calling this process "bleeding" almost makes me think that pruning might be painful for that vine!

Today's verse describes our dependent relationship with the Father and Son. We bear fruit when we are connected to Him just as branches bear fruit connected to the vine. There are seasons when it does not look like much is happening. But our Vinedresser does everything to make us fruitful, making that pruning cut when and where it is necessary. Pruning can seem drastic and losing sap through the "open wound" can seem counterproductive. But He knows what He is doing, using difficulties in our lives to make us even more fruitful.

There are times I know I am "bleeding" and it hurts. It is especially in those times of transition and change that I can feel those shears working on me. But I can trust the hands of my Vinedresser. He will not put me through more than I can bear.

Lord, make me fruitful for You, even if it hurts.

1 Timothy 6:19

In this way they will lay up treasure for themselves as a firm foundation to the coming age, so that they may take hold of the life that is truly life.

My Virtual Reality

I do not think I have ever had such a bizarre experience as seeing a virtual world with this 3D software! Here, I am learning the controls through a tutorial game and you can see in my son's hand what I am seeing. Creating this artificial environment makes it possible to experience anything anywhere. How wonderful it was to walk the streets of Guebwiller, France, and cross the river's bridge and see the flowers of a place so dear to my heart!

Today's verse alludes to a possible confusion between what is considered life and what is "truly life." This passage is encouraging those who are well-off to be rich in good works and generous in their giving. Being willing to share is what lays up treasure in heaven where moth, rust, and thieves will not touch it (Matthew 6:20). But leading a life that is generous does something for us here on earth as well. It allows us to experience a life that is truly life or "life indeed." There is another dimension to life that one can miss.

Living solely for selfish gain is not true life. But when I live for others, life becomes richer. I so need to remember this when tempted to envy. True life is not found in what I possess. True life is found in what I can give away. I find that true life when I give and serve others. Anything else is a life—but without that dimension, not a true one.

Lord, do not let me miss out on true life today!

1 Corinthians 13:7

It [love] always protects, always trusts, always hopes, always perseveres.

Nitpicking

I wonder how much this poor monkey is enjoying the nitpicking part of the daily grooming. The process of having the eggs of those lice squeezed off his head cannot be all that comfortable! The nitpicking that humans do is not all that comfortable, either. We sometimes get overly concerned with details and things that do not really matter in the behavior of others. Details that are not worth mentioning are mentioned, to the detriment of a relationship!

Today's verse is part of the famous "love chapter." Love is described as persevering. It bears the pain of unmet expectations and hurt. It continues on even when disappointed. This kind of love is a committed one that does not give up easily. And true love is a faithful love that believes the best about a person.

Believing the best of a person means that I will not get overly concerned about details or get critical about the small stuff. Believing the best of a person means that I am according them respect. When I am criticized, I am not motivated to change but will instead "dig in my heels" and continue. But when I am faced with a love that believes in me, I want to live up to that belief. Nitpicking can look very much like seeing a speck of dust in another's eye while ignoring the log in one's own (Matthew 7:3). If I want to have an offense overlooked on my part, I surely need to extend that same kind of grace to others.

Lord, keep me from nitpicking today. Make me as gracious as You are!

Psalm 66:12

You let people ride over our heads; we went through fire and water, but you brought us to a place of abundance.

Daffodils

I will never forget visiting this beautiful immense expanse of daffodils with my father. It was breathtaking! They just went on and on as far as the eye could see. Skagit Valley, Washington, is not only known for its daffodils, but also for its tulips. Most all bulb flowers do so well here because the soil is rich with volcanic ash.

Today's verse begins on a negative note. David understands that God is testing him. The context of this verse explains that God tests and tries us as silver is tried (verse 10). The testing included afflictions, being ridden over, as well as going through fire and water. Through all of this, David remains faithful to the Lord. In fact, his response is to go into the house of the Lord to worship Him with sacrifice. Instead of bitterness for a hard life he says, "Come and hear, all you who fear God, and I will declare what He has done for my soul" (verse 16).

What God did for David's soul was to bring him into a wide open place, a place of abundance. Just as those daffodils thrive on volcanic ash in the soil, I too can come to a place of beauty and growth after the fiery trial. This place of abundance is the same place in Psalm 23 that is full of green pastures and still waters that restore my soul. If in bitterness I shun His presence, then I miss out on that abundant place of refreshment! It is there that He reassures me of His love and care.

Lord, help me find that place of abundance!

Proverbs 11:6

The righteousness of the upright delivers them, but the unfaithful are trapped by evil desires.

Martens in the House!

The cute and furry martens in our area of France were a real problem. Because we had a carport rather than a garage, they would burrow up into the car carriage for warmth and chew on the wires! A device with an electrical shock discouraged them. But the parties they would have in our attic were quite another challenge! The only solution was trapping them and letting them go, as they were protected. Thankfully, our landlord lured them into cages with boiled eggs.

Today's verse talks about what will trap those who feel no allegiance to the Lord: their evil desires. What looks innocuous and tasty turns out to be dangerous. Their evil desires promise comfort and warmth, but instead deliver a nasty shock. Those who are in right standing with God are delivered from even wanting what is evil and wicked. Their righteous living keeps them away from entrapment. When the one who is righteous delights in the Lord, his desires change and are no longer evil, aligning with His desires (Psalm 37:4).

It is not always easy for me to determine if my desires are evil and self-serving. My heart can deceive me and my rationale can be flawed. Sin can be sneaky and alluring, and temptation can be very strong. It is only in submitting my desires to Him that I can have any confidence that my desires are lining up with His. He will shine the light of His Word and expose the thoughts and attitudes of my heart (Hebrews 4:12). The discomfort of conviction is a whole lot better than becoming trapped!

Lord, change my desires to be like Yours.

1 Timothy 6:17

Command those who are rich in this present world not to be arrogant nor to put their hope in wealth, which is so uncertain, but to put their hope in God, who richly provides us with everything for our enjoyment.

Silhouettes

My eldest daughter had the terrific idea to make silhouettes of all the countries or states in which she had lived! She framed them all and grouped them around the saying, "Home is where the heart is." The word "silhouette" is actually a family name. Étienne de Silhouette was an eighteenth-century finance controller for the French government. He so sorely taxed the wealthy that they described their reduced fortune as a "silhouette" or a shadow of what once was.

Today's verse speaks of the uncertainty of riches. They are so ephemeral and fleeting that one cannot find security in an account balance. Whether they are reduced by unexpected hospital bills, unemployment, or taxes, there can never be peace of mind in a nest egg. Hoping in riches is a losing proposition. Any number of circumstances can reduce one's riches to a "silhouette."

How much better to fix one's hope in a God who supplies every need! His resources remain constant and untouchable, regardless of the latest economic forecast. He not only supplies but He richly supplies! There is no end to what He does for His own. I know, because I have seen Him come through over and over again. He gives and gives, and He does so to take pleasure in our grateful enjoyment. What a beautiful giving heart He has! What a slap in the face it must be to Him to see His children hoping and depending on themselves.

Thank You, Lord, for your unending daily provision!

Isaiah 31:5

Like birds hovering overhead, the Lord Almighty will shield Jerusalem; he will shield it and deliver it, he will 'pass over' it and rescue it.

The Pied Kingfisher

This is one amazing bird! The pied kingfisher lives in Asia and Sub-Saharan Africa and is referred to as the "king of kingfishers." The black and white markings make him easily recognizable. But it is his specialized hunting skills that make him remarkable. He is the largest hovering bird, scouting his prey from 50–60 feet above water. He uses no air currents but instead will flap his wings eight times a second to hold himself in place.

Today's verse describes God's promise to His people to shield, deliver, and rescue them. They had turned to Egypt for help from their enemies rather than to God. They had turned to the silver and gold idols they themselves had made rather than to God. This promise was made despite their revolt, and with the promise comes a call to turn to Him (verse 6). He is the One who hovers and sees every distress. He is the One who not only surveys from above, but like the kingfisher, descends with amazing precision. Nothing escapes His watchful, loving eyes.

He sees it all. And He uses that knowledge to show me His goodness, mercy, and love. The plan He is unfolding in my life takes into account every tear. He is my "El Roi," the God who sees. He saw Hagar's tears and He sees mine (Genesis 16:13). He hovers. He stays in the place of tender concern. I can be assured that my circumstances, though difficult, are working toward a good that I may not ever see this side of eternity. He has promised.

Thank You, Lord, that your love and protection hover over me!

Ephesians 3:17b–18

And I pray that you, being rooted and established in love, may have power, together with all the Lord's holy people, to grasp how wide and long and high and deep is the love of Christ . . .

Money Grows on Trees!

My parents always told me that money does not grow on trees. Imagine my surprise to learn that there have been found particles of gold on the leaves of some eucalyptus trees! The incredibly long roots of this tree can grow to a depth of 114 feet. In Australia, some of these eucalyptus trees have pilfered gold from ore deposits underground and have transported them to their leaves! The concentration of gold is only 46 parts per billion. Still, it is amazing that some trees have rooted themselves in something so precious!

Today's verse encourages the believer to be rooted and established in something even more precious: the love of Christ. Just as the leaves of the eucalyptus tree reveal secrets hidden underground, so the "leaves" of the life of a believer reveal where he is planted. The love of Christ is so vast and nourishing that our lives reflect Him as He develops His fruit in us.

Being rooted and established in His love is essential. His love is what allows me to grow and thrive. Without it, I would shrivel up. Being grounded in His love makes loving others possible. This immeasurable love is my reason to be. But to be honest, there are times I am not feeling it. In those moments I delve deeper into His Word, taking more time to listen to Him. I watch for those sweet affirmations through prayer. I so need those reassurances and He never disappoints!

Lord, keep me rooted in Your love today!

Romans 12:19

Do not take revenge, my dear friends, but leave room for God's wrath, for it is written, "It is mine to avenge; I will repay," says the Lord.

Revenge

This very bizarre gun is prominently displayed on the wall of my friend's home hair salon. With this gun, it is not just the prey that is hunted, but the hunter himself. Her theme is the jungle, but maybe it is more than decoration. Maybe it is a warning not to criticize her work! In that unlikely scenario, everyone gets hurt!

Today's verse is a clear command against taking revenge. Like the self-directional gun, taking revenge can backfire. Instead of finding peace and closure with the guilty one called to account, our brand of revenge can hold an element of bitterness. Somehow, the hurt continues, and the revenge seems to fall short. That is because taking revenge is taking a role that does not belong to us.

The revenge of the Lord is always timely and completely just. When I leave room for Him to work, I can continue living life without that wrong done to me consuming my heart and mind. I can feel lighthearted and free from the sense of injustice knowing that He will deal with that person. There is peace in leaving that wrong in His hands. He will repay that individual in a way I never could. He promises. God would not be a holy God if He did not act on His perfect sense of justice. He will one day right every wrong, even the ones done in secret. Nothing is hidden. I am reassured that He will bring it all to light and right will prevail!

Thank You, Lord, that I can count on Your justice!

Deuteronomy 13:4

It is the Lord your God you must follow, and him you must revere. Keep his commands and obey him; serve him and hold fast to him.

The Gecko

Meet our uninvited house guest! He and all his friends even faithfully attended our small church in Taiwan one summer long ago. I didn't mind the geckos as they ate all those nasty mosquitos and spiders. And I will admit they were a welcomed entertainment during sermons in Taiwanese that I did not understand. Their ability to scamper up walls and dart upside down across the ceilings had me worried, but holding on never seemed to be a problem!

Today's verse tells us to hold fast to the Lord our God. We hold fast to Him by refusing to follow any other god. It is through revering Him, obeying Him, and serving Him that we hold firmly to our faith. Regardless of what the world around us does, we are to stay true to Him. This charge was repeated by Joshua as his farewell message (Joshua 23:8). He knew the people would feel the pressure from surrounding nations to worship false gods. And he knew that the people would experience blessing and not discipline if they would hold fast to God.

Holding fast to God is a challenge in any century. Resisting the surrounding culture takes firm resolve. Those false gods of money, recognition, or influence can be enticing. But when I am occupied with obeying His Word and serving Him, I am less inclined to let go of Him. Just as God created the toe pads of the gecko to grip ceilings and walls, so He has created me to desire Him. The Lord will not let me fall when I hold fast!

Lord, keep me faithful to You today.

He longed to fill his stomach with the pods that the pigs were eating, but no one gave him anything.

Carob Pods

I have never seen a carob pod growing, although they have been cultivated in California since being imported in 1873. They almost look like locusts the way they hang off a branch, which is why they are also called "locust bean." This tree grows well in the Mediterranean climate and the pods are used to feed livestock, but we enjoy them too. The seeds when pulverized are a great substitute for chocolate. Carob chocolate has only half the fat of regular chocolate, but then I only enjoy it half as much!

Today's verse from a parable describes a young man who was desperately hungry. After asking for his inheritance from his father and then squandering it, he finds himself feeding carob pods to the pigs and wishing he could fill up his stomach with them as well. It is finally at this point that the "prodigal son" comes to his senses and returns to his father. His father, representing our Heavenly Father, runs out to welcome him.

So many are living contentedly on carob pods in the pigsty when they could be dining at their Father's table (and with real chocolate). So many do not come to their senses. And the father did everything right. There was no lack of love or failure to communicate truth. He raised that son perfectly. Yet, the son rebelled. It serves no purpose to second guess or feel guilty that something more could have been done. It is the Lord who does all the "doing" to draw us to Himself. And thankfully, there is always hope that a loved one will return to God's waiting arms.

Lord, keep me hoping and praying.

1 Corinthians 2:10

. . . these are the things God has revealed to us by his Spirit. The Spirit searches all things, even the deep things of God.

The Whimbrel

Half the fun of walking close to the water on Southern California beaches is watching the whimbrel. He is very recognizable with his striped head and long curved bill. When he flies, it will be just over the water or ground. More often I see him running near the water's edge. He uses that long bill to pick and probe in the sand, finding crustaceans, insects, and worms. He will dig deep in the wet sand to reach his dinner.

Today's verse teaches that there are deep things of God that His Spirit searches and reveals to us. These things cannot be physically seen, heard, or even imagined (verse 9). These are things that God has prepared for those who love Him and can only be known through His revelation. No one can know the thoughts of God except the Spirit of God (verse 11). God's thoughts are not our thoughts (Isaiah 55:8), yet His Spirit resides in the believer. And it is only through God's Spirit that we can have even a small inkling of all that God has prepared for us.

When the Spirit reveals the deep things of God it is through His written Word. I need to dig deeper to know Him more. I do not want to be satisfied with surface knowledge. His Spirit wants to reveal more of Himself to me. But too often I am rushed or distracted and do not take the time to dig deeper or listen to that still, small voice. The deep things of God are so deep that it will take all of eternity to know Him. But what an incredible privilege it is to start now!

Lord, keep me going deeper.

Psalm 107:29

He stilled the storm to a whisper;
the waves of the sea were hushed.

High Surf Advisory

It is not uncommon to hear of high surf advisories in our area of Southern California. The National Weather Service uses this term to describe any pounding surf that poses a danger to those in the water. This alert can also mean the presence of dangerous rip currents or "sneaker waves." The sneaker wave is a coastal wave that is much greater in force and height than the ones preceding it. It is unanticipated and takes one by surprise.

Today's verse is reassuring as a reminder of God's absolute control of the waves and the weather. He stills the storm to just a whisper. The waves that looked so menacing are hushed in a moment at His command. What is less reassuring is verse 25 where He spoke and stirred up the tempest that lifted the waves high to begin with. In this psalm, several negative scenarios are described where God allows circumstances that cause people distress. Each time, they cry to the Lord, and each time, with love and tenderness He responds. The Lord allows the difficulty to show Himself powerful. He shows His unfailing love and His wonderful work in a way that would not have been otherwise seen.

Those waves ebb and flow in my life. There are wonderful times of calm, but perhaps more often, the winds are blowing and the waves are rough. But with each storm He is there, ready to show Himself powerful and build up my faith. He is faithful and has never yet failed me. He will not let those waves overwhelm me. He has already overcome the world and I can trust Him!

Thank You, Lord, for Your steady love holding me up!

Luke 24:25

He said to them, "How foolish you are and how slow to believe all that the prophets have spoken!"

The Sloth

These sloths move so slowly they can seem to be holding still even when on the move! It is said that "a rolling stone gathers no moss." However, this slow-moving animal can actually grow algae on their fur, turning a greenish hue and blending in with their surroundings. Contrary to popular belief they do not sleep all day, but only ten hours. They move at such a snail's pace to conserve energy, as their diet of mainly leaves digests slowly and is low in calories.

Today's verse is a reproach from the resurrected Jesus for two of His disciples while walking on the road to Emmaus. These men were sad and discouraged, their hopes dashed that Jesus would redeem Israel. They misunderstood the prophets and they did not believe the testimony of the women and disciples who saw the empty tomb (verses 22 & 24). They were slow to believe. But rather than leave them in that state, Jesus opened their spiritual eyes to His Word and later to His identity (verse 31).

How personal Jesus is to meet me exactly where needed! Just like those two disciples, I can be so slow to believe. With infinite patience Jesus answers my doubts and questions. He reassures me through His Word. He makes His presence felt. And each time He does this, He gives me another opportunity to grow my faith and trust. It is better to be slow than to be at a standstill. But my prayer is that I can respond to keen disappointment with firm belief in His control and goodness a bit sooner each time. He is giving me this opportunity now.

Lord, may I quickly respond with belief!

2 Corinthians 4:16

Therefore we do not lose heart. Though outwardly we are wasting away, yet inwardly we are being renewed day by day.

Ripe Plantains

My husband wanted to help so I sent him out for some groceries, including bananas. He mistakenly came home with these. I do not have much experience with fresh plantains. They did not look so good with their big black spots. After looking at some recipes online, I learned that the blacker they become on the outside, the more edible and sweet they are on the inside. I let them get completely black and then opened them with some misgiving. Sure enough, their flesh was beautiful on the inside and as sweet as could be!

I could not help but think of today's verse. Outwardly and with enough time, we are all wasting away. We do what we can to minimize the effects of age, but eventually we look more and more beat up! Our bodies break down, but that does not have to be true for the inside. Life can be full of hardship and struggle. Like Paul, we may feel that we are "hard pressed on every side" (verse 8) but that does not mean we despair. We may feel crushed by the weight of our trials but we have hope.

I do not want to lose heart, because God is at work creating something beautiful on the inside. Within I am becoming more mature. Inside I am becoming sweeter as I respond to the Lord in faith and perseverance. Despite all of life's bruising, I can be confident that God is using it all to make me more like His Son.

Thank You, Lord for this hope! Keep me focused on what You are accomplishing on the inside.

Psalm 139:5

You hem me in behind and before, and you lay Your hand upon me.

My Shutters

I loved living with shutters in both Germany and France. They completely blocked out noise and light, making it easy to sleep in! When a storm came through, it was great to protect the newly washed windows from rain splatters. During a hot spell, closed shutters kept the house cooler. And for security reasons, shutters were especially helpful. In fact, some insurance plans would refuse to cover for theft if the shutters were open! But the best thing about shutters was the sense of privacy they afforded. I often felt a sense of peace with those shutters closing out the world.

Today's verse describes just how well God's Spirit knows me. He knows when I am sitting, standing, when I go out, and when I return. He knows me so well that He knows what I am going to say before I say it. Rather than this being an uncomfortable thought, it is a truth that is wonderful. His thoughts to me are too numerous to count and they are precious (verse 17). He lays His hand on me in a loving and protective gesture. Like those shutters, He encloses and surrounds me with His presence and His love.

The world often needs to be blocked out. Being enclosed in the Lord's presence is only possible when I retreat from all the noise and activity around me. To be still and listen to His voice often means turning off all the other clamoring distractions. It is shutting the door to the room or closet to pray in private (Matthew 6:6). When I make that effort, He is there, ready to meet me.

Lord, help me to shut out the world today and enjoy Your presence.

2 Corinthians 7:1

Therefore, since we have these promises, dear friends, let us purify ourselves from everything that contaminates body and spirit, perfecting holiness out of reverence for God.

Cat Grooming

If it seems that cats are always licking themselves, you are right, as they spend fifty percent of their awake time in some form of grooming! Their rough tongues and teeth are used to maintain healthy skin and remove loose hair, dirt and parasites. They learn this behavior very early and are often self-grooming by the time they are weaned. But in addition to the obvious benefits, this daily ritual is also "an emotional feel-good behavior."

Today's verse talks about the effort we are to make in being uncontaminated, not only in the body but in the spirit too. Our motivation to keep ourselves morally pure is a special one as our bodies are the temple of God (6:16). He promises to live within us, walk among us, and be a Father to us. Because of these promises, He wants us to keep ourselves holy, or set apart for Him. We keep ourselves pure and uncontaminated from the world by being completely separate from its morals and values. There is no fellowship between light and darkness (verse 14).

Although I am pretty good at noticing dirt on someone else, I do not always see the dirt on myself! My less-than-clean spirit is so well hidden from others that it is easy for me to ignore. I can be asymptomatic but still be contaminated and contaminate others! Keeping myself pure comes as a result of that daily examination and confession. He brings to light those dark places I have swept to the corners. And He so freely and lovingly restores me that this can also be an "emotional feel-good behavior!"

Lord, purify my heart today.

Psalm 145:13b–14

The Lord is trustworthy in all he promises and faithful in all he does. The Lord upholds all who fall and lifts up all who are bowed down.

Bowed Down

I was intrigued to see this odd plant on my walk at the harbor. It is an agave succulent native to Mexico. The nectar or "honey water" from this plant has long been used as a sweetener. Its vertical flower stalk can grow up to ten feet! Because it arches back toward the ground it is sometimes called a Lion's Tail. Though it looks sad, it is producing so many small blooms that the weight of them bows it down.

Today's verse is an encouraging promise. The Lord is trustworthy because He is faithful to all His promises. He promises to uphold all who fall and lift up those who are bowed down. He sees when life becomes a heavy burden and we fall and stumble under its weight. He understands when the struggles we face bow us down so we see only the ground. But He promises to lift us up!

Like this plant, I can still be producing something beautiful even when I am bowed down. When I successfully move out of that depression or funk, I can share with someone else who is struggling (2 Corinthians 1:4). My life can speak to others of the faithfulness of the Lord. He does lift me up when I am down. But even the experience of being down can be turned around by Him to be something beautiful and useful to Him! How gracious He is!

Thank You, Lord, that You are faithful to lift me up!

Proverbs 15:14

The discerning heart seeks knowledge, but the mouth of a fool feeds on folly.

Pelicans

How can something be so majestic and wonderful and yet make me laugh at the same time? The pelican is an impressive bird, soaring overhead with a huge wing span. But up close and personal, that large elastic throat pouch of theirs gives them an odd look. However, God in His creativity designed that pouch to catch up to three gallons of water with their prey. They then throw back their heads and squeeze the water out of the sides of the pouch, leaving the fish ready to be swallowed. A pelican will swallow lots of things from fish and crustaceans to tadpoles and turtles. If they are hungry enough, they might even drown and swallow a seagull! Having all that water with their catch allows them to swallow just about anything!

Today's verse contrasts the one who is discerning with the one who is a fool, swallowing everything! The discerning heart will seek knowledge and wisdom. The fool, however, seems to be satisfied with foolish things. The fool has no discernment and will swallow whatever folly the world presents, whether it is in the form of mindless television, slick magazines, or the latest fad.

I do not want to be a fool. I want to be discerning in what I "swallow." Feeding on God's Word gives me that discernment as it teaches me only what is truth. But it requires effort on my part. I am to seek this knowledge rather than to just mindlessly go through my day. Intentional living requires that I am mindful as to what I will allow myself to accept.

Lord, make my heart discerning as I feed on the Truth of Your Word. Don't let me swallow anything else!

James 5:11

As you know, we count as blessed those who have persevered. You have heard of Job's perseverance and have seen what the Lord finally brought about. The Lord is full of compassion and mercy.

Stalagmites

What an incredible sight to see these stalactites and stalagmites so far underground in the north of France! Our tour guide had to constantly prod us to keep moving. But between the picture taking and the spontaneous singing of our chorale group, we made slow progress! These magnificent cone-like structures are formed by slowly dripping water that deposits calcite. They only grow one-fourth to one-half inch every century!

Today's verse talks about how important it is to persevere in order to appreciate the compassion and mercy of the Lord. The one who perseveres is blessed or happy. Certainly Job did not feel especially blessed when going through all the heartache of loss and calamity. In fact, he argued with his well-meaning friends and questioned God about what was happening. But Job did persevere in staying true to his Lord. Even though he was ignorant of the reasons for his trials, he did not give in to the pressure from his wife to curse God and die.

God finally brought about a positive outcome though it took years and years. I may also be asked to wait for that positive outcome that the Lord in His mercy and compassion brings about. Just as those stalagmites take years to form, so God's plan can take a lifetime to accomplish. I may never understand it all but I can persevere and be true to Him because He is loving and faithful, no matter what!

Regardless of what this day brings Lord, keep me faithful to You.

Hebrews 10:24–2

And let us consider how we may spur one another toward love and good deeds, not giving up meeting together, as some are in the habit of doing, but encouraging one another —and all the more as you see the Day approaching.

Sticking Together

It was not uncommon for us to stop the car in rural France and Germany and gaze at a nearby flock of sheep. For the most part, they seemed unconcerned and just gazed right back! Perhaps they felt that there was safety in numbers. In fact, sheep instinctively band together in large groups for protection. Predators will spot the one who lags behind, wanders off, or isolates himself. Sheep need to have that visual contact with other sheep to reduce stress while being moved or handled. They become very agitated when they are separated from the flock.

In today's verse, believers are encouraged to continue meeting together. Some had given up the habit. But in meeting together we draw encouragement from one another. Without this encouragement, we become lax in showing love and doing selfless acts for others. Just as sheep follow other sheep, we need to follow the good examples of others. If we are not following other believers, then it stands to reason that we unwittingly follow the example of the world.

It can be dangerous for me to isolate myself. I become vulnerable to spiritual attack. The many stresses of life can weigh me down and discouragement can easily set in. I never stop needing the prayers and encouragement of others. And I need to be giving out that same encouragement.

Thank You, Lord, for the encouragement of being part of Your flock.

Psalm 119:103

How sweet are Your words to my taste, sweeter than honey to my mouth.

Fresh Strawberries

There is nothing better than the surprise of biting into an especially sweet fresh strawberry! I am surprised, as I have grown accustomed to strawberries that are not as flavorful being picked too soon. But when they are local and picked at exactly the right time, the flavor is amazing! I will sometimes buy less-than-sweet strawberries for their pop of color and still enjoy them. I will even use frozen strawberries on occasion. But it is never the same as that fresh sweet strawberry with the juice and texture exactly right!

Today's verse likens God's words to that kind of sweetness. His words are like honey for the soul. Whether we hear them from a Bible teacher, a song, or a devotional, it is always sweet. But there is a different more intense flavor when we discover a nugget of truth for ourselves in His Word. The taste is better and sweeter when He speaks to us directly from His Word without any other intermediary. It is just picked. It is fresh and there is a special sweetness.

I am encouraged by others' teaching. God uses the study and clear exhortation of Bible scholars in my life. There is a myriad of wonderful study guides. They are all sweet and have their place. But there is a more satisfying and intense flavor to His Word when I take the time to open it on my own. It is especially sweet when the Lord meets me and speaks to me directly. His Spirit is so personal, guiding me into a truth for that moment and for my exact need.

Lord, I need Your sweet words. Make them fresh for me today.

Psalm 103:10

He does not treat us as our sins deserve or repay us according to our iniquities.

Just "Deserts!"

I really thought I deserved this dessert. I had ordered only fish and vegetables and so I figured I could indulge just a little. After all, it was just dessert. I had no idea it would be quite this big. However, with three others helping, it was no problem! The phrase, "getting your just desert," dates back to the thirteenth century, and its meaning was "a thing deserved," whether good or bad. The original spelling used only one "s" referring to the obsolete meaning of the word "desert," or that which is deserved. Today one sees this phrase with the two "s" spelling. It makes more sense to me, as I sometimes think dessert is deserved!

Today's verse is a wonderful reassurance that I do not get my just desert from the Lord. If I were to insist on the justice I deserve, I would be in big trouble. Certainly, God is just. But His justice was satisfied by Christ's sacrifice for sin on the cross. Because Christ paid the penalty for sin, I am not repaid for my own.

I am so thankful that God does not give me what I deserve! I am spared His wrath and punishment. His grace is amazing! This psalm tells me of His compassion. He is gracious and slow to anger. His love for me is as great as the distance to the heavens (verse 11)! His love is so wide, so long, so high, and so deep that it is immeasurable (Ephesians 3:18)! I absolutely do not deserve that kind of love!

Thank You, Lord, that You do not give me my just desert. Thank you for Your incredible mercy and love!

Romans 12:3

For by the grace given me I say to every one of you: Do not to think of yourself more highly than you ought, but rather think of yourself with sober judgment, in accordance with the faith God has distributed to each of you.

You're So Vain

For a good five minutes, I watched this bird look at himself in the mirror. I have never seen a bird be obsessed with his looks! He/she did not seem to mind that I was just inches away. Perhaps he was just attracted to the reflected light, or perhaps he was enthralled with his own reflection. All he seemed to see was himself.

The behavior of this bird reminded me of today's verse. This verse is addressed to believers in the church. Each one is given his spiritual gift by God Himself. These gifts allow for each of us to contribute our part to the functioning of the church. It may be a more public speaking gift or it may be a behind-the-scenes supportive gift. Each one is important. These spiritual gifts are just that: gifts. We did nothing to deserve receiving them. God distributed them according to His plan.

That being true, I have no cause to boast. My purpose is to glorify Him and not myself. I am not to think that I am somehow higher up in God's favor. My view of myself is to be sober, recognizing the role of grace in my life. When I think of myself more highly than I ought to think, I am forfeiting the grace He promises to the humble. I can pretty much expect to fail and fall when I get too full of myself.

Lord, don't let me become so proud that I miss out on Your glory and grace!

Deuteronomy 33:26

There is none like the God of Jeshurun [Israel] who rides across the heavens to help you and on the clouds in his majesty.

Saint Bernards

One of our favorite places in Switzerland is the Alpine village of Grand Saint Bernard. It is situated in the foothills of Mount Blanc right at Italy's border. The St. Bernard dog used to be bred here by Augustinian monks. In the summer months one can still see these gentle giants at the traveler's hospice for which they were named. This dog is renowned for its capabilities as an avalanche search dog. The small cask of brandy at their neck is a long-standing myth. But the myth is perpetuated for the sake of the tourists and their cameras. The most famous St. Bernard is "Barry," who has saved over forty lost mountaineers.

Today's verse is a beautiful description of the God we serve. He rides the heavens and through the skies to give help to His loved ones. He is majestic and there is none like Him. He saves those who are lost and cry out to Him. He inclines His ear to deliver and rescue us. He is a "very present help in time of trouble."

I can put my hope and trust in Him because His help is timely. He rides the heavens to my rescue and He is never late. He hears me the second I cry out to Him and He never disappoints. Even though there are times He tests my faith and arrives at the very last moment, He has come through for me again and again. Why should I ever doubt or fear?

Lord, give me eyes of faith to see You riding the heavens to be my help!

Galatians 5:22–23a

But the fruit of the Spirit is love, joy, peace, forbearance, kindness, goodness, faithfulness, gentleness and self-control.

Immigrant Fruit

I was surprised to learn that almost every food we eat is an "immigrant." The plant explorer or food spy, David Fairchild, introduced more than 200,000 exotic plants and crops to the USA over 37 years. He traveled to over 50 countries, bringing us apples from Kazakhstan, bananas from New Guinea, oranges and limes from China and new strains of avocados from Chili!

Today's verse describes another kind of fruit which is not native or natural to us. It is the fruit or evidence of the one who is filled with and walking by the Spirit of God. The results of being in close communion with Him are evident in one's behavior and attitude. The fruit comes from Him and not from ourselves. It is not natural to react to stress with calm confidence. It is not even normal to respond with kindness to someone who intentionally hurts us! To have deep-seated joy in the midst of crisis is certainly otherworldly.

I have none of these qualities on my own, especially in tense, stressed moments. But as a believer, I have the Spirit of God, who resides in me. That means that I have the potential to respond with these beautiful characteristics when it does not seem natural. When I see that they are lacking, it is not a matter of "self-help" but turning to Him for His help. The more I confess my inadequacies and turn to Him, the more He responds with this beautiful fruit. These qualities describe to perfection the One I serve. He is slowly (some days very slowly) producing His character or image in me!

Lord, please show Your fruit in me today.

Titus 3:5

He saved us, not because of righteous things we had done but because of his mercy. He saved us through the washing of rebirth and renewal by the Holy Spirit.

Amazing Starfish

Is there anything as colorful and fascinating as a starfish? Their name is slowly changing to "sea star" as in fact, they are not really fish. But whatever the name, they are amazing and a little creepy all at the same time! They can consume prey outside their bodies, and they have no brain or blood. But what impresses me the most is their amazing ability to regenerate limbs. When caught by the arm by a predator, they can leave it behind and grow another!

Today's verse is all about a different kind of regeneration. Being in Christ makes us a "new creation" (2 Corinthians 5:17). The old has passed away, replaced by the new! It is due to the cleansing work of the Holy Spirit. It is all His work in us and has nothing to do with our own good works. He saw our predicament, desperately needing to be saved. Rather than giving us what we rightly deserve, the Lord acted out of His infinite mercy. He changes the heart and makes us new.

Self-help and good intentions will not make me new. Strong resolve or publicly-made resolutions will not change my heart. I may succeed in changing my behavior but I am still the same inside. It is only through His supernatural regeneration that I am truly made new. His Spirit makes it possible. There is newness of life and purpose now. And there is completion of the process in heaven where I will finally become like Jesus (1 John 3:2)!

I am tired of the old me. Thank You, Lord, for making me new!

Psalm 77:19

Your path led through the sea, your way through the mighty waters, though your footprints were not seen.

No Footprints

When walking on the beach, I prefer making my own footprints rather than following the prints of someone else. They may be too far apart or too close, or perhaps going a direction I don't want to take. One set of footprints brings to mind that well-known poem where two sets of footprints change to just one as the Lord carries us through the hard times. That set of footprints is evidence of someone's presence and a reassurance that we are not alone.

Today's verse refers to a time when the Lord's footprints were not seen. The Israelites were led through the Red Sea. God's mighty power brought them out of bondage, but there were no footprints to follow. There was no precedent. It had not been done before. Those mighty waters blocked their way, but they obeyed God's command to enter them.

There may not be footprints to follow as I walk by faith and not by sight (2 Corinthians 5:7). There are times the Lord asks me to go forward without seeing the next step so clearly. He always reassures me of His presence, but I sometimes wonder if I am on the right path. Does He really want me to go through those waters? Isn't there an easier way? I doubt God is really leading me when I see the path strewn with obstacles. Something in me expects the path to be smooth, straight, and relatively easy. But He does lead me through deep waters. He does it to show me His incredible power. He does it to increase my faith. And He does it so that I will depend on Him.

Lord, lead me today, even without footprints.

Blessed is the one who always trembles before God, but whoever hardens their heart falls into trouble.

Macadamia Nut

It seems a bit extreme to open up a macadamia nut with a vise and hammer, but this nut is said to be the hardest nut in the world to crack! Even after being boiled or roasted, it is a very difficult nut to open. Three hundred pounds of pressure per square inch is needed. The effort is worth it as this nut is up to eighty percent oil (the good kind) and delicious! My favorite are those enrobed in chocolate!

Today's verse talks about something that can be just as hard as the macadamia nut: a heart that does not fear God. It would take a very hard heart not to recognize the awesome power that God demonstrates. The person who hardens their heart against God is one who is at risk to fall into all kinds of trouble. That is because a hardened heart is a prideful one, and pride goes before the fall (Proverbs 16:18). The heart of King Nebuchadnezzar became arrogant and hardened with pride. In consequence, God stripped him of glory until he acknowledged God as sovereign (Daniel 5:20). The story never ends well for those in whom pride produces a hardened heart. They become a hard nut to crack!

How much better to fear God and tremble before His majesty! The one who always trembles before God is blessed. Recognizing His power and splendor and my complete dependence gives me the right perspective. My trembling heart will be soft and pliable, ready to obey and serve. Yes, I have confidence to approach God's throne because of Jesus. But that does not mean I will not tremble before His awesome presence!

Lord, keep me from developing a hard heart.

Psalm 33:18

But the eyes of the Lord are on those who fear him, on those whose hope is in his unfailing love . . .

Mona Lisa

Who is looking at whom? The Mona Lisa's mysterious smile and eyes seem to follow the museum visitor at the Louvre. I was surprised to see that the painting is so small, but she fulfilled all my expectations! She hangs in her own private, climate-controlled room under bulletproof glass. This Renaissance oil of Leonardo da Vinci is not only the most well-known work of art, but also the most written about, sung about, and visited. The way her eyes and smile followed me, I am sure she remembers me!

Today's verse has eyes that follow me. These eyes are full of love. The Lord's eyes are following and watching out for all those who fear and reverence Him. From His dwelling place, He watches all who live on earth and considers everything they do (verses 14–15). Nothing gets by Him. He never closes those eyes in sleep. He never turns His eyes away. His surveillance of His own is done in love, ready to protect and deliver. He looks to strengthen those whose hearts are fully committed to Him (2 Chronicles 16:9).

Throughout the Old Testament is the phrase "and he found favor in the eyes of the Lord." Being that the Lord Jesus shows grace, which means unmerited favor, I can echo this phrase. Because of His grace I have found favor in His eyes, totally undeserved. My hope is never disappointed when I look to His grace and unfailing love. He sees me. He knows. And He cares. I can count on it.

Thank You, Lord, for your constant watch over me!

Jeremiah 17:11

Like a partridge that hatches eggs it did not lay are those who gain riches by unjust means. When their lives are half gone, their riches will desert them, and in the end they will prove to be fools.

The Partridge

The only partridge I am familiar with is the one "in a pear tree" as part of the Christmas song! In reading about her, I have learned that up in a pear tree is the last place one would find a partridge. These birds build their nest close to the ground in the fields and hedges of farmland. The partridge hen produces some of the largest "clutches" of any bird species: up to twenty-two eggs!

Today's verse refers to a partridge hatching eggs. Not only is she hatching her own, but those of others. This is not a behavior common to this bird but it makes the point. The partridge produces more eggs than any other bird. Wanting more is a good description of insatiable greed. How many eggs are enough? For some, gaining more and more riches is the goal of life. As acquiring more does not satisfy, one is driven to continue amassing wealth by any means.

How sad to see a life impoverished by ill-gotten riches! Reputations are ruined. Relationships are irreparably broken and life ends up becoming meaningless. The person described here proves himself a fool. My heart's desire is to be someone who puts their trust in the Lord (verse 7)! That way, I will be blessed and rewarded for honesty and integrity. What point is there in more and more riches as "they will surely sprout wings and fly off to the sky like an eagle" (Proverbs 23:5). I want to be content with the number of eggs in my own nest.

Lord, thank You for the blessing and reward that comes from trusting You.

James 3:12

My brother and sisters, can a fig tree bear olives, or a grapevine bear figs? Neither can a salt spring produce fresh water.

The Fig Tree

When I was growing up, the fig tree in our back year was my dad's pride and joy! The whole family enjoyed those green figs and the abundant shade the large leaves provided. In fact, my dad built a round bench encircling the large trunk. Every year, he would lay out those figs for drying, and we could enjoy the dried fruit all year long. In all those years, that tree faithfully bore its figs. Never once did it surprise us with olives!

Today's verse describes a ludicrous scenario. How ever could a fig tree produce olives, a grapevine produce figs, or a salt spring produce fresh water? It is impossible, of course. These images teach us that what comes out of the mouth reveals what is in the heart. What comes out of the mouth is consistent with what is thought and felt inside. Eventually, our hidden nature is revealed by the words we speak.

No one can tame the tongue nor can anyone make themselves new inside. It is only by the work of the Holy Spirit that I can hope to change. When cursing and praise both come out of my mouth, it is a clear signal that I need to do business with the Lord. "This should not be" (verse 10), but unfortunately, it is. I can blame my words on stress or fatigue but what I really need to do is just confess it. I do not want to disappoint or grieve the Holy Spirit. And He graciously offers His self-control so that my life consistently bears fruit that honors Him.

Lord, control my tongue today to consistently honor You.

Hebrews 12:11

No discipline seems pleasant at the time, but painful. Later on, however, it produces a harvest of righteousness and peace for those who have been trained by it.

Shearing Sheep

There was once a silly sheep who disliked shearing so much that she hid in a cave for six consecutive seasons to avoid the ordeal. With the sixty extra pounds of wool she could barely move! Life was getting a bit difficult and it was probably with a sense of relief that she finally gave up and allowed herself to be sheared. Without shearing, that wool fleece became heavy, soiled, and unhealthy.

In today's verse there is a harvest, not of wool but of righteousness and peace. This harvest requires a process that can be as uncomfortable as shearing. The Lord's discipline is unpleasant and painful. But for the believer it is not a question of punishment. Jesus took on Himself that punishment on the cross. Discipline is love in action and a sure sign of belonging to Him (verse 8). Just as a father lovingly disciplines his son, so the Lord corrects and trains through discipline.

When I am experiencing something negative in my life, I can sometimes wonder if it is a "trial" or "discipline." But usually it is clear. I am like that three-year-old who looks sideways at the parent to see if he is watching. There is rebellion in my heart when I refuse to acknowledge that something is wrong. When I stubbornly continue my behavior, the Lord lovingly corrects me for my good. When I finally give up what I know is wrong, that heavy weight on my back is lifted! Like the newly shorn sheep, I can run and jump and move with ease! Peace and righteousness feel good!

Thank You, Lord, for Your loving correction.

Matthew 11:28

Come to Me, all you who are weary and burdened, and I will give you rest.

Tandem Bicycling

Now this is the way to ride a bike! As much as I enjoy bicycling, I am not too thrilled about the soreness or leg cramps that often follow my rare excursions. How much nicer to share the pedaling! The rider in front is called the captain, the steersman, or the pilot. As the stronger and more experienced rider, he is responsible for steering, braking, shifting, changing gears, and keeping the bike balanced. The one in back is called the stoker and only helps with pedaling while listening and following directions.

Today's verse is an invitation from Christ to come to Him for rest. Work does not stop but there is help. Being yoked with Him makes the burden of work lighter and easier to handle. He is gentle and humble and does not force Himself. But when I allow Him be the "steersman," then the load is shared and the result is rest for the soul. Being connected to Christ makes all the difference.

It takes a conscious effort on my part to come to Him and yield to Him the control. It is only when I come to the end of my own strength that I am open to the idea. To relinquish the controls is not always easy. I have my own ideas about how fast or slow I should be pedaling and what direction to take. But His plan is always the better one. There is relief when I allow Him to take charge. There is a lightness of heart when I can look around me and enjoy the journey. There is rest.

Lord, make my burden lighter today by giving me rest for my soul.

1 Peter 1:22

Now that you have purified yourselves by obeying the truth so that you have sincere love for each other, love one another deeply, from the heart.

Kisses

I am not sure if these seals are kissing or just checking each other's breath! Maybe they are siblings making up after a squabble. Perhaps they are long-lost friends experiencing a sweet reunion. I hate to think of it as just an easily explained animal behavior. Rather than believing it an instinctive act, I prefer to see it as a sweet moment of greeting. After living in France for nearly three decades, I grew accustomed to kissing cheeks as a form of greeting. I grew so used to it that often it could become meaningless and routine.

Today's verse talks about love being sincere. It is described as a love that comes deeply, from the heart. It is more than showy grandstanding or flowery speech. It is more than a warm greeting. A sincere love will not be only "with words or speech but with actions and in truth" (1 John 3:18). A sincere deep love is unselfish and without hypocrisy. There is no thought of recompense or some hidden agenda.

There is a progression in experiencing this kind of love. It can only begin with a pure heart. And a pure heart begins with obeying the truth. It is a relief to know that I do not have to manufacture this lofty love on my own. It is a natural outgrowth of the Lord working in me. Obedience to His way will keep my heart pure, unsullied, and able to love. When I am having trouble loving someone, the best remedy is to run to Him for cleansing!

Lord, today make my heart pure and able to love.

Colossians 2:6–7

So then, just as you received Christ Jesus as Lord, continue to live your lives in him, rooted and built up in him, strengthened in the faith as you were taught, and overflowing with thankfulness.

Giant Sequoia

The "General Sherman" sequoia is by volume the largest known living single-stem tree on earth. It stands proudly at 275 feet tall and is 36 feet in diameter. Those standing at its base must feel completely awed by its grandeur. One would think this giant of a tree impervious to the footsteps of us mere mortals. But in fact, a fence is built around the base. It is there to protect its shallow roots from being stepped on and trampled. Damage to its roots could have serious consequences!

Today's verse talks about where we place our roots. We have a choice. We can put down roots in the nourishing soil of Christ's love and so are built up and strengthened (Ephesians 3:17). Or we can plant ourselves in the toxic soil of hollow and deceptive philosophies, based on human tradition (verse 8). Strong, deep roots in Him will be impervious to human foot traffic! Faith remains strong and vibrant when Christ is the object of that faith.

I will not grow strong and firmly planted when I read, see, or listen to prevailing thought that discounts God and His Word. I am surrounded by godless philosophy and it is a struggle to be intentional about what I allow to influence me. The more I compromise, the more shallow and vulnerable my convictions become. Shallow roots mean I am swaying with the next wind storm of trial. I want to stay strong and continue growing deep roots in Him.

Lord, keep me strong in You and in Your Word.

Psalm 131:2

But I have calmed and quieted myself, I am like a weaned child with its mother; like a weaned child I am content.

Other Side of the Fence

It seems to me that the grass is the same on both sides of this fence. But apparently this deer does not think so! "The grass is always greener on the other side of the fence" is a saying with which we can all relate. We tend to want what the other has, thinking that it is somehow better. This old proverb of discontent has been shown to have some basis when looking at grass from a distance, taking into account "optical and perceptual laws" (James Pomerantz). But this deer is up close and does not have that excuse.

Today's verse describes contentment as a calm and quiet attitude. Like a weaned child who is no longer needy, the contented person feels no lack. Instead of that panicked feeling that we are missing out on something, contentment looks around with peace and satisfaction. There is no need to look at that neighbor and compare circumstances. There may be a fence making differences obvious, but there is no unrest about it.

I live in an area that is incredibly well-to-do. I can easily slip into that attitude of disquiet and unrest by looking at what I do not have. However, I also see the unhappiness, stress, and lack of fulfillment in the very same people who have so much. Their grass is greener of course. But the greenest grass is not the point of life. I would rather have a life that finds its fulfillment in relationship. And of course, the most satisfying relationship is with my Creator.

Lord, keep me content in You, forgetting what is on the other side of that fence!

John 8:44b

He [the devil] was a murderer from the beginning, not holding to the truth, for there is no truth in him. When he lies, he speaks his native language, for he is a liar and the father of lies.

Language Lab

This photo takes me back to the early days of learning French in the language lab. The teacher there in Albertville, France could quietly listen in on our progress—or lack of it! Mastering French was quite a challenge. And of course one never stops learning. My motivation kept me focused, as real life usage was just outside the door.

Today's verse describes the devil's native language as being a language of lies. He does not speak anything else. The truth is just not found in him. The devil is called the "father of lies" and his goal is to deceive and to destroy. He is especially adept at mixing in just a grain of truth in order to confuse the hearer and give credibility to his message. Although we do not know what language is spoken in heaven, we do know that the devil's native language will not be heard!

The only way I know to recognize his lies is to know and be convinced of the truth found in God's Word. The devil will try to convince me that I am worth nothing. He will bring up my past and my failures and chain me to feelings of unworthiness. But it will not work. God's Word tells me I am forgiven and no longer under any condemnation (Romans 8:1). How could I be worth nothing when Jesus died for my sin? He loves me with an everlasting love (Psalm 103:17). How fantastic it is that one day, I will never hear Satan's lies again!

Thank You, Lord, for speaking to me the language of truth and love!

Romans 8:6

The mind governed by the flesh is death, but the mind governed by the Spirit is life and peace.

Magic Mushrooms

These mushrooms look innocent enough. But the psilocybin in them can alter the mind just as LSD does. A recent book by Michael Pollan explores the testing of psychedelics as a treatment for depression, fear, and anxiety, especially as a result of a terminal cancer diagnosis. He even went so far as to experiment on himself! His conclusion was that these psychedelics appear to help with what he calls a "psycho-spiritual distress." He also believes that there really is nothing else for people in that situation.

Today's verse talks about two states of mind. One mind is governed by the flesh and one is governed by the Spirit of God. The mind that is governed or controlled by the flesh is the mind without God and without the peace of God. There is not only physical death but spiritual death in store. In contrast, the mind governed by the Spirit is life both here and eternally after death because there is peace with God through His Son, Jesus.

I cannot speak personally about facing death. And I do not want to minimize what that suffering may be like. But it is often in the sobering moments facing one's own mortality that there is a last chance for establishing peace with God through the forgiveness offered by His Son. To take away that last opportunity by altering one's state of mind seems cruel. I know for the believer there is peace and assurance facing death. I have seen it. And when it is my turn, I am confident because He has promised a perfect peace for a mind that is steadfast, trusting in Him (Isaiah 26:3).

Thank You, Lord, that I can live and die without fear.

Job 38:36

Who gives the ibis wisdom or gives the rooster understanding?

The White Ibis

Perhaps the rooster is given understanding to know when to crow. I often wish he was not so understanding! But how is the ibis wise? It could be because he knows to fly in the energy-conserving V formation. Maybe he is wise because he uses his long beak to feel for and capture his prey without even seeing it. I like to think he is wise because he is mostly monogamous! These behaviors are instinctive but they show more wisdom and understanding than some humans do!

Today's verse reminds us that it is the Lord who gives wisdom and understanding. It is given, not earned. He is the source and gives freely to all who ask in faith (James 1:5–6). He not only gives but gives generously and without reproach. Without asking Him, we are not wise. We may think we know the best solution to our predicament. But with His wisdom there is always the potential for something better. That is because there are consequences we do not anticipate. He knows the future. He can see the outcome. Every decision made without His wisdom to guide and direct is suspect.

I am not an instinctive creature. God created me with the ability to ponder, weigh options, and reflect on possible outcomes. But sometimes, these God-given abilities make me an independent thinker. I think I can make decisions just fine without Him. And sometimes things work out. But before long, the Lord will humble me to the point where I see my need to ask Him. How much better to recognize my limits and ask Him in the beginning of that decision-making process!

Lord, thank You for the gift of Your wisdom every day for every decision.

Isaiah 46:4

Even to your old age and gray hairs, I am he, I am he who will sustain you. I have made you and I will carry you; I will sustain you and I will rescue you.

Paragliding

How thrilling it must be to experience paragliding! It amazes me to see these giant colorful "birds" floating effortlessly above. They can reach incredible heights and cover long distances using the air currents and shifting their body weight. The pilot will often use a variometer to find and stay in the core of a thermal. It helps him realize when he is in sinking air and when he needs to find rising air.

Today's verse is such a reassuring promise of the Lord's sustaining power. As my Creator He carries me at just the right moments. He knows when I am losing altitude and lifts me up to where I need to be. This sustaining power carries me right into my old age, allowing me to live life elevated!

How comforting to know that God rescues me when I am starting to fall. But I can avoid that sinking feeling altogether with my own "variometer": God's Word. His Word lets me know where those thermal air currents are. His Word lets me know when I am losing my cruising altitude. It is in following His instructions for life that I can stay aloft. Without understanding and following His way, I risk slowing down and even falling. But oh, the benefits of obeying! Life is less complicated. There is nothing so reassuring as being carried in His strong arms. I can relax knowing that He has my back! I can even enjoy the ride and those beautiful vistas.

Thank You, Lord, for carrying me today!

Isaiah 61:8

For I, the Lord, love justice; I hate robbery and wrongdoing. In my faithfulness I will reward my people and make an everlasting covenant with them.

Robbed!

The nerve of this seagull stealing cake at my grandson's birthday party! He was persistent, returning every time we moved away! The seagull is known for its scavenger habits. These "garbage men with wings" like to hang around fishing boats, picnic grounds, and parking lots. Most of the time they do us a service, but this one had gone too far!

Today's verse reveals God's very character. He hates robbery and wrongdoing and He loves justice. Because He feels so strongly on the subject, He uses His power to right those wrongs. He is faithful and just (1 John 1:9) and will deal with all sin. In His grace He rewards His people with promises of salvation and vengeance for wrong done against us.

I am not unique in living with injustice. We all live with injustice at some point of our lives. We all have stories of being robbed, defrauded, or victimized. I am grateful for courts of law that mete out some justice. But it is not always perfectly done and many times, robberies among acquaintances or family members never appear in courts. Thank God He is just. Thank God He is faithful to eventually punish and reward according to His perfect justice! He has promised to avenge and repay (Romans 12:19) and He will do it perfectly. Rather than let anger consume me at something unfair, I can have confidence that God will take care of it.

Thank You, Lord, for calming me down with reminders of Your perfect justice.

Proverbs 24:14

Know also that wisdom is like honey for you: If you find it, there is a future hope for you, and your hope will not be cut off.

The Persimmon

I recently rediscovered persimmons. Remembering their strange bitter aftertaste, I thought I did not like them. What I had not realized is that there are several varieties. The one I disliked so much was the Hachiya pictured here. They have a pointed bottom and are mushy inside. But the Fuyu variety with the flat bottom is wonderfully sweet and can be eaten like an apple. However, even the Hachiya can be tasty when baked in pudding, cookies, and breads.

Today's verse likens wisdom to the taste of sweetness in honey. Finding wisdom is worth the effort as it will mean a future hope. There is not much hope of a positive future for the fool who discounts God's words. But the one who is wise is the one who treasures His words, finding them "sweeter than honey" (Psalm 119:103). God's Word is what makes wise the simple (Psalm 19:7). And with wisdom one makes the best decisions, starting with obeying His law.

Gaining wisdom is a lifelong process involving not only reading and knowing His Word, but intentionally putting it into practice. His Word does not read like an advice column that one can take or leave. God's Word is not just full of suggestions on how to live. It is authoritative. God's precepts give me not only a good course of action but the very best one! I have no wisdom of my own but I can walk in His wisdom when I submit to His way. Living wisely means there is hope for my future!

Lord, make this a sweet day by helping me be wise.

2 Corinthians 4:8–9

We are hard pressed on every side, but not crushed; perplexed, but not in despair; persecuted, but not abandoned; struck down but not destroyed.

Wooden Cookie Press

These old-fashioned wooden cookie presses are beautiful. I see quite a few of them in French tourists shops, but I am more interested in the older ones in antique stores. The images are so imaginative and are very detailed. The resulting cookie is almost a work of art and a shame to eat! My own experience with these molds has been frustrating! I tend to not press the dough hard enough into the mold for fear of it sticking. But that pressure is needed to set the image. If the dough gets stuck, then a sharp tap on the back of the mold will release it.

Today's verse describes a different kind of pressure. We are hard pressed on every side by different trials and problems. The difficult times are often perplexing because we just do not understand what God is doing. But we do not despair. No matter how hard life becomes, when we belong to the Lord we are never destroyed or abandoned. He is in control and is revealing Himself through all that is happening (verse 10).

All my frustration, all my grief, and all my suffering are intended to form the beautiful image of Jesus in me. Nothing is random. Our God is not capricious or fickle. He is loving and faithful. He is just and true. Even though I do not understand what He may be doing in my life, I can always count on who He is. One day, when I see the finished product, I will understand.

Thank You, Lord, that I can trust You even when I do not understand.

1 Samuel 2:1

. . . My heart rejoices in the Lord; in the Lord my horn is lifted high. My mouth boasts over my enemies, for I delight in your deliverance.

The Ibex

We were privileged to take a very long hike in the Massif du Chablais in the Haute-Savoie. We were just under the tree line at about 6,000 feet. The views were breathtaking, but the most memorable moment was coming across a herd of some thirty ibex mountain goats! As a group, they calmly crossed our path. Their horns appeared impressive and menacing with their prehistoric-looking ridges. The herd was made up entirely of males. In the summers they form groups and hold big battles to establish superiority. In fact, even during our short encounter, two of them started to get into it!

Today's verse begins a prayer of thanksgiving. Hannah had just dedicated her son, Samuel, to the Lord. She is rejoicing in the fact that the Lord has vindicated her before her enemies. She exults that her horn is exalted in the Lord. The horn is a symbol of strength and Hannah recognizes that her strength is in Him. The Lord has made her victorious over those who had ridiculed her for her barrenness.

David calls the Lord "the horn of my salvation" (Psalm 18:2) and Jesus is called a horn of salvation (Luke 1:69). Because He is my strength and salvation, I too can call Him the horn of my salvation! He fought for me and He won. He continues to fight against every foe in my life. Because of Him I can have the victory!

Thank You, Lord, that it does not depend on me. You are fighting my battles!

Psalm 119:130

The unfolding of your words gives light; it gives understanding to the simple.

California poppy

W hat could be more breathtaking than a boring brown field suddenly coming to life with a vibrant carpet of red? The spring rains in California change the landscape into a burst of color with the blooming of this state flower. Not only is it beautiful but it has many uses. Its leaves are used medicinally, its pollen cosmetically, and its seeds are used in cooking. If you pick one, this simple fragile flower will lose its petals almost immediately. And without the sun, the flower folds into itself each night or on a cloudy day.

Today's verse is part of that very long psalm extolling the wonders of God's Word. His Word gives light and understanding, even to the simple. The light of His statutes and commands allows us to be who we are meant to be. Obeying Him and His way warms us and causes us to grow and be beautiful. Without the light of understanding, we close up and shrivel. When the clouds of darkness or disobedience block the warmth of His light, we suffer without even knowing why.

It takes faith and trust to obey Him. My way seems better and easier. Certainly, life would be less challenging if a believer could just do as he pleases. At least that is how I reason. However, the more I compromise His standards, the darker my day becomes. The light of His loving words and counsel to me fall on deaf ears as I close in on myself. But when I choose obedience, despite the cost, then my spirit opens to a renewed closeness to His heart.

Lord, keep me in the light of Your Word!

But whoever does not have them is nearsighted and blind, forgetting that they have been cleansed from their past sins.

The Ostrich

I was surprised to learn that the ostrich does not really bury his head in the sand! It is such an accepted saying that I never questioned it. But in fact, it just looks as if they do, being that they press their long necks close to the ground. They do this to avoid detection, and as their plumage blends in so well with the sandy soil it seems that their heads are buried. No one is too sure where this idea originated, but the saying is well known. Someone who exhibits this behavior figuratively is one who does not face facts.

Today's verse describes a believer who is figuratively nearsighted and blind. This believer has not grasped the reality of true forgiveness. This means he may have trouble adding to his faith all those beautiful qualities listed (verses 5–7). We can easily bury ourselves in thoughts, memories, and self-recriminations from past sins. When we do, we make ourselves ineffective in our Christian walk (verse 8).

I do not need to bury my head in shame. The Lord with His gracious forgiveness lifts my head. He makes it possible for me to live out my faith, adding to it goodness, knowledge, self-control, perseverance, godliness, kindness, and love (verses 5–7). I continually remind myself that as far as the Lord is concerned, my sins are as far away as the east is from the west (Psalm 103:12)! He has completely removed them. Being convinced of this truth makes it possible to live for Him the abundant life He wants to produce in me!

Thank You, Lord, for lifting my head to see Your complete forgiveness!

Psalm 36:8

They feast on the abundance of Your house; you give them drink from your river of delights.

Eden

This hidden gem on the Havasupai Reservation is called the desert's "Garden of Eden." One can only access it by a ten-mile descent by foot or mule. I made this trek as a teenager with a group of others. I can still remember the awe I felt when coming across the cascading turquoise water! It was a welcomed sight after the dry, hot and dusty trail. We had to pack in our own water for drinking, but splashing in the water was a relief from the relentless sun.

Today's verse mentions rivers of delights. The Lord's presence is described as a dwelling place where there is feasting and abundance. His presence quenches the thirst of our souls. His unfailing love (verse 7) is a refuge and a delight. The Garden of Eden was a literal place near four rivers given as landmarks (Genesis 2:10–14). The word "Eden" in Hebrew means "delight." And there, His presence was a delight to Adam and Eve. It was His presence that made it not only a garden but a garden of delight.

That same delight in my Lord's presence is still possible. Because He has paid the penalty for my sin, I can walk and talk with Him in that garden of delight. There is delight when I can forget about past failures. I am delighted to realize that nothing can ever separate me from His love. No other relationship can give me the level of consistent delight that He offers! My Garden of Eden is a deep, peaceful place of relationship. He is always there, waiting for my return.

Help me Lord, to find that place of delight today.

2 Corinthians 10:5

We demolish arguments and every pretension that sets itself up against the knowledge of God, and we take captive every thought to make it obedient to Christ.

Herding Cats

I thought herding cats was impossible! But much to my surprise, I discovered there is actually a Cat Herders Day on December 15! However, my original thought holds true. Cats are just too independent and stubborn to be herded, or cooperate when moving them from here to there. This day is actually to recognize the frustration of trying to "manage the unmanageable." This day is a day for all of us who feel like we are saddled with an impossible task!

Today's verse seems like the impossible task of herding cats. Taking thoughts captive can be much the same scenario. Our thoughts run away with us, leading to wrong attitudes and actions. Those thoughts sometimes just do not cooperate. The thinking of the believer is not to be the same as that of the world (verse 2). But the world's influence is so strong that thoughts just naturally conform to worldly independent thinking, leaving God out of it.

Thankfully, the Lord does not make this task impossible. He has given us His divine power to control and redirect our thoughts (verse 4). On my own, my thinking becomes full of pride and disobedience. But because of His Spirit in me, I am not subject to merely human judgments. As a believer, I have the mind of Christ (1 Corinthians 2:15–16). What a wonderful thought that is! He is there to turn my heart and mind from what is false and harmful. He brings those wandering thoughts back into the corral of His unchanging truth!

Lord, may my every thought today please You.

Romans 8:38–39

For I am convinced that neither death nor life, neither angels nor demons, neither the present nor the future, nor any powers, neither height nor depth, nor anything else in all creation, will be able to separate us from the love of God that is in Christ Jesus our Lord.

He Loves Me, He Loves Me Not

I had no idea until now that the game of pulling off daisy petals has its origin in France! It is called, "effeuiller la marguerite," and the idea of course is to determine if the object of your affection returns your love. The phrase, "he loves me, he loves me not," is repeated with the removal of each petal until with the last petal comes the answer. This phrase exists in thirty-three languages so perhaps this game is worldwide. I remember playing it as a young girl, but this cat does not seem too interested in playing it!

Today's verse reassures us of the permanence of God's love. We never have to play this game with God. Unlike human relationships, there are no games involved. He has made a commitment to love us and He never goes back on His promise. There is no dark power that can interfere with His love. There is no possible event in our future that can change His love. Death itself cannot destroy His indescribable love for us.

Does He love me more today than yesterday? Will He love me more tomorrow than today? As He is love by His very nature, the answer is "no." His love is a perfect love that cannot be improved upon. The answer is always, "He loves me."

Thank You, Lord, for Your perfect love.

2 Corinthians 4:18

So we fix our eyes not on what is seen, but what is unseen, since what is seen is temporary, but what is unseen is eternal.

Promenade Tapestry

This beautiful tapestry called "Promenade" hangs on the wall of the Cluny Museum in Paris. It was made in the fifteenth century and is from a series of six. The flowers and plants all have symbolic meanings, and the scene is meant to depict life on a manor. It is hard to imagine all the long hours it took to painstakingly place each stitch by hand on the loom. I am drawn most to those tapestries with dark backgrounds. The dark blue seems to emphasize the people in the scene, making them more visible.

Today's verse tells us to "see" what cannot be seen. What is normally seen by our physical eyes is only temporary. Paul encourages those going through difficult times to look to the unseen, to look toward what is eternal. The images and beauty of a tapestry are not seen from underneath. Seen from the underside, nothing makes much sense. We do not see how the dark colors are adding to the scene. We do not see what God is doing or how everything will be working out. But He promises to be working in us the very beautiful image of His Son.

Sometimes the Lord is using beautiful silk thread. On rare occasions He may even use gold or silver thread. But sometimes the threads are dark and coarse. I may never understand why God allows excruciating pain or what looks like senseless tragedy. But then my view is incomplete. He is seeing the images emerge on my "tapestry" and it will be beautiful one day!

Thank You, Lord, that I can trust Your unseen eternal work in me.

James 3:17

But the wisdom that comes from heaven is first of all pure, then peace-loving, considerate, submissive, full of mercy and good fruit, impartial and sincere.

Snowy Owl

This pure white plumage on the snowy owl is remarkable! We do not see them too often, as they breed on the Artic tundra and only migrate south in search of lemmings. They are unlike other owls in that they hunt and are active both day and night. But it is their snow white appearance that makes them stand out! The owl has long been associated with wisdom in Greek and Roman mythology and in Aesop's Fables. Perhaps it is because owls are always asking questions!

Today's verse lists several descriptions of wisdom, beginning with the word "pure." Wisdom is first of all pure. That makes sense, as the beginning of wisdom comes from the fear of the Lord and following His precepts (Psalm 111:10). The one who is wise is the one who is careful to follow God's way. That purity demonstrates itself in the list of characteristics that follow.

Funny, I do not usually link the words "wise" and "pure" together. Like so many, I think of the wise as educated, successful, well-respected, well-read, and continually learning. But fearing the Lord and the purity that comes from obeying Him is the "wisdom that comes from heaven." It may not be the wisdom widely recognized by the world, but who am I trying to please? It is not what I know but Who I know that gives me the possibility of living wisely. He is the source of true wisdom and a life well-lived.

Lord, thank You for giving me wisdom to live life Your way.

Psalm 103:2

Praise the Lord, my soul, and forget not all his benefits.

Forget-Me-Nots

This sweet blue flower was described by Henry Thoreau as "unpretending" and "modest." Their name is said to come from an old German legend where God named all the plants. But this tiny one cried out, "Forget me not, O Lord!" So God replied, "That shall be your name." They are small, being only one centimeter or less in diameter. King Henry IV used this flower as a symbol during his exile in 1398. And ladies in medieval times wore this flower as a sign of faithful love.

Today's verse tells us to "forget not" all His benefits. This passage goes on to list just a few including forgiveness, healing, redemption, love, compassion, and satisfaction. David is reminding his soul to praise the Lord for what He has done for him and to remember. David knew of God's ways with Moses and His miraculous deeds with the people of Israel. He also experienced God's grace in his own life. But like so many of us, his soul was forgetful and needed reminding.

How could I forget these incredible benefits in my own life? It is really very easy. I forget His forgiveness when I am plagued with guilt. I forget His healing when doubt clouds my prayers. When I feel worthless, I forget that He thought enough of me to redeem my soul. I forget His love when I beat myself up. When I wonder if He cares what I am going through, I am forgetting His compassion. I forget that only He satisfies the deepest longings of my soul when I look for that satisfaction elsewhere.

Lord, do not let me forget today.

Matthew 19:5

For this reason a man will leave his father and mother and be united to his wife, and the two will become one flesh.

Termites

The termite can wreak havoc in Southern California as they feast on the wood of our homes. They seem secretive and destructive. There are three kinds; workers, soldiers, and reproductive termites. Only the reproductive ones are able to fly. Both the young kings and queens will fly from their home in a large swarm as they search for a mate. Each new royal pair will emerge from the swarm together and establish their new home, breaking off their wings as they settle down!

Today's verse is the answer Jesus gave to the Pharisees seeking to trap Him with questions on marriage. He quotes what God established in the beginning in Genesis 2:24. The step of marriage is to be binding. The commitment it requires is much like those termites breaking off their wings. The original and best plan for marriage is that it be exclusive and permanent. One new flesh is created from two. Tearing apart the two can cause excruciating pain. The Lord in His love and compassion gives us the best plan to avoid that kind of pain.

God's plan for marriage can seem restrictive. But to give love the best chance to flower and last is within that safe place of total commitment. We endure whatever pain or inconvenience there may be by "tearing off our wings." It shows that we are serious to stay together. The world says that one is somehow missing out. But I know differently. It is through many years of ups and downs, trials and joys that my love for my husband grows.

Thank You, Lord, for giving me the strength and power to tear off my wings and stay.

Psalm 119:31–32

I hold fast to your statutes, Lord; do not let me be put to shame. I run in the path of your commands, for you have broadened my understanding.

Slow Progress

These runners were given a strange place to run. Their path took them right through the mud. The slipping and sliding have them covered with it. If the goal was to get as dirty as possible, then they nailed it! It only makes sense that for the serious runner, the ground chosen would be free from mud or any other kind of obstacle that would slow progress. That piece of lifted concrete, that hole or dip in the ground, or that unfortunate rock can trip us up and we fall flat on our face.

Today's verse mentions running in the path of God's commands. This path has none of those unfortunate obstacles. It is smooth and flat. The path of God's commands may be challenging, but there is nothing that God places there to trip us up or cause us to fail. He is interested in our success. He wants us to reach great speeds and distances. Maybe we can even enjoy the endorphins of the "runner's high!"

The more I run according to His way, the more He broadens my understanding of what He wants and why it is the best course. To be on that path with others is a tremendous encouragement but sometimes it feels as if I were running all alone. Regardless, I do not want to follow a more popular path and be put to shame. I want to remain resolute and determined to obey, regardless of the cost.

Lord, keep me from veering off Your path today.

And I pray that you, being rooted and established in love, may have power, together with all the Lord's holy people, to grasp how wide and long and high and deep is the love of Christ.

Nasty Gopher

My dad grew extensive gardens with award-winning irises. As an adult, I can understand the war he had with gophers. But as a young girl, I was on their side. I was horrified that Dad would run the hose through their burrows and flush them out with water. When the root-eating rodent popped out, my dad would be ready with his shovel. There are more humane methods to be rid of them. But they sure are a menace to enjoying all those beautiful cared-for flowers.

Today's verse talks about being rooted and established in God's love. Having roots is essential to grow in faith and enjoy good spiritual health. But then there are those nasty gophers. They burrow underneath where we cannot see them and gnaw on those roots. We start to doubt His love. Before long what is happening below the surface starts to be visible in the flower that droops. God's love has not changed but we are no longer drawing from it.

God's love for me is wider, longer, higher, and deeper than I can realize on my own. I need His power to really grasp this truth. But when I do, His love nourishes me and makes me strong. When I live out the truth of His love, my faith and confidence flourish. Those gophers do not have a chance to erode anything. The Lord is so good to continually reassure me of His love. Regardless of how I feel, His love is constant and true.

Thank You, Lord, for holding me up with Your love.

1 Corinthians 2:9

However, as it is written: "What no eye has seen, what no ear has heard, and what no human mind has conceived"—the things God has prepared for those who love Him—

Fall Colors

The colors of fall can be breathtaking! And the colors in God's palette continually amaze me. His use of color is bold and startling. I have trouble putting red and orange together, but not Him! Our God is creative and masterful with color. And how amazing it is that He should take such creative care in something so temporal. It makes me wonder about the colors that are eternal in heaven. As He will be the only source of light there, it's difficult to imagine what different hues and new colors He will create!

Today's verse speaks of our limitations in understanding what is prepared for us in heaven. Our earthly senses and even our imaginations cannot fully grasp the colors, light, and sounds of our eternal home. But the passage goes on to say that believers can have some spiritual understanding because we have residing in us God's Spirit. Our physical senses and our mental imaginings can only go so far in understanding spiritual truth. We need the revelation of His Spirit. It is because of His Spirit we can understand what He has so freely given us (verse 12).

So much of what He has so freely given to me is in my future. But He has painted my world with the beautiful colors of His love now! I see that color with spiritual eyes. Surely, the color of His faithfulness is a bright cobalt blue. And the color of His forgiveness? It must be dazzling white!

Lord, heighten my spiritual senses to see and hear and feel all You have given to me today!

1 Corinthians 10:31

So whether you eat or drink or whatever you do, do it all for the glory of God.

Classical Music

I was surprised to learn recently that one of our daughters does not enjoy classical music. I grew up with courses in music appreciation, piano, and in a home filled with the sounds of classical music. When I asked her why she does not like it, her answer actually made sense. She resents getting in a calm peaceful place with one movement, only to be shaken up with the next movement in a faster tempo. I understand this sentiment, but most every piece, regardless of its different moods and movements, will have a theme that is always repeated in some form. I enjoy listening for it and recognizing its reappearance.

Today's verse can be a theme that reoccurs throughout a life. Whatever a believer does, it is to be to the glory of God. That covers a lot of movements and moods. There are moments of the day where there is frenzied activity and one can hardly catch one's breath. Then there are calm slow relaxing times. Always appreciated are the pauses and rests. There are discordant parts of life where the melody can sound abrasive, only to be followed by some soothing sounds. Regardless of the style, a theme ties it all together.

If something as mundane as eating or drinking can be done for God's glory, then most anything in life can be done for Him. This is the recurring theme I want for me! I do not want my life divided into sacred and secular. Every one of my activities can be done with Him and His glory in mind.

Lord, may You be glorified in every mood and every movement!

Hebrews 5:14

But solid food is for the mature, who by constant use have trained themselves to distinguish good from evil.

The Flamingo

The brilliant pink and orange of the flamingos never fail to fascinate me. This social bird with long legs and long curvy neck looks so stately and graceful. But it is their color that makes them stand out. As newborns, they are a bland white and gray. But because of their shrimp and algae diet high in carotenoids, they turn this beautiful vibrant pinkish orange. I guess the saying is true then: "You are what you eat!"

Today's verse refers to a diet of "meat," meaning the more profound truths of Scripture. The one who has a steady diet of meat is the one who is trained in righteousness (verse 12) and can distinguish good from evil. It is a process over time and constant use. Meat is not just knowledge or citing verses by memory. Meat and spiritual maturity come from a constant use of God's Word in daily life. Over time the meat-eater will be able to teach and mentor others (verse 12).

It is not difficult to see who are mature in their walk with the Lord. A long steady diet of God's Word slowly changes believers, giving them wisdom to choose the right path. Our spiritual maturity is not measured in years but in consecrated time in His Word and in intentional application. Obeying God's Word and hiding it my heart slowly changes me from the inside out. If I am what I eat, then what color am I? Am I still white and gray, pale pink, or the most brilliant pinkish orange?

Lord, keep me motivated to read and apply Your Word today!

He cuts off every branch in me that bears no fruit, while every branch that does bear fruit he prunes so that it will be even more fruitful.

Plane Trees

These plane trees are a common sight in France, often lining a country road. They do not look like much here; however, when they leaf out, they are beautiful and give welcomed shade. But during the pruning season they are cut back so far they look as if they may not survive. The knobby ends to those branches make the tree look so strange and forlorn. Yet if they were not cut back so aggressively, they would become thin and scraggily with their old growth.

Today's verse refers to the pruning of vine branches to produce more and better fruit. But the idea is the same: that old growth needs to be removed before new growth can happen. The one who does the pruning is the Father or the gardener. He does not want me to be content with the fruit He has already produced. He wants me to cooperate with His pruning shears in order to produce more fruit that is richer and more excellent.

Pruning does not feel so good. It is a painful process. Just after pruning, the plant does not look so good either. But when the Lord allows the hard times in my life, He has in mind to produce new growth in me. Every painful circumstance He can use. There is new dependence on Him with every failure and with every disappointment. I may not see the new growth for a while, but He has promised a beautiful result: a fruitful life.

Help me, Lord, not to question your pruning shears. Help me to trust what You are doing in my life.

Psalm 90:17

May the favor of the Lord our God rest on us; establish the work of our hands for us—yes, establish the work of our hands.

Ladybug

When a ladybug lands on me, I don't usually brush it off. Many cultures consider it good luck! In France it is called "bête à Bon Dieu," meaning insect of a good God. Farmers encourage them, as they protect their crops by eating aphids. I just enjoy them for their bright red and black design, even if they are part of the beetle family. Their name originated in the Middle Ages when farmers prayed to the Virgin Mary for crop protection. When these insects arrived, they were called "Beetle of our Lady." Eventually it became shortened to "ladybug."

Today's verse recognizes that favor in our lives has one true source, the God of the universe. We are told that "every good and perfect gift" originates with Him (James 1:17). How incongruous to attribute any good in our lives to dumb luck! For the believer, His favor rests on His own all throughout their lives. In His gracious beautiful favor He establishes the work of our hands. He even promises that our labor in the Lord is not in vain (1 Corinthians 15:58). What is done for His glory will have eternal significance, regardless of how mundane it may seem.

All labor is vain without Him, whether it is building homes, guarding gates, or what I do in a day (Psalm 127:1). How amazing that the Lord wants to be involved in every part of my life, including work, projects, and hobbies! He blesses and He guides my hands and thoughts. He confirms and makes my efforts successful. He gets all the glory and that is how it should be!

Lord, help me recognize your favor and goodness today!

Matthew 6:33

But seek first his kingdom and his righteousness, and all these things will be given to you as well.

Sandcastles

I doubt that this sandcastle was built by a small child. It seems too involved and complicated, needing some special molds and skills. Sandcastle-building has become quite the art form with annual competitions all over Southern California. In Corona Del Mar, they have been holding competitions for over fifty years! The entries are elaborate and take painstaking precision. The results are impressive but no longer there. These fantasy castles and kingdoms are eventually reclaimed by the ocean. What a shame to see all that creative work washed away!

Today's verse speaks of a kingdom that is eternal. It does not erode with time. What effort is invested in this kingdom will endure. We are promised that when spending our lives living for God's Kingdom, we will be able to live our lives without worrying about tomorrow (verse 34). The mundane pursuits of food and clothing become less important. Life is more than food and the body more than clothes (verse 25). Seeking His Kingdom means living for Him and for values that are eternal.

The most important component of any kingdom is its king. Seeking God's Kingdom is to live as His subject and submit to His rule. When I live for Him and His purposes, this gracious King takes care of the details. But I sometimes get distracted by building my own little sandcastles. I want my own kingdom, however small, in the hopes of having some say and control. I want to be the one in charge! But my pathetic kingdom is never as good as His. And I do not want to waste my time on what will not last!

Lord, keep me focused on living for You.

Philippians 4:6

Do not be anxious about anything, but in every situation, by prayer and petition, with thanksgiving, present your requests to God.

Nail Biting

I wonder if this feline is feeling anxious. Probably not, as nail biting is part of normal cat behavior. Our Tiger does it too, even though we try to keep up with trimming those nails. But for humans, nail biting is considered an oral compulsive habit. Some research shows that thirty percent of children and forty-five percent of adolescents have a problem with this compulsion. Most outgrow it, but five percent of these young people continue the habit into adulthood. What starts as a stress reliever can so quickly become a mindless habit!

Today's verse addresses the problem of anxiety. That gnawing feeling of unrest and worry can drain us of energy. Anxiety can also become a habit, causing the believer to doubt God's control and goodness. Being anxious is a sure sign of a lack of trust. But this verse tells us there is no situation that warrants anxiety. Whatever I am anxious about, the answer is to bring it to God in prayer.

It seems odd to see the "with thanksgiving" phrase as part of that prayer. I used to think it was there to assure that my prayer would not seem so demanding! But in fact, when I thank the Lord for all of what He has already done in my life, I start to feel the anxiety lessen. In enumerating all His gifts and blessings, and all the ways He has come through for me in the past, my heart begins to relax.

Thank you, Lord, that I can relinquish to You every anxiety and enjoy Your peace!

Proverbs 4:11–12

I instruct you in the way of wisdom and lead you along straight paths. When you walk, your steps will not be hampered; when you run, you will not stumble.

Shoeing Horses

It looks like it hurts. But when done correctly, the shoe can be nailed in place without pain. The hooves of a horse are similar to our human nails but much thicker. And the horseshoe protects the feet of the horse much like shoes protect our feet. Before nailing the shoe there is a whole procedure to follow: carving, trimming, and leveling surfaces. Good shoeing will result in a symmetrical hoof, which is so important to unhampered steps!

Today's verse is part of instruction from a father to his son. His encouragement is to get wisdom and to hold on to understanding. In doing so, paths will become straight, steps will not be hampered and stumbling can be avoided. It is God's wisdom that keeps us balanced and walking the way we should. When we do not allow God's Word and wisdom to trim and carve away what does not belong, our walk becomes painful. We need constant "maintenance" or unchecked pride grows and we become wise in our own eyes (Proverbs 3:7)!

I love to read God's Word. I even appreciate His commandments and warnings as they are spoken in love. But the independence in me is strong. When I start doing life without Him, my steps begin to look a bit foolish and off. My footing is not as sure and there is potential for falling. It is His wisdom that makes my steps firm and purposeful. I can trust His hands to cut away my pride and wrong thinking.

Thank you, Lord, that Your wisdom makes my steps sure!

1 John 4:1

Dear friends, do not believe every spirit, but test the spirits to see whether they are from God, because many false prophets have gone out into the world.

Frog Legs

The French are much more courageous than I am in what they choose to eat! We went to a restaurant recently that specialized in frog meat! Not only could you eat it off the bone, but you could order it without bones deep fried or on a pizza. I guess it is an acquired taste, or perhaps it is just the idea of it that bothers me. In any case, those trying this "delicacy" often say that it "tastes like chicken!"

One thing can be very much like something else. An undiscerning palate is one thing, but failing to verify teaching can be very harmful. Today's verse talks about the possibility of confusing true prophets with false ones. They can seem quite similar when they use the same religious vocabulary. Both false and true prophets use Scripture. There may even be miracles involved. Perhaps there is a huge following. How does one discern if a spirit is from God or not?

He does not leave me to wonder. The most telling test follows in the next two verses. Those spirits who deny Jesus is God are false teachers. No matter how popular the speaker may be, how many books he has written or how persuasive his speech is, I am not to listen. This one amazing truth, that Jesus is God, is the most polarizing. It separates sheep from goats (Matthew 25:33), believer from nonbeliever, and false teacher from true. There is no other name under heaven by which one can be saved. There is no other gospel.

Help me Lord, to be discerning. Thank you that You make the test so very clear.

Psalm 84:3

Even the sparrow has found a home, and the swallow a nest for herself, where she may have her young—a place near your altar, Lord Almighty, my King and my God.

Swallow's Nest

There is a city ordinance in San Juan Capistrano, California, that prohibits knocking down a swallow's nest! Their bird droppings may be annoying, but they are protected. The return of the swallows in March is celebrated every year with a parade and their likeness is sold in the town's souvenir shop. These swallows build their mud nests clinging to the ruins of the Great Stone Church of the Mission. The arches of the vaulted ruins are bare and exposed, making it the perfect place for their nests.

Today's verse speaks of another perfect place for a nest. The swallow builds her nest near God's altar. When one thinks of a nest, there is the thought of comfort, care, and protection. A nest represents home and hearth. And the altar of God represents His presence. It is a place of adoration and worship. The psalmist cannot even mention the word "altar" without praising His name! Those who dwell in His house are ever praising Him (verse 4).

A nest may be built of all sorts of bits and pieces. It could include mud, feathers, twigs, and leaves. But the most important factor is its proximity to God's altar. My nest could be feathered well with all kinds of creature comforts, but does it include God's presence? Dwelling in His presence means there is happiness and praise for Him. More than anything, I want my "nest" to be His dwelling place where His presence is felt.

Lord, may my home be marked by happiness, satisfaction, and praise to You!

Hebrews 12:11

No discipline seems pleasant at the time, but painful. Later on, however, it produces a harvest of righteousness and peace for those who have been trained by it.

Green Gold

No wonder the pistachio is referred to by the name "green gold." This nut is prized not only for its taste but appreciated for all the intensive labor needed to harvest it! It is true that the partially-opened shells are hard and sometimes uncooperative, but at harvest time there is also a hull that needs to be removed from the seed. Some small growers put the pistachios in a sack and roll it around with their feet to loosen that hull!

Today's verse speaks of the fruit of righteousness and peace. It comes as a result of painful discipline. Every believer goes through it from time to time. The Lord disciplines those He loves. And He does it for our good so that we can share in His holiness (Hebrews 12:6 &10). We can be sure that He is not exacting punishment as He took that on Himself at the cross. But discipline is proof that He loves us and that we belong to Him (Hebrews 12:8). Out of love, He uses it to correct and teach. Nevertheless, it hurts.

Tumbling around in that sack, I can trust Him that He knows what it will take for me to have this fruit. It is such a long process of removing that "hull" of sin. And I do not want to prolong it further by not responding the way He intends. I want to be "trained by it" and see the good result. When He uses the hard times to mature me and produce fruit, He also graciously reassures me of His love.

Thank you, Lord, that You love me enough to discipline me.

Four things on earth are small, yet they are extremely wise . . . hyraxes are creatures of little power, yet they make their home in the crags . . .

Rock Hyrax

These little creatures are no bigger than a guinea pig, yet they are called "the little brother to the elephant!" He can boast to being the elephant's closest living relative, having similar teeth, toes, and skull structure. He makes his home in the rocks and the niches of sheer cliffs. But he does not come out of his rock shelter during rainy cool weather. He comes out when the sun does and he starts his day with several hours of sunbathing!

Today's verse comes from a passage describing four small living creatures: the ant, hyrax, locust, and lizard. They all have two things in common: their small size and the fact that they are wise—extremely wise. The hyrax knows when to run to the rocks to hide himself. He knows he is small and vulnerable. He knows his limitations. He does not have the size and strength of his "big brother." Without this wisdom to know when and where to run, he would be in mortal danger!

I have no power of my own. It is no weakness to admit my weakness and cry out to Him! It is even a mark of wisdom. When my heart grows faint I need to be led to the Rock that is higher and more powerful than I am (Psalm 61:2). In the middle of crises, I am not even sure where He is. I need to be led through His Word and through prayer to trust and lean on His powerful presence. He is solid and unmovable regardless of any panic I feel. I am wise when I run to Him!

Lord, lead me to the Rock today.

Proverbs 4:11

I instruct you in the way of wisdom and lead you along straight paths.

The Cockpit

It was an exciting moment for our two grandsons to be invited into the cockpit of the plane! How sweet of these pilots to take the time and even let little William wear the hat! That cockpit is usually off-limits and a bit of a mystery. What actually goes on there is often surmised from television and film. Yet, every time I board a plane, I am trusting that the pilots have a competent control of the plane. I am trusting their instruments and education to lead me safely to the right destination.

Today's verse gives me that same kind of confidence. I am trusting that following the way of wisdom will lead me to where I want to be. The way of wisdom is quite simply following God's way rather than our own. Obedience to God's timeless precepts and commands is wise, allowing us to avoid all kinds of pitfalls, pain, and detours. Wisdom comes from fearing God enough to take Him at His word (Proverbs 9:10).

The Lord does not often invite me into the cockpit. He wants me to live by faith rather than by the sight of all those controls and gauges (2 Corinthians 5:7). He knows what He is doing in my life even when I do not understand. He asks me to trust Him. He asks me to give over all the controls to Him. He is leading me to the best destination. He is leading me with His light and faithful care to His holy mountain, to where He is (Psalm 43:3). What destination is more important than that? I would rather trust Him than myself.

Thank you, Lord, that Your control is completely trustworthy.

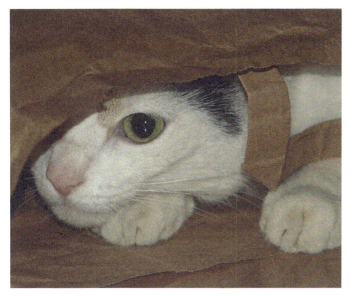

Ephesians 5:11–12

Have nothing to do with the fruitless deeds of darkness but rather expose them. It is shameful even to mention what the disobedient do in secret.

Curious Cat

We have all heard the saying, "curiosity killed the cat." The lure of the bag is a temptation too strong for most felines, our Tiger included. Their little cat brains must curiously ask themselves what that bag or box might hide. Tiger's favorite thing to do was to run into an empty bag on the kitchen tiles and slide across the floor in it! Sometimes the handle would end up around his neck and the bag would hang on him as he tried (and failed) to walk away with his dignity intact.

Today's verse is surprising. Not only are believers to have nothing to do with evil deeds of darkness, but we are to expose them to the light of His goodness, righteousness, and truth (verse 9). We expose them by living a contrasting life, as "children of light," seeking to please the Lord. What is surprising about this verse is that we are not to even mention what the wicked do in secret! As part of holy living we are to rid ourselves of "filthy language" (Colossians 3:8).

It seems extreme. But there is a subtle danger in speaking of what goes on in secret. Doing so can desensitize me to the seriousness of sin. I eventually lose any sense of shock. I can slowly move toward acceptance of what is evil or immoral. And discussing the details of any sin can pique my interest and stimulate curiosity. As my mouth reveals what I am thinking about, I want to be sure to think on what is true, honest, just, pure, and lovely. Then I will not be interested in discussing the evil surrounding me (Philippians 4:8).

Lord, keep my thoughts and my mouth pure and full of light!

Proverbs 20:24

A person's steps are directed by the Lord. How then can anyone understand their own way?

Monkey Puzzle Tree

What a funny name for Chili's National Tree! Its name came from the quote, "It would puzzle a monkey to climb that." Its leaves are very thick and tough with an average lifespan of twenty-four years. But that is nothing compared to the longevity of this tree, living as long as one thousand years! Its reptilian branches and its symmetrical appearance make it easily recognizable. But that does not help the poor monkey trying to navigate it!

Today's verse acknowledges that the Lord directs the steps of those who belong to Him. But often, the one directed has no idea of His direction! The question expresses what is often felt: How can anyone understand their own way? It often is puzzling. We do not have the same vantage point and we can never understand it all. We are told in any case not to lean on our own understanding but to acknowledge Him so that He can direct us (Proverbs 3:5–6).

Because I cannot see what lies ahead, I need to trust the One who is already there and knows the way. If I were to wait until I understood the reasons behind every directive, I would be at a standstill and make no progress! But I can be confident of my direction even without full understanding. That is because I trust Him. His eyes are always on me and the twists and turns are not random. He has a loving purpose in every change of course. His direction is always toward a more loving relationship with Himself!

Lord, help me to trust You completely!

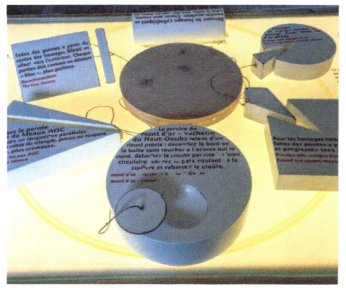

When Your words came, I ate them; they were my joy and my heart's delight, for I bear your name, Lord God Almighty.

Cutting the Cheese

W hile living in France, it was a little intimidating to be the first to cut the cheese when offered that cheese platter. For the French, nothing stinks more than someone who has not cut the cheese properly! This display in Alsace at the Munster Cheese Museum gives the correct method for each form of cheese. There is a certain logic to the rules as everyone gets an even piece in size and rind. When rules are followed, the presentation will stay beautiful and leftovers will keep better.

Today's verse likens the experience of reading God's Word to the pleasure there is in a really good French cheese. So many of them I consider a joy and delight to my taste buds. Here, the Word of God can be a joy and delight to one's heart. Jeremiah was known as the "weeping prophet" as his message was one of judgment for his own people. One does not usually associate the words "joy" and "delight" with Jeremiah. Yet, even knowing that his people would reject God, he could still find gladness in his own relationship with the Lord. He knew he belonged to the Lord God Almighty.

There are precious loved ones in my life who also reject God's message of salvation. There is no avoiding heartbreak over that hard reality. Yet, God does not want me to live my life in sadness. He wants to give me joy and delight through His Word and through my relationship with Him.

Lord, lift the weight of that sadness and replace it with Your joy and delight.

Psalm 62:11

One thing God has spoken, two things I have heard: "Power belongs to you, God . . ."

The Woodchuck

This woodchuck seems unconcerned about the answer to the riddle: "How much wood would a woodchuck chuck if a woodchuck could chuck wood?" He really does not need to count, as these marmots do not normally chuck wood at all! They are regionally called groundhogs, and as such, are great earth movers creating their burrows. One wildlife expert tried to answer the question by using the equivalent in weight of dirt displaced! There are five "w" words and five "ch" sounds in this tongue twister that teach the difference between "would" and "could."

In today's verse, David proclaims the power of God. With the Lord, there is never a question of whether God "could" do something. By His power He created everything we see (Colossians 1:16). With God all things are possible (Matthew 19:26). Nothing is too hard for Him. David had seen God's power up close and personal in his own life and could say this with conviction. He had even heard God speak it to his heart. But there was a second truth David heard, revealed in the next verse, "and with You Lord is an unfailing love."

The words, "would" and "could" are often and unintentionally interchanged in prayer. But there is a huge difference in their meaning. I never need to ask God if He could do something for me or someone else. The question in prayer is always, "Would You?" Nothing is outside His scope of power, but something I want may well be outside His will. And when He answers "no," I can be confident of that second truth. In His unfailing love He knows what is best.

Help me, Lord, to trust Your love.

Hebrews 12:11

No discipline seems pleasant at the time, but painful. Later on, however, it produces a harvest of righteousness and peace for those who have been trained by it.

Wisteria

Our neighbor's wisteria below our Alsacian home is at its peak. I can hardly tear my eyes away from it as it is so full. It practically bends the fence with the weight of its blooms. I do remember seeing our neighbor pruning it, and this is the beautiful result. But not all wisteria vines flower well. There is the story of a lady who, after twenty years of fertilizing and pruning, finally gave up on her wisteria. She cut off the branches, poured gasoline on the trunk and burned it. From then on the wisteria started blooming every spring!

I could not read that story without thinking of our verse for today. The Lord does discipline and train His children. Our Heavenly Father is perfect, and so is His correction. For the believer, judgment and punishment have been taken care of on the cross. But we do need His discipline and it is always done in love. Although it is painful, it is always done for the goal of producing in us the beautiful blossoms of righteousness and peace.

Discipline can last a long time when I do not respond to His correction. Thankfully, He never gives up on me. Of course, not all suffering is discipline. But when repentance is called for, how much better to quickly fall to my knees in humble confession! What hope to know that what follows may be the most productive time of my life!

Thank you, Lord, for producing in me Your peace and righteousness.

Ephesians 4:3

Make every effort to keep the unity of the Spirit through the bond of peace.

Globe Skimmer Dragonfly

Who would have thought that this one-and-a-half-inch insect could travel nonstop between India and Africa? For some of these globe skimmer dragonflies, their transcontinental flight is a "suicide mission." What could possibly motivate them to make such an arduous journey of 4,400 miles? They migrate from the dry season to a wet one in order to mate. The large surface of their wings allows them to glide and conserve energy. And having two sets of wings working independently means they do not have to beat them as often.

Today's verse tells us that believers have harmony and oneness because of God's Spirit. He provides peace, and that peace gives us power to accomplish much! Just as those two independent sets of wings work together to cover long distances, so believers need one another. Through the power of the Spirit, we have the same mind and the same love. We can be united and intent on one purpose (Philippians 2:2). But this unity is something we strive to keep and it is something to be preciously guarded. It is not our natural tendency to work together.

Which wing is the most important of those four? Which one is in the front and which in the rear? Working together can only happen when I am humble, gentle, patient, and loving (verse 2). When I worry about who gets the credit, then I am out of sync. When I am easily annoyed with someone else's lapse, or am harsh in correcting another, then I lose ground. I might be content with the result, but maybe we could have gone much, much further.

Lord, keep us together!

Isaiah 48:18

If only you had paid attention to my commands, your peace would have been like a river, your well-being like the waves of the sea.

Peaceful River

There is something so restful about water. It has such a calming effect on the spirit. The reflections on the surface of the still water can make me sigh. And the repetitive sounds of the waves gently lapping the shore lull me into a sense of well-being. Stay long enough and tensions leave the body, and time seems to stand still. The water mesmerizes me, and when I leave it, I somehow leave refreshed.

Today's verse describes our peace and well-being like a river. That peace comes as a result of following God's way. His way includes leading us by quiet waters and restoring our souls (Psalm 23:2). His commands are designed for our good. He teaches us what is best for us (verse 17). But in our independent spirit, we do not pay attention to how He leads—or if we do, we think we know better! That peaceful river eludes us as we move away from the Lord of peace.

When I am listening and obeying God's voice, I experience peace with Him. There are sweet times and a clear sense of His pleasure when I am not fighting Him. Submitting to Him can be a struggle, but worth the effort when I can feel that deep heart peace in the middle of turmoil around me. He calms my spirit and anxious thoughts. Regardless of my circumstances, the still waters of His peace get me through, guarding my heart.

Lord, keep me obedient and close to the quiet waters of Your peace.

Open my eyes that I may see wonderful things in your law.

Newborn Puppy

The Italian Greyhound puppy looks so tiny and vulnerable sitting on outstretched hands. This breed of dog, as its name suggests, comes from Italy and is the smallest of the greyhounds. All puppies seem especially vulnerable and helpless during their first few days. They are not only blind but deaf, toothless, and unable to regulate body temperature. To cuddle their mother and siblings and to nurse, they depend on their sense of touch and smell. Their eyes do not open until their second week. Life gets suddenly much larger when these tiny puppies can begin to explore and discover their world.

Today's verse describes eyes that are opened to wonderful things in God's law. Our eyes can miss what is positive in God's commandments. Those wonders can easily escape us. This verse is a prayer that God would open spiritual eyes to see His law differently. This entire psalm goes on to extol and praise God's law. The author's eyes have been opened to see a long list of wonderful things: blessing, purity, delight, strength, understanding, knowledge, good judgment, freedom, and comfort, to name just a few! God answered the author's prayer.

I do not often feel this way about God's law. Instead of seeing "wonderful things," in His law, I sometimes see it as negative and restrictive. My eyes need to be opened! I want to see those same wonders in His law, especially the comfort and blessing! God's law is given with love and with the desire to make life work for me. I need my eyes open to explore and discover how God wants me to live and to see it as wonderful!

Open my eyes today, Lord.

Psalm 19:8

The precepts of the Lord are right, giving joy to the heart. The commands of the Lord are radiant, giving light to the eyes.

Water Lilies

Water lilies fascinate me! Their beautiful white and pink flowers look as if they bloom effortlessly as they serenely float on the surface of the water. They can be seen on lakes or ponds whose waters are still, and they can root up to seven feet deep. If left undisturbed, they can cover hundreds of acres of water. Because they float, they access the sunlight unhindered by taller plant species. Their leaves lie flat on the water, soaking up all that light. The result is beautiful!

Today's verse tells us that the commands of the Lord are radiant. They give all the light needed to grow and thrive in life. His commands refresh the soul and make simple people wise (verse 7). They give joy to the heart. Each and every direction God gives is right and completely trustworthy. Obeying His laws makes our lives beautiful.

I do not normally think of rules and regulations as a source of joy. But just as a child can feel unloved and neglected without parental boundaries, so we too can feel as if God does not care if He had not given us His commands. They are a sign of His love. He cares that I succeed in life and He has shown me how. His commands and precepts are designed with my welfare in mind, not to limit me or restrict my freedom. They can give joy to my heart when I see them as proof of His tenderness and care.

Lord, keep me in the still water, soaking up the light of Your presence today!

Romans 8:17

Now if we are children, then we are heirs—heirs of God and co-heirs with Christ, if indeed we share in his sufferings in order that we may also share in his glory.

Royalty

Meet King Henry III, my twenty-first great-grandfather! Thanks to the years of research done by my sister, we can trace our family back to the early 1200s. Although he was kindhearted, history portrays King Henry as weak and ineffectual during his reign starting in 1216. His effigy can be seen at his tomb located in Westminster Abbey. We are also direct descendants of the King Edwards I, II, and III. But will this discovery garner me more respect??

Today's verse reminds me of my identity in Christ. I am not only a subject of the King, I am a child of the King. What an amazing thought! As His child I have access to the throne room of the King of Kings and the Lord of Lords (Hebrews 4:16)! I belong there! Because of the grace shown by Christ's sacrifice, God extends to me His scepter, just as King Xerxes did for Queen Esther so long ago. His throne is called a "throne of grace" because there He dispenses His mercy and help in time of need. Isn't that all the time?

I am not so sure I like the part about suffering. But in our fallen world, suffering is inevitable, especially for doing the right thing. However, I have hope and can look forward to sharing in His glory! Would that I remember that my allegiance belongs to the King and not to the world. He is a King full of love and grace, welcoming me to His throne room.

Lord, help me remember that I am Your child and heir.

Psalm 98:7

Let the sea resound and everything in it, the world and all who live in it.

Sea Lion

We heard Diamond, the sea lion, long before we saw him. His bark was loud and deep and seemed to echo off the walls of his Sea World habitat. The workers told us he was easily the loudest of the sea lions. This playful, intelligent mammal is known for its noisy barking. I remember hearing sea lions bark when living near the beach in Southern California. Late at night when traffic noise subsided, the noise of their barking floated up to the house quite clearly most every night.

Today's verse is a beautiful poetic passage describing the reaction of creation at the Lord's return. Not only does every living thing in the sea shout for joy, but the sea itself will shout as well! Because the rivers clap their hands and the mountains sing in unison before the Lord, the earth will be shouting for joy along with the sea (verse 8). Why all this exuberant response? God comes to judge (verse 9), and when He does, everything unfair will be made fair.

There is a certain deep satisfaction when seeing right prevail. When watching a film where the tension builds, there is often a concluding scene where evil is thwarted and justice prevails. If not literally, I am at least jumping up inside and shouting for joy! I want to see the "bad guys" lose. Part of belonging to the Lord is hungering and thirsting for righteousness (Matthew 5:6). One day that longing will be completely fulfilled when He comes to judge. God will right every wrong. Everything done in secret will be revealed (Luke 12:2). The unrepentant heart will face His exacting justice.

Thank you, Lord, for Your perfect justice and the forgiveness You have given me.

Psalm 143:8

Let the morning bring me word of your unfailing love, for I put my trust in you. Show me the way I should go, for to you I entrust my life.

The Morning Glory

This beautiful flower is just like its name. At night it closes, perhaps to keep in the moisture, perhaps to keep out damaging insects. Then with the light of dawn, it opens its petals and appears in all its glory! The name morning glory actually refers to over 1,000 species of flowers that do this same thing. The species pictured has blossoms shaped like funnels and come in purple, pink, or white. They grow on vines that climb all over a fence or trellis.

Today's verse looks to the morning, not only as the start to a new day, but also to the hope of God's unfailing love. It is a hope that is never disappointed as God is faithful to all His promises. Our trust is well placed in His unfailing love. No other love is so constant. No other love is so wide, long, high, or deep as His love (Ephesians 3:18). And He demonstrates His unfailing love for us by showing us the way we should go. His love guides and protects in that brand new day.

The word of his unfailing love may not always be found in my circumstances. The word of His unfailing love may not always be found in my feelings. The word of His unfailing love is most consistently found in the Bible. Starting my day with the reminders of His love reassures me that He is there. He is waiting for me to wake up so He can show me again. Because I can trust His love, I can entrust to Him my life!

Thank you, Lord, that Your love never fails me.

Galatians 6:2

Carry each other's burdens, and in this way you will fulfill the law of Christ.

Pregnant Male

This creature is unlike most any other in nature. It is the male seahorse who carries the eggs for the female! The female will deposit her eggs in a special pouch he carries. There, he fertilizes the eggs with his sperm, and carries them for two to four weeks until he gives birth. Their babies are called "fry" and there can be as many as 1,000 at a time. The female has it easy. Her part is to swim up to the male each morning during gestation and give him a special greeting!

Today's verse talks about helping each other to carry our burdens. Doing so fulfills the law of Christ, which is to love one another. These burdens are the unfortunate result of our sin (verse 1). They are different from His burden, which is light (Matthew 11:30). Rather than look askance at the one fallen in sin, thinking we would never do that, we are to do all we can to lift him up and lighten his burden. We all carry around the memories of past failures. Understanding how the Lord has forgiven us helps us extend that same grace. In love, we want to help with words of encouragement and affirmation.

It costs me something to help carry the burden of another. It means that I take time out to pray, give godly counsel and practical help. It might mean hours on the phone. Sin can complicate a life. The consequences can be very burdensome with broken relationships and poor self-image. But that burden can be lighter when I come alongside. It is one of the best ways to show love!

Lord, help me to be willing to carry another's burden.

Philippians 2:14–15

Do everything without grumbling or arguing, so that you may become blameless and pure, "children of God without fault in a warped and crooked generation." Then you will shine among them like stars in the sky.

Counting Stars

It seems an impossible task, to count the stars. But who among us has not at least tried as a child? I was surprised to learn that there is an answer! 9,096 stars are visible to the naked eye if one could see both hemispheres at once! So of course, we have to divide that number in half. Maybe the number 4,548 seems underwhelming but in fact that number becomes even less impressive with poor visibility or in lighter skies over cities. However, with only a three-inch telescope that number jumps to about five million!

Today's verse describes those who do not grumble or argue as shining stars in the sky. Perhaps it would not be so difficult to count these stars! Someone who does not grumble and argue stands in stark contrast to everyone else. And the light from even just one of these stars pierces the spiritual darkness around it. People notice when there is a sweet uncomplaining spirit in the face of adversity. I know because my mother was one of these stars. Even though at ninety-five she had to depend on others, lose her mobility, and suffer all kinds of indignities, she did not grumble.

I often wonder how best to "let the light shine" (Matthew 5:16) so that people see and God is glorified. This answer seems too simple. But I find it is one of the hardest to live out. Thankfully, it is God who works in me to bring about what is not natural (Philippians 2:13)!

Lord, make me a star! Keep me positive and uncomplaining today.

Psalm 22:6

But I am a worm and not a man, scorned by everyone, despised by the people.

The Earthworm

Earthworms are disgusting whatever their size! But this one is small compared to the one discovered in South Africa at twenty-two feet! There are 2,700 different kinds of this slimy creature but their role in nature is amazing. They till and aerate the soil, making it more fertile. They have no lungs, breathing through their moist skin. There is no love lost for the worm on my part, but they have love to spare, having no fewer than five hearts! And of course, fish love the taste of a fat worm!

Today's verse sees King David in a pity party. He felt as lowly as the worm, scorned, and despised by the very people he serves. He was insulted and mocked, and the people shook their heads at him. Like Christ would later experience on the cross, David felt abandoned and forsaken by God. But the pity party is short-lived as David turns his troubling thoughts into a plea for strength, deliverance, and rescue (verses 19–21). David begins this psalm feeling like a worm, but then realizes that God has not despised or scorned him (verse 24).

I remember singing as a child the Worm Song: "Nobody likes me, everybody hates me. Guess I'll go eat worms . . ." I have not felt sorry enough for myself to resort to eating worms, but I can relate to what David was feeling. When I feel misunderstood or ill treated, I can easily fall into that unhappy "poor me" state. How gracious the Lord is to care and lift my head (Psalm 3:3). His love for me is from everlasting to everlasting (Psalm 103:17), and remembering that changes everything!

Thank you, Lord, that Your love lifts me up.

Revelation 3:17

You say 'I am rich; I have acquired wealth and do not need a thing.' But you do not realize that you are wretched, pitiful, poor, blind and naked.

The Amaryllis

I love the burst of vibrant red color in the amaryllis. The color is especially surprising, as it can bloom indoors in the middle of a dark cold winter. Each bulb produces 2–12 funnel-shaped flowers. This flower goes by many names: Belladonna Lily, Jersey Lily. March Lily and Easter Lily. But the amaryllis is not directly related to the lily even though it is shaped like one. Because of its long leafless stems, it is commonly called "Naked Lady."

Today's verse talks about a nakedness that is spiritual. What is so sad is that the person described does not realize his nakedness, nor his poverty nor blindness. Being wealthy has caused this person to feel self-sufficient and not in need of anything. But Christ proposes a remedy. Along with salve for the eyes to restore spiritual sight and true eternal riches, Christ gives us white clothes to cover our nakedness (verse 18). Those white clothes are a symbol of His righteousness obtained for us.

I may stand proud and colorful like the amaryllis, but in fact, I am poor, blind, and naked without the Lord. My pride keeps me from realizing my need. As a matter of fact, the word "amaryllis" means pride! And instead of answering His knock (verse 20), I mistakenly think I am fine on my own. I need to let go of my pride and denial so I can open the door to His knock. I am so grateful that He waits there, ready to forgive and begin anew an amazing love relationship!

Lord, may I always realize my need and open the door to You.

Proverbs 26:23

Like a coating of silver dross on earthenware are fervent lips with an evil heart.

Outdated Silver

In a modern household, it is no longer the style to have many silver-plated items in drawers or on tables. I was offered my mother's silver-plated dessert tray but turned it down. I knew that there would be lots of maintenance to keep it clean and shiny. Silver can so easily become tarnished and dark, losing its shine. With proper care, silver can be an eye-catching piece of decor. However, I could not see myself buying special cleaning products and taking time to polish the silver!

Today's verse talks about a different kind of silver. Not only is it of inferior quality, but it is covering something mundane and of little value. Silver dross is used as a symbol in Scripture for what is base and worthless. This silver includes impurities that float to the surface in the melting process. It catches one's attention, but flaws are seen on closer examination. Fervent or smooth-talking lips are just like that silver. Flattering words can hide an evil heart.

A vow of friendship. A declaration of love. A promise made. Or a pretense of good will. It can all be "silver dross" hiding a much different agenda. The hurt caused by this kind of duplicity can be life-changing. We all have stories. We have all been victims. But there is One who will never be untrue. His Word is always trustworthy. He calls me His friend (John 15:15). He affirms for me an unending love (Psalm 103:17). He keeps every promise (2 Corinthians 1:20). And His plans for me are good (Jeremiah 29:11).

Thank you, Lord, that Your Word is pure silver and always trustworthy.

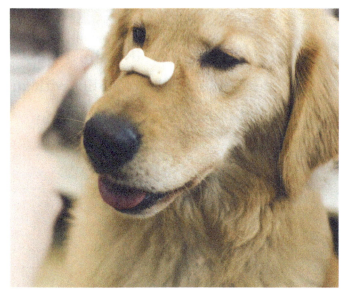

Titus 2:12

It [grace] teaches us to say "No" to ungodliness and worldly passions, and to live self-controlled, upright and godly lives in this present age . . .

Doggie Discipline

This dog understands the word "No!" I am amazed at his self-control sitting there with that treat on his nose. I wonder how long that lasted? With smelling it, seeing it, and imagining that first bite, the dog must be trembling with the effort to refrain from gobbling it up in a moment! I do not think the owner was too far away as the tension mounted.

Today's verse is surprising. The grace that normally comes to mind is the grace that offers salvation, that amazing unmerited and undeserved favor from God (verse 11). But this grace is a grace that teaches. This grace allows the believer to live a godly life that pleases the Lord. And like saving grace, it is completely unmerited. We do not earn the ability to live a self-controlled life. It is a gift that is part of the evidence of the Holy Spirit in our lives (Galatians 5:23). We cannot take credit for staying away from sin. We cannot take credit for our obedience to God.

I am so thankful for the gift of self-control without which my life would be a mess. His Spirit enables me to say "no" to temptation. His Spirit gives me the power to turn my back on ungodly desires and choose obedience. And despite the occasional slip, He has changed my heart to want what is right. My highest desire is to honor Him with my choices. And it is with His help that I can achieve that desire even just a little.

Thank you, Lord, that Your self-control is another evidence of Your grace!

Isaiah 61:3b

They will be called oaks of righteousness, a planting of the Lord for the display of his splendor.

The Acorn

It is pretty amazing that this small acorn can grow to be a mighty oak. It seems such an insignificant beginning to this towering tree which has so long been a symbol of strength and endurance. I do not give much thought to those acorns littering the ground, although people do eat them. They are eaten as nuts after leeching out the bitter tannins. They are also used to make flour and oil. But if the acorns are correctly planted and cared for, some species will produce an oak measuring as high as ninety-eight feet!

Today's verse uses the oak tree as an image of the righteous, displaying the splendor of God. He is the One who plants that acorn to become the mighty oak. He chooses the best spot for good soil and sun exposure. He plants that small acorn at the right depth in the soil and watches over it, guarding it from pests. He displays His righteousness through His followers so the planting is exactly right.

The only way to become that oak is by His righteousness. On my own, I stay as little and insignificant as the small acorn. I know myself. I cannot produce righteousness on my own. "This righteousness is given through faith in Jesus Christ to all who believe" (Romans 3:22a). I have right standing with God because of Christ. My position is secure in Him. But I want my daily walk to reflect right living too. Right choices and obedience will make me stand tall, firm, and fruitful. He has planted me exactly where He wants me, to display the splendor of His righteousness!

Lord, may Your splendor be seen in my life.

1 Samuel 16:7

But the Lord said to Samuel, "Do not consider his appearance or his height, for I have rejected him. The Lord does not look at the things people look at. People look at the outward appearance, but the Lord looks at the heart."

The Oyster Toadfish

We saw some interesting fish at the Woods Hole Aquarium in Cape Cod, Massachusetts, this oyster toadfish among them. He was so ugly that he fascinated me with a face only a mother could love! But these fish have proven quite useful. Biologists have sent the oyster toadfish into space to study the effects of gravity on our balance system! These experiments were part of an effort to understand motion sickness, important for the astronaut. Although they taste good, their grotesque appearance keeps humans from readily eating them.

Today's verse reminds us that outward appearance is not the most important value. Samuel was to choose the first king for the Israelites under God's direction. Samuel was naturally drawn to the tallest, most handsome son of Jesse. But the Lord reminded Samuel that appearance is not everything but the heart is. As with many of the Lord's principles, we get this one totally backward. The appearance and image is everything, whereas the hidden unseen heart takes second place.

I am so influenced by what is on the outside. If someone has their hair, makeup, and clothes together, I automatically think that everything is in order on the inside. I can easily adopt this attitude toward myself as well. Then comes the surprise of conviction when the Lord taps me on the shoulder and tells me that my heart is ugly with sin.

Lord, make me beautiful on the inside where You are looking.

Proverbs 3:5–6

Trust in the Lord with all your heart and lean not on your own understanding; in all your ways submit to him, and he will make your paths straight.

Leaning House

Perhaps the Leaning Tower of Pisa is not so unique! This house, used as a hotel, is found on the Blau river in Ulm, Germany. The Guinness Book of Records named it the most leaning hotel in the world in 1997. It was built around the fifteenth century in the Fisherman's Quarter of the city. I cannot imagine staying there. I would be afraid that I would roll out of bed!

Today's verse is a loving warning against leaning on one's own understanding. When a believer counts on his own reasoning rather than trusting in God's unveiled plans, he leans as precariously as this house. Our own understanding is flawed and limited. We never see the big picture. Leaning and trusting in only what we can understand makes us lean away from the sure foundation that He is! In limiting ourselves to what we can surmise or figure out, we become unstable. We teeter and sway, rather than standing firm with a wholehearted trust in His direction. He has promised to lead the way and make our paths straight.

My own understanding sure gets me in trouble. I assume the wrong thing. I read a situation incorrectly without even knowing it. I think I know, and I do not. There is only One who knows the future, who knows what is best for me. The Lord not only knows, but He has the power to bring it about! If I lean at all, I want to lean into Him and His strong arms.

Lord, keep me trusting in You with all my heart.

Job 34:3–4

For the ear tests words as the tongue tastes food. Let us discern for ourselves what is right; let us learn together what is good.

Good Taste

This cat is enjoying ice cream almost as much as I do! Our Tiger never tasted the stuff because I was always unwilling to share. However, I have given him a taste of yogurt and he was thrilled. I imagine many cats enjoy foods that involve milk or cream. But I still remember the veterinarian warning us that the digestive system of an adult cat does not take too well to drinking milk. Although the taste is delicious, it is not so good for him.

Today's verse records the advice of one of Job's three friends. Elihu was eager to help Job discover the reason for his troubles. He had a lot to say, but it was off the mark. Certainly, we are to test what we hear and listen with discernment. Just as we taste food to see if it has a pleasing flavor, so we "taste" what we hear to decide if it rings true. The problem is that we all have differing taste buds. What seems right and good to one can seem wrong and sour to another. Our subjectivity gets in the way of finding absolute truth.

Thankfully, I do not have to discern for myself what is right. It is not up to me to come to some sort of consensus. God's law goes beyond individual opinion or cultural norms. God's law does not change with the times. Surveys and votes do not change what God has put in place. And not only does it taste good, but it is good for me!

Help me Lord, to discern what You call good and right.

Isaiah 61:3

. . . to bestow on them a crown of beauty instead of ashes, the oil of joy instead of mourning, and a garment of praise instead of a spirit of despair.

Super Bloom

This incredible "super bloom" in Southern California is breathtaking! The once barren hillsides and scrub lands are bursting with color and people are descending in droves to experience the beauty. After all the rain we have had, it is a welcome sight. But in some areas there is an additional reason for this super bloom. The wildflowers are especially spectacular in areas affected by the Woolsey fire where 97,000 acres were burned. It is truly a "miracle of nature" to see the blackened ash-covered ground recover itself in vibrant color!

Today's verse, spoken by the prophet Isaiah, is a declaration of what God would do for the Israelites. He promises to replace the ashes on their heads with a crown of beauty. Those ashes, along with the sackcloth, were a sign of sorrow and repentance for sin. That itchy rough garment of despair concerning their sin would be replaced with a garment of praise. Joy would replace mourning. God's forgiveness changes everything!

I do not always feel much sorrow over my own sin. But when I do, it can feel like a crushing weight. Thankfully, He promises to be near the one who is brokenhearted over sin (Psalm 34:18). His forgiveness turns my ashes into a crown of beauty! When I humble myself and go to Him in confession, the black ugliness of sin disappears. Despair over my past mistakes and failures is transformed into beautiful colorful praise for the new start He gives me! He is faithful and just to forgive every single time!

Thank you, Lord, for turning my ashes into beauty.

Romans 12:3b

. . . Do not think of yourself more highly than you ought, but rather think of yourself with sober judgment, in accordance with the faith God has distributed to each of you.

Nesting Dolls

Although the nesting or "matryoshka" dolls originated in Russia, they are also made by French Alsacians. We see them all year long in France, but they are especially popular at the Christmas markets. The number of dolls in a set can vary anywhere from five to several dozen. A number of different themes are used, including fairy tale figures, animals, and religious or political figures. I am partial to the traditional "little matrons." But they all show beautiful artistry in the elaborate and detailed painting.

Today's verse came to mind in thinking of the different sizes of these dolls. Each one has its place in the set. Each one belongs to the other and is needed to be complete. Paul encourages his readers not to think of themselves more highly than they should. Whatever size we think we are, we are not to look down on someone else. Whatever talents we have are a gift from our Creator. Each capability is a grace from Him.

Each believer has received a special talent or gift to serve Him. When I think about myself with sober judgment, I realize that any success in life ultimately comes from Him. It is all grace. If there is any boasting to be done, it is boasting in what the Lord has done and not myself (1 Corinthians 1:31). Pride is a sneaky temptation, but I do not want to disqualify myself from serving Him by allowing it to poison my thinking.

Lord, thank you for all your gifts to me! Keep me from taking any credit.

1 Corinthians 15:2

By this gospel you are saved, if you hold firmly to the word I preached to you. Otherwise, you have believed in vain.

Giant Clam

It is called a "giant clam" for good reason. This is the largest of the mollusks on earth. It can grow up to 500 pounds and can measure up to four feet! Just think of all the clam chowder it could produce! The giant clam is not endangered although it is classified as vulnerable, as it has been over harvested for food and decoration. What struck me is that the giant clam has only one chance to choose its home. Once it has fastened itself to a spot on a reef, it will sit there for life.

Today's verse encourages the believer to hold firmly to God's Word. By the gospel or "good news" of salvation we are saved from the punishment our sins deserve. It is on the truth of God's Word that we take our stand (verse 1). When we commit our lives, our future, and our eternal destiny to what God says, we flourish and grow. There is no reason to attach ourselves to some other philosophy or system of thought. His Word gives hope, encouragement, and all the nourishment our faith needs to grow and thrive.

Trusting in my own ideas and reasoning gets me in trouble. The waves of the sea or the blowing winds can toss me about making me unstable (James 1:6). But when I put my entire confidence in what the Lord says about a matter, I know I am on firm footing. The decrees of the Lord are firm (Psalm 19:9) and make me firm as well. I want to attach myself to Him and make His truth my home!

Lord, keep me in Your Word and remembering Your truth today.

Colossians 3:12–13

Therefore, as God's chosen people, holy and dearly loved, clothe yourselves with compassion, kindness, humility, gentleness, and patience. Bear with each other and forgive one another if any of you has a grievance against someone. Forgive as the Lord forgave you.

Silk Floss Tree

We have one of these silk floss trees growing right down the street from us. Their blooms are beautiful and inviting, resembling the hibiscus. And their pods are full of a cotton-like fiber that some use in making upholstery. But their trunks and branches are covered with these thorn-like growths. Some tree owners even put a barrier up so the passerby does not inadvertently knock into it.

Today's verse reminded me of this tree. A believer can seem pleasant and inviting by wearing mercy, kindness, humility, gentleness, and even patience. But without the grace to bear with each other's faults, we become harsh. Without forgiveness, we are like those prickly thorns and people keep their distance. Our motivation to forgive others is the realization of how much the Lord has forgiven us.

Forgiveness has got to be one of the hardest things the Lord asks of me. When I have been wronged, I feel it is my right to harbor ill will, at least until that person shows some remorse. But letting go of the hurt seems nearly impossible until I am able to forgive the one who caused it. True healing can only happen when I let that person off the hook, regardless of their attitude about it. Jesus died for my sins while I was still His enemy (Romans 5:6–8). If I am to forgive like He forgave, then I need to extend forgiveness, whether deserved or not!

Lord, I need Your help to forgive.

Philippians 4:12

I know what it is to be in need, and I know what it is to have plenty. I have learned the secret of being content in any and every situation, whether well fed or hungry, whether living in plenty or in want.

Lap Cat

This is not our cat. Tiger would never consent to sit in our laps, let alone relax and sleep there. I tried so hard to make him a lap cat, but he would have none of it! There is something soothing about having that little heater rest on one's knees. But when a cat is that relaxed and contented I feel pinned in place, not wanting to disturb him by getting out of the chair.

Today's verse is about experiencing contentment regardless of our circumstances. Having every need and desire fulfilled is no guarantee to having contentment. Nor is experiencing lack a recipe for discontent. Paul knew what he was talking about as he lived both of these scenarios. What is encouraging is that contentment can be learned. It is not always our first reaction, but with enough practice it can be. There is a secret to learning this contentment and that secret is found in our relationship to Christ. He gives us the ability to find contentment in Him.

What this suggests to me is that when I am feeling disgruntled and deprived, I just need to crawl back up into His lap! Rather than focusing on the negatives in my life, I turn to Him. Reminding myself of who He is and all the blessings He has already given me helps me find that lap of contentment. For me, it is really a choice as to where I am focusing my thoughts.

Lord, help me to find that elusive contentment in You.

Colossians 1:16b–17

. . . all things have been created through him and for him. He [Christ] is before all things, and in him all things hold together.

Desert Soil

The views in the Utah National Parks are truly breathtaking! Around every corner is another amazing scene of cliffs, arches, and odd rock formations. One thing that seems unimpressive is the unforgiving soil being so dry and barren. But in fact, it is teeming with activity, due to the microscopic cyanobacteria one-eighth of an inch below that surface. There are signs to keep off this fragile crust. This bacteria is binding the sand and soil particles together, creating a place for algae, moss, and fungi to grow.

Today's verse is a powerful statement to the absolute creative control Jesus has in every part of nature. Despite what one believes about how this Earth came into being, these verses say categorically that Christ was involved in the process. Everything created has been created through Him and for Him. No power is above Him and in Him and that power, all things hold together. From the exact tilt of our Earth to the crust on the desert floor, He holds it all together.

Because He can and does hold things together on such a grand scale, I can be confident that He holds me and my life together as well. His creative power holds me squarely and securely in His hand (John 10:28). Nothing is out of His control today, even if I feel like things are flying apart. He even scrutinizes the path ahead, knowing what is around the next corner (Psalm 139:3). When I am feeling overwhelmed, He holds together what I cannot. He knows the end from the beginning and I can trust Him with every detail.

Thank you, Lord, for holding me together.

1 Corinthians 3:3

You are still worldly. For since there is jealousy and quarreling among you, are you not worldly? Are you not acting like mere humans?

Not Feeling It

My poor husband recently had a rotten tooth extracted and with the local anesthetic, he felt and looked much like this dog! But the upside is that there was no pain during the procedure. He did not feel a thing! Feeling physical pain is sometimes easier than dealing with strong feelings and emotions. Over the years I have often heard it said that "feelings are neither good or bad." They are somehow neutral and natural. It is what we do with them that can result in something negative or positive. Feelings are the motor behind so much in life.

Today's verse seems to support the idea that our feelings are normal and natural. When we feel jealousy, we are following our normal human inclination. However, some feelings, though understandable, are absolutely wrong in God's sight. Jealousy is one. Our God is a jealous God but we are never given that right. Hate is another. The hate does not even have to lead to action to be wrong (Matthew 5:22). When one lusts for someone other than a spouse, it is as wrong as the actual act of adultery (Matthew 5:27–28). Feelings do matter.

Of course, not all feelings are wrong. But just because it feels normal does not mean that the Lord approves. My heart is deceitful and ready to excuse every feeling for whatever reason (Jeremiah 17:9). My heart is all about those feelings that motivate and shape my life. Controlling them, dealing with them, and sometimes confessing them is only possible through His Spirit!

Lord, help me evaluate my feelings in the light of Your Word.

John 12:24

Very truly I tell you, unless a kernel of wheat falls to the ground and dies, it remains only a single seed. But if it dies, it produces many seeds.

Nurse Log

How strange to see a tree growing out of the remains of another! This tree grows in the Cathedral Grove of Vancouver Island. But throughout our Pacific Northwest, nurse logs can be seen. When a whole row of trees are growing in a perfectly straight line, they are probably marking the place where an old tree fell. These chunks of dead wood become cradles for new life! That is because they give a head start to young seedlings as they decay, providing water, moss, leaf litter, disease protection, and nutrients.

Today's verse includes the same principle of having more impact dying in the service of others than living for one's self. The next verse explains that those who love their lives lose them. But the one who hates his life will keep it. The nurse log has literally died as has the kernel of wheat in our verse. However, our dying as believers has more to do with giving up rights and privileges in serving others. Picking up our cross and following Jesus involves the daily denying of ourselves in the interest of others (Mark 8:34).

This is just as hard as it sounds and for me, proves to be a daily struggle. My needs, my wants, my preferences take center stage but I am not to hold on to them too tightly. If by putting myself second I can encourage someone else, then I am being a "nurse log." Enough of these selfless acts will add up to creating a legacy that lives on even after my actual death!

Lord, make me a servant today!

Romans 5:1

Therefore, since we have been justified through faith, we have peace with God through our Lord Jesus Christ.

The Gavel

The tapping of a gavel in a courtroom can mean different things. When tapped twice, everyone is to rise. When it is tapped three times, all are to be seated. There can be repeated vigorous tapping to restore order. One tap may be used to declare a matter settled and finished. With the tap of a gavel comes all the power of that court. When that gavel is brought down, there is a decision made. And that symbol of authority brings with it a certain finality.

In the courts of heaven, the gavel comes down with unquestionable authority. God has every right to proclaim someone guilty or not guilty. He is our righteous Judge, and all His judgments are true and just. Today's verse is a wonderful assurance for the one who has placed their faith in Jesus. There is no fear of that gavel coming down. The believer is justified, or declared righteous, not because of our own deeds but because of being credited with His righteousness (Romans 4:22–25). The just punishment that we rightly deserve has been fully met by His death on the cross. The righteousness Jesus achieved has been laid to our account!

It has been decided. The gavel has already come down. I do not have to live in fear and doubt. He declared, "It is finished," on that cross. How amazing that I can stand before Him, declared righteous! There is peace with God now and throughout eternity. My heart is not troubled because of my guilt and sin. His forgiveness and declaration has established heartfelt peace, relief, and the joy and hope of heaven!

Lord, how can I ever express my gratitude!

Ephesians 5:15

Be very careful, then, how you live —not as unwise but as wise.

Sting Ray Shuffle

There have been numerous stories lately about stingrays on the California beaches. All records were broken when 156 stingray injuries were reported in just three days! Normally, I think of this problem as only being on the Atlantic side. But apparently, the low tides and warm water have brought these unwanted visitors close enough to be a problem. The prevailing wisdom is to shuffle your feet when entering the water. The sand kicked up when walking this way will alert and scatter them.

Today's verse tells us to be wise by living and walking carefully. We walk through life with a purpose. We walk in a manner that is worthy of our calling, pleasing the Lord (Colossians 1:10). We do not walk courting disaster as the unwise would do. Rather than wondering just how far one can go in a particular behavior before it becomes sin, we need to walk with a healthy fear of danger. So much heartache can be avoided when we walk through this life the way the Lord has prescribed. Walking carefully is walking within His will, making the most of every day (verses 16–17).

Walking my way instead of His does not seem so bad. My problem is that I do not see that stingray in my path, as it can blend in with the sand. The only way I can be confident of my next step, and the one after that, is to know I am walking to please Him. No decision is too small or unimportant to bring to Him for counsel (Psalm 73:24). He guides me through His Word which touches every area of my life.

Lord, show me how to walk today.

Psalm 77:2

When I was in distress, I sought the Lord; at night I stretched out untiring hands and I would not be comforted.

Night Blooming Cereus

How amazing that this cactus flower only blooms at night! This flower is either white or a pale color, opening after nightfall and wilting by dawn. It is native to Arizona and the Sonora Desert and is short-lived in that harsh environment. But it is beautiful and fragrant in its temporary glory. I find it incredible that our Creator would fashion such a beauty, seemingly for His own enjoyment! And the older the plant, the more blooms there will be.

Today's verse by Asaph, thought to be King David's director of music, describes the distress he was feeling in the middle of the night. He sought the Lord. He cried out to the Lord, but at the same time, he refused to be comforted. His soul must have resembled the dry, thirsty desert. He was feeling those thorns of the cactus choke out the comfort he so needed.

When the lights are out and the house is quiet, there is ample opportunity to focus on the distress I have pushed to the corners of my mind during the day. Like Asaph, I can turn to the Lord in those sleepless moments. What seemed hopeless and without comfort transforms itself into something fragrant and beautiful: praise. Like Asaph, I can remember what God has done for me. Remembering His faithfulness in the past gives me courage to face the future. No one sees that flower of renewed faith and intimacy with the Lord. It blooms at night, and as I grow older, there are more opportunities for blooms to appear!

Thank you, Lord, for Your comfort and reassurance in the night.

Galatians 3:28

There is neither Jew nor Gentile, neither slave nor free, nor is there male and female, for you are all one in Christ Jesus.

The Cardinal

It is not fair. The male cardinal gets all the attention with its bright red plumage, whereas the female is largely overlooked. And yet, although the colors are more subtle, she is beautiful too. Normally among songbirds, the male is the only one to sing. He will sing to defend his territory and during courtship. However, the female cardinal also sings. She sings mainly during the spring, during courtship, and while sitting on her nest. Her song is a bit longer and more complex than his.

Today's verse downplays the differences between races, between social status, and between the sexes. These words describe a coming together that is not so natural. Believers can achieve oneness in Jesus Christ. Regardless of our differences, followers of the Lord can have a unity that is remarkable! Unlike the "birds of a feather who flock together," the body of Christ is incredibly diverse. People who would not normally come together find themselves sharing a deep bond in our shared love of Jesus!

What a beautiful testimony to find this unity in a world that is so divided! Love that reaches across generation, gender, and race is the mark of a Christian (John 13:35). It is not natural. I want that mark on my life, but it can only happen with the fruit of the Spirit in me. It helps to remember that down deep, my soul is exactly the same as my neighbor's. I see differences but the Lord looks on the heart (1 Samuel 16:7).

Lord, thank you that You can bring together what the world cannot!

Psalm 119:45

I will walk about in freedom, for I have sought your precepts.

Enjoying the View

I imagine that anyone with a fear of heights would give this overlook a wide berth. This view of canyons and mountain peaks is a panoramic one, going in all directions. The overlook affords a dizzying view of the valley below. But this open plateau edge drops suddenly away 1,600 feet above the valley floor! If it were not for that sturdy rail going around the perimeter, I would not feel free to walk very close to the edge and I would miss out on those amazing views.

Today's verse puts two words together that normally one would not think to do; freedom and precepts. Prevalent thinking equates freedom with no rules or restrictions at all. But God's law is like the railing. Because of its presence I can freely walk about and enjoy incredible vistas. God's law provides safety and protection. They are there, not to restrict and be a burden, but rather to free us to walk in confidence. God's law even alleviates our anxiety. "Great peace have those who love Your law, and nothing can make them stumble" (Psalm 119:165).

The author of this psalm cannot say enough about how he loves God's law. He describes it as giving comfort (verse 52). God's statutes and precepts reassure me of the right direction my life is taking. I never have to wonder if another way is better or more exciting. I do not miss out on anything except what will harm me. His law is an expression of His love for me. Following it gives me the best kind of life there is!

Lord, keep me walking in the freedom that following Your law brings!

James 4:1

What causes fights and quarrels among you? Don't they come from your desires that battle within you?

Locked Antlers

The bull moose antlers are impressive with a spread of up to six feet! They can weigh as much as forty pounds. Each year they are shed and grown anew until old age. Their size shows their status and strength, especially during mating season. They are made of bone and are one single structure. Two bull moose with similar sized antlers will face off and lock antlers over a female. How sad when they get their antlers so entangled that they are unable to free themselves, and die!

Today's verse was addressed to believers in the church. These early Christians struggled with the very same thing we do today. Desires battling within eventually show themselves in tensions and quarrels without. The desires mentioned here are probably the result of "friendship with the world" (verse 4). They desired what they did not have. Praying for their desires would not have resolved the situation. That is because they were asking with wrong motives and would spend what they received on themselves (verses 2–3). Their desires needed to change.

Most of my desires would probably fall into this same category. I wish I could say differently. The pull of the world is strong, and so is envying what others have. In my heart of hearts I know that possessions do not bring me true joy, but it sure is easy to be distracted! And when my selfish desires get in the way of a relationship I know it has gone too far.

Lord, may my desires be honoring to You.

Psalm 56:8

Record my misery; list my tears on your scroll—are they not in your record?

Lily of the Valley

In France, bouquets of lily of the valley are offered to friends on May first to wish them luck and happiness. This day (their Labor Day) is called "Fête du Travail" or "Fête du Muguet" meaning lily of the valley. I love their delicacy and sweet smell. Legend has it that these are the tears of Eve as she was banished from the Garden of Eden.

Today's verse tells us there is a scroll belonging to the Lord that records our tears. With this beautiful imagery we understand that God knows about every deception and every sorrow. The Lord is aware of and records every tear drop. King David had plenty of occasions to shed tears. When he wrote this psalm he was on the run for his life. His enemies were constantly after him. Apparently, real men DO cry. But he was confident the Lord knew of his circumstances and his feelings. When David cried out, he was reassured that God was with him and for him.

He sees my tears too. Although this is poetic imagery, I like to think of Him saving every drop. It shows me that I am precious to Him. He even sees the unshed tears that stick in my throat. God's awareness of my circumstances and emotions would be meaningless if He did not also care. But He not only cares, He has the power to do something about it! He consoles like no other. He comforts. He sees and understands. He reassures me that He is on my side. No one else can dry my tears like He can.

Lord, thank you that one day there will be no more tears.

Jeremiah 32:17

Ah, Sovereign Lord, you have made the heavens and the earth by your great power and outstretched arm. Nothing is too hard for you.

Magic or Miracle?

Our grandson on his fourth birthday was front and center with that magician, mesmerized by the seemingly impossible feats performed. Lately, he has been drawn to all things magic, including hats, capes, and wands. But the awe on all of their sweet faces was priceless. These little boys were properly amazed but the parents were impressed as well with the sleight of hand. Who doesn't like to be astonished by what looks to be impossible?

Today's verse describes not magic, but the miraculous. God's power is evident in the creation of the heavens and the earth. No tricks or sleight of hand were needed, only His incredible outstretched arm. The heavens and earth testify to His great miraculous power. By seeing and appreciating His power in creation, we can be assured that absolutely nothing is too hard for Him!

I have evidence of God's power all around me. And yet, I am sometimes so accustomed to it that it no longer seems miraculous. Sure, the sun will rise tomorrow morning. Of course principles of gravity will continue to hold true. However, everything that God does is miraculous. Anything produced by the power of God is a "miracle." But when His miracles become commonplace to me, I begin to wonder if something could be too hard for Him. I need to have that childlike wonder when seeing a caterpillar or gazing at the stars. When I do, then my faith grows as I realize that NOTHING is too hard for Him to accomplish in my life!

Lord, help me to trust Your incredible power!

Galatians 6:1–2

Brothers and sisters, if someone is caught in a sin, you who live by the Spirit should restore that person gently. But watch yourselves, or you also may be tempted. Carry each other's burdens, and in this way you will fulfill the law of Christ.

Caring Dolphins

A while back, I took my daughter whale watching but all we saw were dolphins. Neither of us was disappointed though. They are so much fun to watch, jumping, frolicking, and following our boat. Dolphins are such intelligent mammals and often will "bow-ride," swimming alongside a ship to conserve energy. But what is really surprising is their altruism! A dolphin will stay by another ill or injured dolphin, even helping them to the surface to breathe!

Today's verse is addressed to those who are living and walking by the Spirit. Restoring a fellow believer who is broken with sin is more than just altruism but a command. This act of love and caring is done with kindness, tenderness, and a gentle spirit. When we restore someone to a close relationship with the Lord, we listen, we cry, we share, we pray together, and we encourage confession. How amazing it is to see God's forgiveness make one whole again!

There are really two prerequisites to restoring a believer caught in sin. The first is to be in right relationship with the Lord myself. The second is to care—to care and love so much that I am willing to be involved, even long term. To care that much means being a servant with my time. It also means caring enough to risk misunderstanding and perhaps a broken relationship as a result of speaking truth. But what a privilege to be used by Him to bring someone back!

Lord, make me willing to care that much!

The precepts of the Lord are right, giving joy to the heart. The commands of the Lord are radiant, giving light to the eyes.

Indoor Herb Garden

My grandsons were pretty excited to help their daddy put a herb garden together! They started with pots of rosemary, cilantro, and basil and have since added several more. When "helping" their mommy make dinner, they are much more likely to eat that strange dish when they have picked the herbs for it. But to begin with, the herbs did not do so well in the living room. They did not have much light there. It was not until they were placed in brighter room full of light that there was growth.

Today's verse describes God's commandments as light to the eyes. His precepts are radiant with light and can even make us joyful when obeyed. He has made His light to shine in the heart of the believer. That light comes from the glory displayed in the face of Christ (2 Corinthians 4:6). Following His commands and precepts places us in the light of His presence. Being there produces the "fruit of the light": goodness, righteousness, and truth (Ephesians 5:9).

I can tell when I am trying to produce these fruits on my own. The goodness starts to wilt. Righteousness and truth are looking a bit peaked. Without His light I am not so robust, but a bit tired. Everything is an effort and it all seems too much. Whether the image is light or being connected to the vine, without Him I can do nothing. But in His light I can grow and thrive. When I feel discouraged and lacking motivation, I just need to get back into the light of His presence!

Shine on me today, Lord. Help me stay in Your light.

Joshua 24:15

But if serving the Lord seems undesirable to you, then choose for yourselves this day whom you will serve . . . But as for me and my household, we will serve the Lord.

Bald Eagle's Nest

The nest or aerie of a bald eagle is the largest of any North American bird. They can measure up to thirteen feet deep and eight feet wide! Along with sticks, the eagle uses moss, grass, plant stalks, lichens, seaweed, and sod. The bole area for their young is lined with softer material and down feathers. Recently, the public was reminded to keep the areas in their vicinity clear of trash. Apparently, the eagles will sometimes make use of the trash on the ground to build up their nests.

Today's verse is part of a charge Joshua gave the Israelites just before his death. He admonished the people to fear the Lord and serve Him faithfully by throwing out the gods of their ancestors. Joshua challenged them to choose! Then comes the declaration that he and his household choose to serve the Lord. There will be no compromise by allowing the trash of false gods to cross his threshold.

I want to have that same resolve as Joshua. One would think that false gods would not really be an issue. But a "god" can be anything I prioritize and value more than my Savior. In allowing other things to take His place, my nest or house might grow larger and more impressive to some. But it is foolish to be building my house on what is essentially sand (Matthew 7:26). It is by wisdom that a house is built (Proverbs 24:3). And when I am fearing and obeying Him, I am being wise (Psalm 111:10). May all who enter my house see exactly who we choose to serve!

Lord, I choose You.

Deuteronomy 32:4

He is the Rock, his works are perfect, and all his ways are just. A faithful God who does no wrong, upright and just is he.

Delicate Arch

The Delicate Arch is one of the over 2,000 found in Arches National Park in Utah. Other notable arches have names like Landscape Arch, Double Arch, and Broken Arch. Their odd formations are the result of centuries of erosion carving layer and layer of rock away. They look like they could last forever with their impressive height, this one standing 46 feet tall. But in fact, each arch is fated to one day fall, as did the Wall Arch in 2008.

There is another Rock that will never fall or face erosion. Today's verse describes our God as a Rock. His perfection will never change. Everything He does is perfect and just. Most of all, this Rock is faithful and can be counted on to always and forever be there, strong and solid. He will never do wrong, as He is upright and just. He is THE Rock and there is no one like Him (Psalm 18:31). Because He is my rock, "I will never be shaken" (Psalm 62:2). "He is my rock of refuge to which I can always go" (Psalm 71:3). And most of all, God is the "Rock of my salvation" (Psalm 95:1).

How reassuring to be reminded of His permanence. Nothing will ever change Him or His promises to me. Even when I am unfaithful, He will always remain faithful and true to Himself. In a world where everything is in a constant state of change, He continues perfectly unchanged. I can run to Him for everything I need. Being a rock, He gives me the stability I need.

Thank you, Lord, that I can always count on You!

Ephesians 6:18

And pray in the Spirit on all occasions with all kinds of prayers and requests. With this in mind, be alert and always keep on praying for all the Lord's people.

Praying Mantis

This mantis looks to have been interrupted in his prayers! These alien-looking insects got their name from their prayer-like stance. These strange creatures are the only insects that can turn their heads 180 degrees! They may look like they are praying but in fact they are very alert and highly visual, noticing any disturbance in their environment. Even when flying at night, some are able to avoid bats, detecting their echolocation sounds.

Today's verse encourages the believer to pray on any and every occasion. This verse closes out the passage talking about how to fight the spiritual war. The battle we wage is not fought individually but in concert with others. Of course we pray for ourselves. We want strength, protection, and greater faith. But we are also to be praying for all of the Lord's people facing the same challenges we do.

I am told to be alert. I need to have my "antennae" up and sensitive to needs around me. All it takes is to turn my head in a half circle to see someone who needs prayer. My prayers can lift up and encourage a fallen soldier. Praying for another encourages them to get back in the battle and to persevere. I sometimes feel that praying for others is not as important as some of the other ways I serve Him. How often I have heard (or said), "Well, I guess all I can really do is pray for her." Are not our prayers the most important thing we can do?

Lord, make me a faithful prayer warrior today!

1 Corinthians 15:51–52

Listen, I tell you a mystery: We will not all sleep, but we will all be changed—in a flash, in the twinkling of an eye, at the last trumpet. For the trumpet will sound, the dead will be raised imperishable, and we will be changed.

Jacaranda Trees

I love the time of year when the Jacaranda tree is in bloom. Their purple color is so vibrant it almost looks unreal, like something from Dr. Seuss! When several of these trees line a street, their blooms resemble a sea of lavender. And when their blossoms drop to the ground, their beauty continues as a lilac carpet. It seems appropriate that their flowers are in the shape of a trumpet, as they herald the coming of summer!

The trumpet in our verse today has a very special meaning. Sounding it will signal the resurrection. It does not say who will blow this trumpet—perhaps an angel—but it will be heard all over the world. When it is blown, those believers who have died will receive their new incorruptible bodies. Those believers still living at the time will also be changed. Death will forever be swallowed up in victory (verse 54)! What a day that will be!

One future day I will hear a trumpet sound that will announce the end of time. Death will no longer sting, and sin will be powerless. My body will be changed to be imperishable. Knowing this helps me to stay steadfast, immovable, and involved in what He wants me to do. He has promised that my work for Him will never be futile or in vain (verse 58). Thinking about what is to come keeps me motivated and encouraged!

Lord, keep me listening for that trumpet!

John 10:4–5

When he has brought out all his own, he goes on ahead of them, and his sheep follow him because they know his voice. But they will never follow a stranger; in fact, they will run away from him because they do not recognize a stranger's voice.

Calling All Cows

Seeing these cows on my walk reminded me of thirty black and white dairy cows in Normandy. In 1943, their owner left them in a field as the Germans were advancing. He was able to return for them but some French opportunists had taken them for their own. They challenged my friend's grandfather to prove the cows were his. So he told them to call the cows over. Of course, the cows just looked at those interlopers and did not budge. But when the true owner called them, they all immediately got up and approached!

Today's verse describes the same phenomenon but with sheep. Jesus was addressing the Pharisees, but they were not understanding His meaning. Jesus then identifies Himself as the Good Shepherd who lays down His life for His sheep. Those who are His sheep know and recognize His voice and follow Him.

Not only is the Lord's voice recognizable, but He calls each sheep by name (verse 3)! And when He speaks to me, I will know it is Him. He will never say anything in opposition to what He has already said in His Word, the Bible. His voice does not condemn as he has already laid down His life as payment for every sin. His voice will never accuse or tear down. His words are full of love, even when He says something difficult to hear. His voice is soft and tender as He draws me closer to Himself.

Lord, let me hear Your voice today.

Ephesians 4:29

Do not let any unwholesome talk come out of your mouths, but only what is helpful for building others up according to their needs, that it may benefit those who listen.

Impatiens

I tried growing impatiens in our long narrow yard while living in Grenoble, France. They seemed to really thrive in the climate and soil. But I eventually gave up, as our rabbit kept thinking they were his lunch! This flower is said to be a symbol of motherly love, as they easily release and scatter their seed at the slightest touch. It certainly is not indicative of motherly love with its other names; "touch-me-not" and "snap weed."

Today's verse would be great on the wall of every family room! Somehow, the standards in this verse are especially difficult to live out with those closest to us. Within those four walls we feel free to speak our mind without any filters. We allow ourselves to snap at others or use our words to distance ourselves from those around us. However, the standard for our words is that they be helpful and beneficial to those listening. And we are to build up and encourage others in a way that speaks to their needs.

More often than not, my words are expressed according to my need to say them. I often am unaware or uncaring as to the needs of the listener. But with that attitude, conversation is usually cut short. If my words are not building up, they are perhaps subtly tearing down. How much does it really cost me to compliment or encourage? I want my words to be sweet to the soul and healing to the bones (Proverbs 16:24). I want my words to be kind, compassionate, and forgiving.

Lord, make my words as gracious as Yours.

Proverbs 17:24

A discerning person keeps wisdom in view, but a fool's eyes wander to the ends of the earth.

Walking the Dogs

In walking our daughter's dogs, there are two different lengths for the leashes. Both dogs are fairly obedient, but Paco, the smaller black one, needs the shorter leash. He was an abandoned stray, and we are not sure what he lived through before becoming part of the family. But whatever it was, he thinks he can take on any other dog he sees and lets them know it! He also is very distracted by any and every smell he encounters, which makes for lots of pulling on that leash. His cooperation does not come easily!

Today's verse describes a fool whose eyes wander away from what is wise. Wisdom is like that shorter leash that keeps the discerning person from wandering. The fool is easily distracted away from wisdom. Wandering aimlessly is how the adulteress is described and she does not even know it (Proverbs 5:6). Some wander away from the faith because of their love of money (1 Timothy 6:10). Without the shorter leash of wisdom, we wander all over the mountains and hills, following the wrong shepherds and forgetting where to find our resting place (Jeremiah 50:6).

Christ is the wisdom of God (1 Corinthians 1:24). I know that connecting to Him is wise. He is the One who keeps me on the right path. The problem is that I am "prone to wander . . . prone to leave the God I love." I am so easily distracted. I pull on that leash to go check something out and end up going in the wrong direction. When I trust in my own understanding or ideas, I am out of step with Him. His direction and His pace are always the best.

Lord, make me wise by following You.

Philippians 3:12

Not that I have already obtained all this, or have already arrived at my goal, but I press on to take hold of that for which Christ Jesus took hold of me.

Driftwood

There is no mystery at all as to why "driftwood" is called driftwood. It is simply wood that has drifted. The wood comes to be in the water through flooding or storms breaking off tree branches. Or it could be there as a result of logging. In any case, the wood drifts aimlessly at the whim of the waves. When and where it washes up on to shore seems completely arbitrary. Just like for some people, circumstances push and prod to move a body from here to there with no clear goal in mind.

In today's verse, Paul lives his life with a specific goal in mind. He wants to gain Christ (verse 8), to be found in Christ (verse 9), and to know Christ (verse 10). Paul not only wanted to know Jesus and His power, but he was also ready to suffer for His sake. He was willing to completely deny himself and take up his cross to follow Him (Luke 9:23). His goals would last a lifetime and make his life significant. There would be no aimless drifting through life for him!

What is my purpose? Because I belong to Him, I want the goals in my life to match up with His for me. Knowing Him is the most worthwhile purpose there is! And God prepared in advance a whole plan of good works for me to accomplish (Ephesians 2:10). I, like every believer, have a purpose. I do not want to waste time and just drift through life! And I am confident He will give me what it takes to "press on."

Lord, keep me from drifting today.

Philippians 3:13b–14

Forgetting what is behind and straining toward what is ahead, I press on toward the goal to win the prize for which God has called me heavenward in Christ Jesus.

Elephants Never Forget

It is a common adage that "elephants never forget." There have been many scientific studies done and it has been established that although they don't remember every little thing, elephants do have remarkable memories. The older females leading a herd are especially likely to remember previous watering holes. They remember the urine smells of up to thirty other elephants in their herd, distinguishing friend from foe.

Today's verse talks about the value of forgetting something very specific. Paul is saying that to make any progress in our Christian growth, we are to FORGET what is behind. I always assumed, knowing Paul's past of persecuting the Church, that he meant his past sins. However, the context of the passage speaks of his Jewish lineage, his zeal, and his righteousness. He counted his religiosity and good works as rubbish in order to know Christ and to have the righteousness which comes from faith in Him.

Do I pride myself in past accomplishments in the realm of good works? Am I on "cruise control" in my spiritual journey, thinking what I've already done for the Lord can somehow carry me along? Or am I motivated to keep on keeping on? It is a sobering thought to realize that any spiritual pride or SELF-righteousness will keep me from moving forward. Better to forget even the good things in my past if they cause me to be complacent in the present. The Lord wants me to keep pressing on to a deeper and more satisfying relationship with Him.

Lord, keep me motivated to press on.

Isaiah 44:3

For I will pour water on the thirsty land, and streams on the dry ground; I will pour out my Spirit on your offspring, and my blessing on your descendants.

Twisted Garden Hose

Is there anything more frustrating than having to retrace one's steps and straighten out that hose? It seems that the longer the hose, the more likely it is to develop a kink and suddenly stop the flow of water. I hurry to get to the problem because I know that the sudden release of that water when straightening the hose will make the end fly all over the place and spray what it shouldn't: the window, the car or me! It is usually a moment I would rather others not see!

Today's verse talks about God's Spirit and how He can quench our thirst just as water does. His presence gives life and health. With Him and His power, we flourish and grow. He wants to bless those who belong to Him and even their families! Without Him we will eventually wilt, dry up, and bear no fruit. But like a kink in a hose, I can sometimes cut myself off from that source of water; His Spirit.

The flow of water is interrupted through no problem on His part! The water blockage comes from my own pride. I see the good things in my life and very quickly take credit for them. I pat myself on the back for all the good decisions I have made. Rather than recognize the source of everything good in my life, I somehow feel I had something to do with it! My family genes, my financial acumen, or my level of education take center stage rather than His goodness!

Lord, help me see that it is from You that all blessings flow!

Matthew 18:12

What do you think? If a man owns a hundred sheep, and one of them wanders away, will he not leave the ninety-nine on the hills and go to look for the one that wandered off?

Black Sheep

We enjoyed meeting our friend's small herd of sheep in the German countryside. I found it odd that most of them were black, as normally they are more rare. Back in the day, the black sheep was less valuable, as their fleece could not be dyed. Being the "black sheep" of the family could have been a phrase originating with this in mind, denoting a member who was worthless, or a nonconformist, wandering away from the group.

Today's verse describes that individual sheep who, unlike the rest of the herd, wanders off and goes his own way. I love how the shepherd goes after that one who is different and does not conform to the behavior of the group. To our Good Shepherd, each sheep is valuable and worthwhile. The following verses describe the joy of the shepherd in finding that nonconformist sheep. There may be disapproval and disdain from the other sheep, but to the Shepherd, there is unconditional love and acceptance!

How do I see my fleece? Is it black or white, and does it matter? All are sheep and all have wandered off from the Shepherd (Isaiah 53:6). How silly of me to think that I am any better or any worse than the other sheep around me. I was lost and He cared enough to go after me and find me. He has brought me into the fold as He has done with each of us who have responded to Him in faith. We are all the same, in need of being found!

Lord, forgive my critical spirit when looking at other sheep.

Haggai 1:6

You have planted much, but harvested little. You eat, but never have enough. You drink, but never have your fill. You put clothes on, but are not warm. You earn wages, only to put them in a purse with holes in it.

Fear of Holes

These lotus seed pods do not mean to be frightening. But for those who suffer from "trypophobia," or a fear of holes, the sight of them can trigger all kinds of symptoms, including discomfort, goosebumps, eye strain, distress, crawling skin, panic attacks, sweats, nausea, and body shakes. This is not a phobia that is officially recognized. But as with other phobias, the preferred treatment is exposure therapy in an attempt to change one's response.

There was a response that needed changing in today's verse. The returned exiles were to rebuild their temple. But instead of making this a priority, they concentrated on building up their own homes. Somehow, the time was never right to work on God's house (verse 2). There was always something more to do for themselves. The prophet Haggai spoke to them God's Word: "Give careful thought to your ways." Because of their selfish living, they were not experiencing God's blessing! They could never have their fill. There were holes in their purses.

I can fall into this same way of thinking. How easy it is to put myself and my own comfort and convenience first! But when I do, that elusive contentment with what I have is nowhere to be found. "Holes in my purse" drain away any sense of fulfillment. The Lord calls me to put Him first (Matthew 6:33). Living for Him brings such blessing that everything He gives me can be enough. I want Him and His incredible love to be my "enough."

Lord, help me to put You first today.

Luke 12:24

Consider the ravens: They do not sow or reap, they have no storeroom or barn; yet God feeds them. And how much more valuable you are than birds!

Ravenous Ravens

I don't appreciate seagulls, but ravens even less so. They are big, black, shaggy, and noisy. Recently their numbers have increased in California. They prefer building their nests along sea cliffs, being close to the water and being near a variety of food sources. When their territory overlaps with the seagull, it can get noisy! In referring to a group of them, old expressions used the term "unkindness" or "conspiracy" rather than a flock of ravens. The raven is known for being intelligent and opportunistic in finding its food.

Today's verse talks about our God being a God who cares for His creation, including the ravens. Birds do not need to plant for the coming season or hoard their food for the lean times to come. Yet, they do not go hungry. God cares for their short little insignificant lives. By contrast we, being created in God's image, are of so much more value to the Lord. He is intimately involved in every little aspect of our lives.

I need to remind myself that God will take care of what I eat, what I drink, what I will wear, and every other detail. For Him it is just small stuff. Those who do not belong to Him are consumed with these issues. The food and fashion industries encourage us to "seek after these things." But as a believer, I want to have different priorities. I want my mental energies to be spent on His Kingdom and what is of eternal value! He has always provided all that I need.

Thank you, Lord, that Your care shows me that You value me!

Mark 12:30

Love the Lord your God with all your heart and with all your soul and with all your mind and with all your strength.

Little Heart Cockle

The scientific name for this shell is "corculum cardissa" but I prefer the common name, "little heart cockle," as it certainly resembles a heart! This mollusk lives in the Indio-Pacific region, which is why I have never seen one. The shells vary in color but they have a pattern formed from transparent mass and nontransparent mass. Much of their shell is thin and translucent, making them fragile. Yet they are often found intact on the surface of the sand among coral debris and broken shells.

Today's verse is the response Jesus gave to a teacher of the law who asked Him which is the greatest commandment. Following this commandment would make all other commandments a nonissue. When the Lord has all our heart, soul, mind, and strength, then He also has our obedience to all other commands.

My tendency, though, is to keep parts of my heart separate. It is difficult to give Him all of myself. There is fear for what He may ask of me. There is selfishness in wanting to go my own way. What if He asks me to give something or someone up? My goals, my desires, my hopes and dreams are in that part of the heart that is difficult to relinquish. However, giving Him all of my heart poses no risk at all. I can trust Him with the deepest part of myself. He does not hurt my heart and He never disappoints. He has already given all He could for me. My only reasonable response is to give everything back to Him!

Lord, take all of my heart and make it Yours today.

Psalm 119:45

I will walk about in freedom, for I have sought out your precepts.

Free Range

I like the idea that chickens can roam freely to graze and forage for food. The label "Free Range" for poultry implies a freedom of movement in outdoor spaces. It is said that if they do not have the opportunity to peck at the ground, they will often peck at their own feathers. Of course, allowing them to freely graze outdoors does not mean they can run around where they like. They are cage-free but for their own protection they are not barrier-free!

When I think of liberty and being free, I do not normally think of something or someone telling me what to do! But in today's verse, walking in liberty is equated with following God's law. It seems a paradox. How can I walk at liberty and be seeking His law at the same time? This liberty is not freedom to do whatever we please. It is a liberty from the sin that enslaves and entangles us. It is a liberty that allows us to follow Him. Sin can have the power to keep us in chains, obligating us to do evil. But because of what Christ did on the cross, I have the choice to follow His law.

To be honest, I do not always use my liberty like He intends. The pull of the world, my old habits, and just my ugly sin nature all conspire to convince me that I have no choice! But as a believer, I have the power of the Holy Spirit living within me. And where the Spirit of the Lord is, there is freedom (2 Corinthians 3:17). His precepts are the arms that enclose and protect me for my good!

Thank you, Lord, for making me free!

Isaiah 44:3

For I will pour water on the thirsty land and streams on the dry ground; I will pour out my Spirit on your offspring, and my blessing on your descendants.

Cranberry Bog

It about took my breath away! We were driving the back roads near Plymouth, Massachusetts, when we rounded the corner and saw a shimmering field of red! The cranberry bog was being flooded with water and the brilliant October sun was hitting it just right. The farmers flood the area with up to eighteen inches of water to free the cranberries from the vine. Then, because of the small pocket of air contained in the cranberries, they float to the surface, ready to be harvested.

Water is, of course, essential to growing most anything but with "wet harvesting" it also plays an important role in getting access to the fruit. Today's verse pictures God's Spirit like that water so important to fruit production. Without His work we remain a thirsty land. Without His blessing, we continue life as dry ground. But oh, how it all changes when the Holy Spirit moves and works in people's hearts!

When I try producing fruit and good works in my own strength, I am using thirsty land and dry ground. I need the Holy Spirit to flood my efforts with His life-producing water and power. I can do nothing in my own strength. It is not how busy I am doing things for others. It is not how many Bible verses I know. It is allowing Him to work through me as I depend on Him. It is getting my ego out of the way and being about His glory.

Lord, please pour out today the blessing of Your Spirit.

Romans 6:13

Do not offer any part of yourself to sin as an instrument of wickedness, but rather offer yourselves to God as those who have been brought from death to life; and offer every part of yourself to him as an instrument of righteousness.

Musical Instrument

Fascination with musical instruments can start awfully young, as proven by our grandson. Even before the age of two, this little guy was drawn to all kinds. He will spend inordinate amounts of time on the piano. He strums his dad's guitar, his ukulele, or his "air guitar" if nothing else is available! And being separated from his toy saxophone is a painful experience! When hearing music played by an orchestra, he calls out the violin, the flute, the trumpet, and the drums!

Today's verse talks about the different parts of our body as being instruments, either used for righteousness or wickedness. Being a disciple of Jesus means offering one's whole body to Him in complete surrender (Romans 12:1–2). To do this is a reasonable response to the gift of being brought "from death to life." Because our bodies are the temple of His indwelling Spirit (1 Corinthians 6:19), they are meant for the Lord and the Lord for our bodies (verse 13).

I love that my body can be used as an instrument of righteousness. I can be His hands when I share with others in need. I can be His feet when I approach those who are hurting and offer His comfort. I can use my energy to do what will glorify Him. Sometimes I get discouraged with the unending temptations that seem to come with this body. But through Him and His strength, this body can be an instrument He can use.

Lord, make my body an instrument You can use today.

Romans 15:5–6

May the God who gives endurance and encouragement give you the same attitude of mind toward each other that Christ Jesus had, so that with one mind and one voice you may glorify the God and Father of our Lord Jesus Christ.

Bougainvillea

Our bougainvillea is climbing all over our back fence, and its vibrant red color is gorgeous! There are equally vibrant colors of orange, fuchsia, pink, and yellow, but my favorite has always been the red. There are over 300 varieties worldwide and they can grow from 3 to 40 feet tall. But what is surprising is that the actual flower is a small white blossom one sees in the center. The bright colors actually come from the surrounding bracts, which are modified or specialized leaves. Because they are positioned below the flower, I mistake it for the actual flower.

Today's verse talks about collectively glorifying God. The point of the believer's life is not to draw attention to one's self but to Him. We are that small insignificant white flower. But because of pointing people to Him, there is vibrant color in our lives. He makes us beautiful because He is beautiful. And together with other believers, we can be united with one mind and one voice in this purpose of glorifying and praising Him.

Drawing attention to myself, taking credit for what God has done in my life or wanting to take center stage keeps me like that small insignificant white flower. It takes a humble heart to be more about His glory and His name. But with His help I can have that same attitude Christ did (Philippians 2:5). Along with encouragement and endurance, He gives me the desire to give all praise and glory to Him.

Lord, may today be all about giving You the glory You deserve.

Hebrews 6:10

God is not unjust; he will not forget your work and the love you have shown him as you have helped his people and continue to help them.

The Dung Beetle

There is good reason why this is called a "dung beetle," as these little guys feed on feces! They can be seen rolling balls of it bigger than themselves. They will roll it long distances to bury them for the eggs they will hatch. Seeing one of these struggling uphill reminds me of the Greek mythological figure, Sisyphus. His punishment in Hades was to roll a large boulder uphill. At the summit it would repeatedly roll back down so that the struggle began again.

Today's verse is an encouragement to keep on keeping on! God sees and takes note of every work done to help other believers. These good works are in response to the needs around us. But they are done with a motivation that is pure and unsullied. They are done to show the Lord how much we love Him. Believers are to be diligent (verse 11) and not give in to the temptation of letting go (verse 12). These verses remind us that there is reward for our diligence.

It can be discouraging to feel that we are not seeing any result for our work. It can feel like pushing that boulder uphill. But God is not unjust. He sees and remembers each and every act of service I do out of love for Him. It may not be recognized or appreciated here. Regardless of people's response, my motivation is to please and honor Him out of my love for Him. Meeting the needs of others is a concrete way I can show the Lord my love.

Thank you, Lord that You see, You remember, and You reward.

Psalm 78:19

They spoke against God; they said, "Can God really spread a table in the wilderness?"

Table Settings

I love a pretty table setting! Somehow, all that attention to detail makes the food taste better. When I have company over, they may ask to help set my table. But that is something I always reserve for myself. However, this outlet for creativity can be overdone. This table looks a bit crowded as there seems to be no place for the dishes. And sometimes the flowers are too tall to see other table guests!

Today's verse talks about the Lord Himself spreading a table. It was no picnic being in the wilderness year after year. The Israelites complained and repeatedly put God to the test. How gracious He was to rain down manna, called the "grain of heaven" and the "bread of angels" (verses 24–25)! They gorged themselves on meat that He provided. Yet, their hearts were not loyal. Though He provided for their needs again and again, they continually forgot His power (verse 42). How exasperating it must have been for the Lord to hear the question posed in our verse when He had proven Himself over and over.

I imagine that though the Lord loves me, He must sometimes be exasperated with me. Can He really meet this need? Will He come through for me this time? Can I completely count on Him for that? To even have such thoughts reveals that I have forgotten His power. He has already shown Himself faithful time after time. Yes, He can and does spread a table even in the wilderness! When all seems dry and desolate, He provides above and beyond all we can ask or think (Ephesians 3:20).

Thank you, Lord, for spreading a table for me and meeting my every need!

1 Corinthians 15:25–26

For He must reign until He has put all enemies under His feet. The last enemy to be destroyed is death.

The Condor

This vigilant squirrel is right to keep an eye on the condor flying overhead! But perhaps he does not need to worry too much, as the condor will only feed on a carcass. They are scavengers and I suppose they have their place in the scheme of things. But to me they are disgusting because of their eating habits, not to mention their grunts, growls, and hissing! There are two species of vultures to which the condor refers and they are associated with death in Scripture.

Today's verse speaks of death as an enemy. It is an enemy that touches everyone, and each time brings with it unspeakable sorrow. It is an enemy mankind has brought on ourselves by our own sin and rebellion against God (Romans 6:23). But thankfully, death will one day be vanquished forever. There will be a time when there will be no more mourning or death (Revelation 21:4). The pain and sorrow of separation will in the future be a distant memory. Death will take its rightful place, fully vanquished and overcome under His feet.

I know this is true, as Jesus has already vanquished death for Himself when He rose up from the grave. And God has already made me alive spiritually when I was dead in my sins (Ephesians 2:5). But what is true in a spiritual sense will one day be true in a physical sense as well! I will enjoy a new body that will never wear out (1 Corinthians 15:54), and death will be "swallowed up in victory"! No more funerals, obituaries, or burials! And best of all, no more goodbyes!

Thank you, Lord, for the coming victory over death.

Colossians 3:15

Let the peace of Christ rule in your hearts, since as members of one body you were called to peace. And be thankful.

Silkworm Cocoons

We had the privilege of visiting a silk-making factory in Taiwan and seeing all those larvae in their cocoons. The process has been around for almost five thousand years in China. The resulting silk is not only beautiful but soft and silky to the touch. But how strange to think it all starts with worm spit! The unwrapping of each cocoon supplies one long strand of 1,000 feet, three of which are needed for a single thread. In fact, it takes 2,500 cocoons to make one pound of silk. No wonder silk is thought to be such a luxury.

Today's verse points out that believers, though many, form one body. Christ is our head and as the Church we are the body (1 Corinthians 12:12–13). Just as there are many cocoons and strands of thread to make up silk, so we as Christ followers form together just one entity. This does not happen outside of the supernatural peace Christ gives. When we allow that peace to rule and govern attitudes and actions, we can enjoy not only our unity but the beautiful results!

My little strand I add to the whole may not seem like anything. On my own I do not amount to much. But added together with all the other strands I become part of that one beautiful body giving glory to Jesus! I am called to peace by the very One who provides it. And that peace is a direct result of loving and forgiving others (verses 13–14). Loving and forgiving can sometimes seem impossible, but "how good and pleasant it is when God's people live together in unity" (Psalm 133:1).

Lord, help me live this peace.

Genesis 4:7

If you do what is right, will you not be accepted? But if you do not do what is right, sin is crouching at your door; it desires to have you, but you must rule over it.

Tantrums

This sweet little boy is losing it! What toddler has not gone through the temper tantrum stage? The angry emotions become too much to handle and spill out. It can be frustrating or cute, depending on how much sleep the parent has had. But there is a place where temper tantrums are encouraged: the Tantrum Club for women in London. There, one can scream, shout, rant and rave, jump up and down and bash things. The club welcomes this behavior with support because as they say, "You deserve it!"

Today's verse is a warning from the Lord to Cain. Cain's emotions have reached the boiling point. Much more serious than a child's tantrum, his anger is about to erupt in violence. God does not tell Cain to swallow or suppress his emotions. He tells Cain that he must rule over them in order to avoid sinful behavior. As strong as his anger was, Cain always had a choice.

I often rationalize that I deserve to feel the way I do. It is understandable. But I do not have to be the victim of my emotions. They do not have to lead me to sin, not if I can rule over them. There is always a choice whether or not to give in to the anger or frustration. My problem is that I cannot rule over my emotions on my own. There is often a tantrum going on inside. How thankful I am to have the fruit of God's Spirit, offering me self-control.

Lord, rule over my emotions today!

1 John 4:18

There is no fear in love. But perfect love drives out fear, because fear has to do with punishment. The one who fears is not made perfect in love.

Tarantula

My grandson loves spiders. The bigger and hairier the better! A tarantula certainly qualifies! Their size and appearance are frightening, and I would not relish even the idea of them crawling all over me. This off-putting creature burrows into the ground and does not bother with webs. They will sometimes spin a trip wire at the approach of their burrows. The venom in their bite is weaker than most typical bee stings but that does not stop them from provoking fear in most people.

Today's verse talks about fear having no place in a perfect love. In fact, this is a love that drives out fear. The one who struggles with fear of punishment does not have that complete and perfect love. Because God showed His love by sending His Son to die in our place (verses 9–10), we can know and rely on the love God has for us (verse 16). The punishment for sin has already taken place for those who put their faith in Christ.

How awful it would be to try to love and serve the Lord out of fear of pain and punishment! That is not love at all but obligation and coercion. But because He took the initiative and paid for my sin, I can enjoy a complete, undivided, and sincere love for Him. I am not weighed down with guilt and shame. There is no doubt that He loves me. He has paid the price for my sin and guilt forever! I am free to love Him completely and enjoy His love without fear.

Thank you, Lord, for Your perfect love without fear.

Psalm 112:4

Even in darkness, light dawns for the upright, for those who are gracious and compassionate and righteous.

Poinsettia

I love seeing the red and green of the poinsettia at Christmas time! This native flower to Mexico is referred to as "Flower of the Good Night." The reason for this term is the way the poinsettia becomes so colorful. It is only after twelve to fifteen hours of darkness a day for a period of three months that the leaves (or bracts) become a vibrant red.

Today's verse is a wonderful reassurance that the darkness the believer experiences will not be indefinite. Those who belong to the Lord are upright because of Christ's righteousness. And we are assured that eventually there will be a dawn. Often in Scripture, darkness represents calamity and light represents well-being. No one is exempt from dark times. Regardless of education, wealth, health, or status, we all face some kind of crisis or suffering. But for the believer, there is a dawn coming! For the one made righteous through Christ, there is hope.

What is amazing to me is that even in the darkness, there is blessing. The Lord is actively at work in that darkness. He is using all the negative in my life to test and refine my faith. Every hurt and disappointment, He uses to grow me more like Him. He does not waste any pain or difficulty but He utilizes it all to change me. What a comfort to know He is in control! When I finally exit that time of darkness, I am different. Because of His work and grace, I can emerge more colorful. Perseverance, endurance, and stronger faith are the colors He produces through that dark time.

Thank you, Lord, that you know what You are doing and I can trust You.

John 14:2

My Father's house has many rooms; if that were not so, would I have told you that I am going there to prepare a place for you?

Pet Adoption

I could never visit an animal shelter. I would want to bring at least half of the animals home with me! I have the same problem when visiting a pet store. As tempting as it is, one thing that keeps me grounded is knowing that I have not prepared for one. There are so many considerations, including whether the pet will fit with my lifestyle, and whether my living arrangements will be suitable.

Today's verse talks about a place that is being prepared for the eventual arrival of the believer to his eternal home. Every consideration has been taken. The One preparing this place knows about every desire, preference, and need. That is because He is the Creator and knows us better than we know ourselves. This place will be exactly what we did not know we wanted! And when we finally arrive, this prepared place will immediately be "home" more than any other place we have ever lived.

The particulars are not so important to me. The details will be fabulous, but what will make this place He has prepared so special is the fact that it is in His house! He will be residing there as well. His continual and uninterrupted presence will make this place "home." It will be my forever home, and that illusive contentment I have been chasing all my life will be mine! What other home could be decorated with perfect love, peace, joy, and satisfaction? It is there waiting for me to move in, and when I do, I will feel settled for the very first time.

Thank you, Lord, that You love me enough to prepare a place for me!

Proverbs 2:7–8

He holds success in store for the upright, he is a shield to those whose walk is blameless, for he guards the course of the just and protects the way of his faithful ones.

Bumper Bowling

Maybe I would feel differently about bowling had I grown up using these bumpers. Imagine no more gutter balls! But I did not have this luxury, and I was on my own trying to get that uncooperative ball to reach any of those bored pins. It was not as if my dad did not try to teach me. He was in a bowling league at his work and had his own ball. He and his team won trophies, and of course no serious bowler would consent to using these bumpers. But I love the idea of having that little edge to correct the course of my wayward ball.

Today's verse is beautiful! The Lord God wants us to succeed, but true success is only found in a relationship that follows His course. None of His commands are arbitrary. They exist for our good and for our protection. Through His Word, He speaks and guides. When we obey and follow His perfect way, we enjoy the blessing of intimacy with Him.

I look at those bumpers as His grace to forgive, correct, and restore. Even with the best of intentions I fail. I am "prone to wander" off His path. But because I belong to Him, He does not let this silly sheep stray too far. Sometimes that corrective bump can be a bit of a shock and not at all comfortable. But it is just what is needed to get me back on course.

Lord, I want to always be one of Your faithful ones. Keep me on that path of righteousness today.

Psalm 71:20

Though you have made me see troubles, many and bitter, you will restore my life again; from the depths of the earth you will again bring me up.

Bitter Melon

Bitter melon looks nothing like a melon! It looks more like a cucumber and it is not only its taste which can discourage a try but also its bumpy warty skin! This very bitter fruit is grown in tropical areas of Africa, Asia, the Caribbean, and South America. It is also known as balsam pear, bitter squash, karela, and goya. The bitter melon is believed to aid digestion and improve overall health. It is even believed to help in treating diabetes and cancer, although the research is not conclusive.

Today's verse talks about many bitter troubles. David has had his share with his enemies seeking to kill him. He has also lived with some very unhappy family relationships. Yet he remains confident that his troubles will be short-lived. He looks to the future with hope that God, though allowing the bitter trouble, will restore and lift him up once again. David can say this as he has already seen the Lord do just that for him. This psalm is full of testimony to God's wonderful, faithful care.

Although I enjoy God's blessings, I am not spared "many and bitter troubles." And Peter tells me not to think it strange to experience fiery trials (1 Peter 4:12). But like David, I do not want to allow something difficult and even bitter to make me bitter! He is there through all of it and is ready to restore and lift me up from the depths of disappointment, dashed hopes, and depression. In fact, He is the only One able to do it!

Thank you, Lord, that You are my hope and comfort!

Leviticus 19:18

Do not seek revenge or bear a grudge against anyone among your people, but love your neighbor as yourself. I am the Lord.

Naming Cockroaches

These cockroaches have a name: the Madagascar hissing cockroach. But for those who keep them as pets, they probably have an additional name, such as Bob or Linda. And for the equivalent of two dollars, you can name a cockroach at the Hemsley Conservation Centre near London for Valentine's Day. No, the cockroach is not the love of your life but the EX love of your life! The first names appear on a roach board next to the cockroach enclosure. Participants who exact this revenge receive a certificate and a half-price entry!

Today's verse can be convicting. It is repeated throughout Scripture that we are not to take revenge (Romans 12:19). That job is done much better by the Lord who sees hearts and is righteous. However, holding a grudge is something that we feel entitled to do, reminding ourselves that it is not okay what was done to us. Unfortunately, holding a grudge just keeps the memory alive and keeps the offender at arm's length.

So often, the guilty one is unaware of that unforgiving spirit I harbor. It certainly does nothing to him. The pain I continue to feel becomes self-inflicted and can become more important than the original offense. But to forgive and forget seems as if I am letting that person get away with something. The closer the offender is to me, the deeper the wound. It is impossible to forgive and let go without the Lord. Because He forgives me and does not hold a grudge, He empowers me to do the same. It can only happen as I continually give it to Him.

Lord, help me to relinquish my hurt to You.

Psalm 107: 28–29

Then they cried out to the Lord in their trouble, and he brought them out of their distress. He stilled the storm to a whisper; the waves of the sea were hushed.

Sea Sickness

These poor men! This photo is from a postcard of American soldiers suffering from seasickness on the deck of the USS Powhatan during World War I. The misery on their faces says it all! Not all of them seem to be affected. And the waves cannot be too awfully strong as the deck remains level. But it does not take much motion for the sensitive stomach to churn.

Today's verse talks of merchants who were used to life on the sea. But this time, the Lord Himself stirred up a tempest that created huge waves (verse 25). Their courage melted away as they staggered around like drunkards. This was outside their normal area of expertise. Even so, it was not until they were at their "wits' end" (verse 27) that they cried out to the Lord. And when they did, He brought them out of their distress, stilling that storm and hushing the waves. Coming out of it, they were thankful for the calm.

I take the calm in my life for granted—that is, just until the waves grow large! I am like these sea merchants in thinking I can handle the sudden storm. But I quickly realize that I cannot. What starts as a queasy stomach can turn into full-grown panic as my small efforts do not seem to amount to much. How good and faithful He is to respond to my cry! Whether that storm is of my own making or a test from Him, my first thought should always be to humbly ask for His help.

Thank you, Lord, that You can still my storm.

1 John 3:19

This is how we know that we belong to the truth and how we set our hearts at rest in his presence.

Restless Dogs

This poor pug looks grumpy and sleep-deprived! Have you ever seen a dog circle and circle his bed before finally lying down? Or there's the dog that paces back and forth. The restless dog will repeatedly adjust his sleep position, unable to lie still. The reason for this behavior could be the pain of arthritis or a sign of doggy anxiety. But this restlessness is not just a problem for dogs! Everything can be positive in life and yet one can still have a restless spirit.

Today's verse talks about a heart that is at rest. When we know and are convinced that we belong to the truth, there is a resting settled feeling in our hearts. In His presence, we feel His peace, knowing that we belong to Him. No longer are our hearts restless, wandering, or searching. When we belong to Him, our hearts can no longer condemn us, as He is greater than our hearts (verse 20). We can have confidence before God as He knows everything and He knows our hearts better than we do ourselves! When we believe in God's Son, Jesus Christ, our hearts are finally at rest (verse 23).

When my heart is at rest, there is a confident peace. He does not want my heart to be restless or troubled (John 14:27). His Spirit testifies with my spirit that I am God's own (Romans 8:16) and reassures my heart. How good He is to give me that heart at rest! And how much I want that for friends and family members who live restless lives without Him.

Lord, may I feel that heart rest today.

All things are wearisome, more than one can say. The eye never has enough of seeing, nor the ear its fill of hearing.

Something Missing

This bizarre bronze statue was created by Bruno Catalano and can be seen in Marseilles, France. The artist, having been a sailor for twenty years, created in his art his idea of a world citizen. Every time he personally left a place, he felt he left pieces of himself behind. Perhaps most everyone can relate, as "Everyone has missing pieces in his life that he won't find again." This is a much more artistic way of expressing the lyrics of "I Left My Heart in San Francisco"!

Today's verse is something a world traveler may eventually feel. In the beginning of exploring our world, there is much to see, hear, and experience. King Solomon had all the resources needed to experience life to the fullest. Every desire to see and hear was fulfilled. And yet those experiences did not fulfill him. The desire to see more is always there. The longing to hear more is never satisfied. There is something missing. The search for something new, exotic, and different becomes wearisome. It does not fulfill something deep within. There is still an emptiness.

I suppose one could call me a world traveler after having visited close to twenty-five countries. I am privileged to have seen and heard a lot! I know a number of people who are "minimalists," decrying the accumulation of things and instead filling their lives with seeing and hearing experiences. But eventually it all becomes wearisome without that relationship with the Creator. He is the One who fulfills my life, filling in all the empty places.

Thank you, Lord that You are more satisfying than anything I can see or hear!

Psalm 57:3

He sends from heaven and saves me, rebuking those who hotly pursue me—God sends forth his love and his faithfulness.

Chased by a Moose!

Some snowboarders at a ski resort in Breckenridge, Colorado got the surprise of their lives when chased by a moose! The animal looked calm enough, but at one point must have felt threatened as they zipped by on their boards! Just before charging, the ears of a moose are laid back and the hairs on its hump are raised. If pursued by a moose, it is recommended to either run or take cover behind something solid like a tree.

Today's verse speaks of being hotly pursued. David is running from an enemy who is intent on destroying him: Saul. Unlike a moose whose charge is sometimes only a warning, this pursuit was to the death! David cries out to the Lord for mercy. He takes cover in a cave, and God protects David out of His love and faithfulness. Because David's heart is steadfast, he can sing and make music in the middle of disaster (verse 7). His trust and confidence is so strong that he describes God's love as reaching to the heavens and His faithfulness to the skies (verse 10).

I am amazed at David's trust in God while being so relentlessly pursued! Rather than respond with fear or complaint, David looks past his circumstances to the love and faithfulness of God. His situation sure did not stimulate this praise. And sometimes, neither does mine. It can be hard to praise Him when faced with unnerving conflict and injustice. But when I call to mind His love for me I can be confident. When I remember His faithfulness, my heart can take courage. He will fight for me. He will vindicate me.

Lord, remind today of Your love and faithfulness.

Acts 1:11

Men of Galilee," they said, "why do you stand here looking into the sky? This same Jesus, who has been taken from you into heaven, will come back in the same way you have seen him go into heaven.

Looking Up

Do you see what I see in these clouds? A friend took this photo and she did not even have to suggest what was there. Facing to the left of the picture is what looks like a huge gorilla head. She calls it a monkey blowing kisses! Perhaps one has to use the imagination. But I love looking up in the clouds and seeing different shapes and what they suggest.

Today's verse was addressed to the disciples by two angels at the occasion of Christ's return to heaven. They had just seen Him taken up into the sky and then hidden by a cloud (verse 9). These angels reassured them that He would be coming back, and in the same manner. Somehow at Christ's return, clouds will be involved. Jesus Himself foretold that He would come on the "clouds of heaven" (Matthew 26:64). And one day, every eye will see Him coming with the clouds (Revelation 1:7).

Whether I see strange clouds or not, I want to keep looking up. It is then that I am reminded of His faithfulness, which reaches to the skies (Psalm 36:5). That huge expanse of sky is His creation, and nothing is too hard for Him. He always keeps His word and I can trust Him. What He says, He will do. When I see those clouds overhead, I want to say with firm conviction, "Maranatha," the Lord is coming! He has promised.

Lord, keep me looking up today.

Psalm 20:7

Some trust in chariots and some in horses, but we trust in the name of the Lord our God.

Loving Horses

The bond between a horse and its owner can be so special. Through lots of time and patient training, the horse and owner can have a relationship like no other. It may be that a horse races up to see you, neighs a greeting at the sight of you, or follows you everywhere, wanting your attention. Their loyalty and intelligence is impressive. After much time spent together, a high degree of trust can be established and they can remember you after months of separation.

In today's verse, one can choose to place their confidence in their horses and chariots or in the name of the Lord. I am so glad that now horses are not used so much for war, but in biblical times they were important to battle effectively. Victory or defeat was largely determined by who had the sturdiest chariots and the swiftest horses.

The choice presented in this verse is basically the same today. I can choose to place my trust in my own efforts and resources, or I can depend on the strength of the Lord. It is the Lord who gives victory with the power of His right hand (verse 6). To trust in myself is no guarantee of victory. It is trusting in His name and who He is that changes the outcome of my battle. However, I cannot trust who I do not know. It is only through a close relationship with Him that I can develop that trust. The more I get to know Him, the more likely I am to absolutely depend on Him. The more time I spend with Him, the more I am convinced of just how trustworthy He is!

Lord, keep me close and trusting You.

Proverbs 18:10

The name of the Lord is a fortified tower; the righteous run to it and are safe.

Eiffel Tower?

This reproduction of the famous Eiffel Tower sits at a round point down the street from us in the small town of Buhl, France. No one would mistake it for its huge counterpart but I wondered why it was built there. I learned that the Eiffel Tower could very well be called the Koechlin Tower as Maurice Koechlin, born in Buhl, was the one who had designed it as an employee of Mr. Eiffel. As this monument is said to be the most visited in the world, it is too bad that Koechlin did not get his name associated with the tower.

Today's verse speaks of the name of the Lord as a different kind of tower, a fortified one. His name represents all that He is and His character. Running to Him as our tower of safety is an image of placing all our hope and faith in His power to protect and deliver. This is in stark contrast to the rich who imagine that their wealth is a wall too high to scale (verse 11).

His name is Faithful and True (Revelation 19:11), and He has promised safety and protection from the wicked (Psalm 37:17). When I run to Him, it is in faith, knowing that He will be true and faithful to His Word. I am safe knowing that no evil can touch me without His knowledge and permission. And certainly, no evil can touch my soul, that which I have committed to Him. He is able to keep my soul against that day (2 Timothy 1:12). What comfort this is in a world where sometimes it seems that evil has the upper hand!

Thank you, Lord, for being my safety and security!

Satisfy us in the morning with your unfailing love, that we may sing for joy and be glad all our days.

Black Hole

Theory has it that falling into a black hole would stretch one out like a long piece of spaghetti! These strange phenomena in space cannot really be seen, being black. But scientists know they are there from the gravity pulling on the stars and gases surrounding it. They are thought to be the result of collapsed stars, and their gravitational pull is extremely powerful. The black hole grows enormous as nearby dust and gas fall into it. It grows larger but never becomes full!

Today's verse describes where satisfaction is to be found. God's love does not change or falter. It is unfailing and can be the best beginning of the day. God's love satisfies the relentless searching of our souls. When we are satisfied with His love, our lives are marked by songs of joy and gladness. Without His love, the search for satisfaction can be like that black hole. We can grab at whatever we can grasp to fill the hole inside ourselves. But nothing else can quite fill that void. We are made for a close intimate relationship with our Creator.

The minute my eyes fly open in the morning is the best time to appreciate and revel in His love! Before the distractions and obligations of the day begin, I want to acknowledge His love and care. He has given me another day of life. He is there to walk through the day with me, His presence being my security. His love will never fail me. He has promised. Thinking on this truth brings satisfaction to my day before it even begins!

Lord, satisfy me today with Your love.

Psalm 127:2

In vain you rise early and stay up late, toiling for food to eat—for he grants sleep to those he loves.

Let Sleeping Dogs Lie

I never thought of a dog as being a sleep aid! But in fact, a study by researchers at Canisius College in Buffalo, New York, found that women sleep better with a dog in their bed! Apparently, both cats and humans are equally disruptive to a woman's sleep. I can think of some other disruptions too! But dogs are less likely to wake their owners. And dogs provide a feeling of comfort and security.

Today's verse comes from a psalm written by Solomon, who has lots to say about vanity. It is vain to make life all about acquisition. He should know, as he did not deny himself any possession or pleasure (Ecclesiastes 2:10–11). Yet when he surveyed all that he had toiled to achieve, it was meaningless. God chooses to bless His loved ones and does so apart from our own toil, even in sleep. The Bible is full of verses on being a good conscientious worker and not a sluggard. But toiling incessantly is not the goal of life.

Living with a constant stress that interferes with sleep is not God's plan. This world is so fast-paced, seeming never to stop. One is always in a hurry to do more, be more, and produce more. But when I put God's Kingdom above everything else, God blesses me with everything needed (Matthew 6:33). I belong to Him and I trust His care and provision. I can rest easy, knowing He is faithful to provide. He is the One who provides even those feelings of comfort and security.

Thank you, Lord, that there will be sweet sleep tonight, knowing You love me.

Job 23:12

I have not departed from the commands of his lips; I have treasured the words of his mouth more than my daily bread.

Bread Box

This ornate bread box served such a humble purpose, keeping rats and pests from entering and munching its contents. It is called a "panetière" and it comes from Arles, France. It now graces a corner of a museum in Massachusetts. When it was used in the eighteenth century, it hung on the wall and added to the elegance of a room. The rich walnut wood and the carving elevated something that was a daily necessity into a treasure!

Today's verse gives a glimpse of the closeness and intimacy Job enjoyed with the Lord. Job was an upright man who carefully obeyed and feared God. But even more than that, Job hung on God's every word. To Job, the words of God's mouth were not only a daily necessity like bread, but a treasure! Job had the same regard for God's decrees as David had years later when he said they were more precious than gold (Psalm 19:10).

I want to esteem God's Word as just that precious! I do not want it to be just ornamental but something I use daily. His Word is a treasure because in keeping it, "there is great reward" (Psalm 19:11). No other book on earth is as true, practical, or uplifting! And His Word will never pass away as it is eternal (Matthew 24:35). What other book could ever make that claim? But I can be cavalier about this treasure, forgetting its Author and its import. I have been spoiled by its ready availability and sometimes desensitized by familiarity.

Lord, don't let me lose the wonder and awe of what I hold in my hands!

John 5:39–40

You study the Scriptures diligently because you think that in them you have eternal life. These are the very Scriptures that testify about me, yet you refuse to come to me to have life.

Big-hearted Giraffe

How regal the giraffe stands! Being the tallest of the land animals at between fourteen and nineteen feet, these stately animals have to have strong hearts. And they do! Their two-foot-long heart is equal to fifty human hearts! The giraffe's exceptional twenty-five-pound heart is able to pump blood where it belongs. Being that their necks are six feet long, their blood pressure is two times stronger than other animals in order to push that blood all the way from heart to head.

Jesus' reprimand to the Pharisees in today's verse addresses the distance between heart and head. These men were admirably using their heads, searching out the Scriptures. But unfortunately, they were missing the point. They closed their minds to the truth that the Scriptures were pointing to Jesus as the Messiah, and they refused to come to Him. Their hearts were not involved. And rather than come to Jesus for the life He promised, they preferred to continue searching the Scripture apart from Jesus Christ.

It is said there are eighteen inches between a human's head and heart. That is a long distance in the spiritual realm. One can agree to spiritual truth intellectually without that truth ever touching the heart. My own experience bears this out as I can agree in my head that God's way is best and at the same time stubbornly follow my own! Jesus understands how I am made, and so commands me to love Him with all my heart, soul, and mind (Matthew 22:37). He wants all of me!

Lord, make my heart soft and obedient to all You have taught me.

A quarrelsome wife is like the dripping of a leaky roof in a rainstorm; restraining her is like restraining the wind or grasping oil with the hand.

Leaky Roof

This happened! After a month-long absence I woke up to the sound of raining in my closet! It is not that it was such a strong storm, but our flat roof would not drain properly. I called on God first. Wailed, if truth be told. Then I called my out-of-town husband, a roofer, and our insurance company. Thankfully, the water did not reach my clothes. But it was maddening to hear the slow and constant dripping well after the rain had finished.

Today's verse describes a quarrelsome wife like that constant drip. Each complaint from her lips and each nagging session can be as annoying as those continual drops of water. Because the verse is speaking of a wife, one can assume the description comes from the husband. In contrast to the Proverbs 31 wife who speaks with wisdom (Proverbs 31:26), this wife provokes argument with what comes out of her mouth. She speaks her mind without any self-restraint. Any attempt at correcting her is as futile as restraining wind or grasping slippery oil.

Being quarrelsome can seem quite reasonable and even expected after a hard day. When taking care of the needs of others means lost sleep or when the toilet backs up, a bit of nasty temper seems just the thing to blow off steam. When pressure builds, it is often on those closest to me that I unload. The danger for me is that being contentious can too easily become a habit. I would much rather be characterized by a quiet gentle spirit, making me consistently approachable!

Lord, keep me sweet and peaceable despite my circumstances.

James 3:7–8

All kinds of animals, birds, reptiles and sea creatures are being tamed and have been tamed by mankind, but no human being can tame the tongue. It is a restless evil, full of deadly poison.

Walking the Cat!

When our cat, Tiger, was young, we were worried about him running away. We tried putting a leash on him so he could be with us while we worked in the garden. You can imagine how that worked out! He was more likely to hang himself on it than be safe in the yard. But I suppose like Pavlov's dogs, any animal can be trained to some extent. There are some cases where cats will consent to the leash, but not ours!

Today's verse talks about the impossibility of taming the tongue. Unlike animals, there is no taming it. It is wild and unpredictable. It is full of evil and poison. The potential it has to destroy people is sobering. The fact that it is restless suggests to me that it is very often in motion, almost looking for trouble. What comes out of the mouth reveals what resides in the heart (Matthew 15:18). No man can tame the tongue because the root problem is a heart issue.

Too many times I have tried and failed to control my tongue. Too late, I see the look of hurt and disappointment on another's face. My regret does not call back those words. They hang in the air and echo in my memory. But there is hope with the Creator of that tongue. God's Spirit offers His control for the uncontrollable. He changes the root problem: my heart. And He gives me the ability to check my tongue and control that outburst!

Lord, tame my tongue today.

Luke 10:40

But Martha was distracted by all the preparations that had to be made. She came to him and asked, "Lord, don't you care that my sister has left me to do the work by myself? Tell her to help me."

Director's Chair

I like the idea of the director having his own personal chair. It is elevated to be above the others and the role is clear. The director directs. He tells everyone else what to do. The first known use of the word "director's chair" was in 1953 on a movie set. But the design of the chair can be traced to the fifteenth century.

In today's verse, it would seem that Martha would be the most likely to have a chair like this. She is overworked and overwhelmed with preparing the meal for a houseful of guests, including the Lord Jesus. She is not relaxing like her sister, Mary, who is listening to their most important guest. Instead, Martha is stressed and distracted by all the work. Even so, she does not hesitate to direct Jesus. Martha tells Jesus what He should do to show His care for her.

It seems a bit audacious of Martha to direct Jesus. But I find that sometimes in my prayers I do the same thing. In approaching the Lord with my request, I will direct Him on the best way to answer me. When He does not do it my way, I can doubt His care. If I really want to understand just how much He cares for me, I need to drop what I think is so important and sit at His feet. When I do, I am less likely to try to direct Him.

Lord, help me to get down from that chair and allow You to direct me today!

Proverbs 18:10

The name of the Lord is a fortified tower; the righteous run to it and are safe.

Towers

These towers were all over the island of Sardinia, off the coast of Italy. I was there recently, singing with my French Gospel Chorale. Our guide explained how vulnerable the island was to multiple attacks over the centuries. Archeologists have found the ruins of seven thousand towers, although they believe there were originally as many as ten thousand. Most of the ones still standing today are more recent from the 1500s and served a similar function of defense and communication.

I love the description in today's verse that portrays the Lord's name as a fortified tower. We never have to worry about this tower being in disrepair or in pieces. It stands tall and beckons the believer to run to it for safety and security. There may even be a small window from which we can watch the Lord take down our enemies! There is opposition to His name now, but one day, every knee will bow, and every tongue will confess His name (Philippians 2:10–11).

The righteous can run to it for safety. The righteous? Could that mean me? I am given Christ's righteousness as a gift. I can run to that tower with confidence that I will not be turned away or mistaken as the enemy. In fact, it is in believing in that precious name of Jesus that I am saved from the punishment of all my wrongdoing. "Everyone who calls on the name of the Lord will be saved" (Romans 10:13). Whatever opposition I face, He is there to protect me and fight for me. His name and presence are stronger than any of my feeble attempts.

Lord, keep me running to Your arms.

Hebrews 3:7–8a

So, as the Holy Spirit says: "Today, if you hear his voice, do not harden your hearts . . ."

Penguin Cries

The courtship rituals of the Emperor penguin are fascinating! I find it sweet that they bow to one another before mating. But what is really interesting are their cries. In large nesting colonies, the male will call out to his female partner from the previous year. If she is there at the same time they will find each other in this huge sea of black and white. They are able to reunite as each cry is distinctive and recognizable.

Today's verse speaks of a voice that is also distinctive and recognizable. It was a voice heard and ignored by the Israelites in the wilderness, wandering for forty years. They rebelled against that voice and their hearts became hardened with sin (verse 13). It is not that they could not hear His voice or recognize it. It was that they did not want to obey it. Hearing His voice is not always a comfortable experience. His voice sometimes nudges believers when we are disobedient. His voice calls for deeper commitment and faith. But His voice also speaks words of love and encouragement, hope and reassurance of His control.

I want my heart to stay soft and responsive toward Him. And I want to be able to recognize which voice is His. There are so many conflicting voices vying for my attention. But I know it is His voice when He speaks to me through prayer and the reading of His Word. His voice spurs me on to greater trust and obedience. Condemnation is not heard, but rather forgiveness and love. That is a voice I want to hear. That is a voice I need to hear!

Please Lord, let me hear Your voice today.

1 Timothy 1:19

. . . holding on to faith and a good conscience, which some have rejected and so have suffered shipwreck with regard to the faith.

Iceberg

I can understand these people getting as close as they dare to this iceberg. It is impressive, especially with its beautiful blue tint. However, there is more to this iceberg than meets the eye! I would be concerned that some jagged piece of it hidden below the surface may capsize the boat! This iceberg is termed a "bergy bit" as it is roughly the size of a house. But, of course, this is only the tip of the iceberg as about 90 percent of an iceberg is found under water.

Today's verse is Paul's charge to young Timothy. Although Timothy had been raised by a believing mother and grandmother, he is encouraged to hold on tight to the faith with a good conscience. The possibility of "shipwrecked faith" was a danger for Timothy, even though he was a leader in the church. The believer is never exempt from the threat of wrong doctrine or the temptation to sin. All that is needed to be vulnerable to shipwreck is to think that it could never happen!

I want to hold on tightly to my faith. There are so many unseen and hidden dangers that can put me at risk when I become overconfident. I want to hold on tightly when I am rocked by circumstances that make no sense and tempt me to doubt. I need to hold on firmly to the word of life so as not to capsize (Philippians 2:16). I do not want to be stuck on a sandbar and out of commission. I want to finish this journey right to the end!

Lord, keep my faith strong and my conscience clear.

1 Corinthians 8:1

Now about food sacrificed to idols: We know that "We all possess knowledge." But knowledge puffs up while love builds up.

The Elephant Seal

This seal looks as if he has an oblong balloon attached to his face! He is called an "elephant seal" as his snout can inflate and resemble a trunk. When putting on a mating display, the male will inflate his nose with lots of air and then compete with other males in a snorting contest! For some northern species, the trunk can extend as much as a foot. I am not too sure why snorting attracts the female!

Today's verse describes a knowledge that can puff us up. Knowledge can make us arrogant. Knowledge can make us so prideful that we end up tearing others down. Usually, knowledge in Scripture is presented in a positive light. It is often mentioned with wisdom and understanding. All the treasures of wisdom and knowledge are found in Jesus Christ (Colossians 2:3). But this knowledge is one without love. That kind of knowledge makes us ugly. Someone who is puffed up with knowledge always has to be right and everyone has to know about it. The person puffed up with their knowledge makes others feel small and foolish. It is a poisonous attitude that isolates us.

My own spiritual pride says that this is a real problem in OTHER people! I never see myself as puffed up. The following verse says, "If anyone supposes that he knows anything, he has not yet known as he ought to know." No one has a corner on knowledge except God Himself. Rather than focusing on how knowledgeable I am, my concern ought to be loving others. If that is my focus, my size stays the same!

Lord, forgive my pride and make me loving.

Psalm 59:16

But I will sing of your strength, in the morning I will sing of your love; for you are my fortress, my refuge in times of trouble.

Building Forts

Kids can make a fort out of just about anything! All that is needed is a little imagination and a few props. There was not only room enough in this fort for my two grandsons but their mother as well. Surprisingly, she stayed in there after the boys lost interest. Maybe not so surprisingly! It was quiet and peaceful there. It was even warm with the protection from drafts. After even just a few minutes inside, she came out looking happily refreshed!

Today's verse describes God as a fortress and refuge. David's house was being watched by Saul's men as they lay in wait to ambush and kill him. David prays for deliverance not only from his enemies (verse 1), but from their slander, curses, and lies (verses 10 & 12). He recognizes that God is his strength and that he can rely on Him (verse 10). David's confidence in God being his strength, fortress, and refuge is so strong that he can sing! He praises God in song for His strength and His love.

In times of trouble, I need the warmth and protection of His strength and love. Actually, I just need Him all the time. But it is when faced with hard times that I realize my need. His presence fortifies and strengthens my resolve to stand firm and resolute. His love reminds me that He is in control and will not allow me to be overwhelmed. His strength can be mine when I run to Him for shelter. I am His. I belong to Him and whatever I am facing, nothing is too hard for Him.

Lord, I will sing today of Your strength and love!

He lifted me out of the slimy pit, out of the mud and mire; he set my feet on a rock and gave me a firm place to stand.

Mud Bath

Although these majestic creatures are so huge and ugly, I am saddened to think that they soon could be extinct. The horn of the rhinoceros, because of its purported medicinal properties, make them a target for poachers. When the rhino is not foraging or resting in the shade of a tree, he can be found wallowing in the mud. The mud cools them down in a hot climate and it also protects them from insects. The mud works as a sun block as well.

Today's verse gives a different view of mud. Along with the mire it is a slippery place for human feet. David cried out to the Lord when he found himself figuratively in that slimy pit. There was no way out and the Lord did not respond immediately. David waited patiently (verse 1). In that time of waiting he did not turn to the proud or to false gods for help (verse 4). David continued to trust while waiting. And he praises the Lord for lifting him out of the mess and giving him a firm, stable place to stand.

It often feels as if the Lord does not immediately come when I cry to Him. He sometimes asks me to wait as well. Of course He hears me cry to Him. He sees my predicament and He cares. But He also wants my faith and trust in Him to grow and strengthen. So many times it is in the waiting that this happens. And His delay means that others see and can praise Him with me when rescue comes (verse 3)!

Lord, help me wait with patience.

For you have been my refuge, a strong tower against the foe.

Castle Keep

This castle keep is part of the Arundel Castle in West Sussex, England. Built in 1067, it is of particular interest to me as my ancestors lived there in the mid-1200s! It was bequeathed by the King to Richard Fitzalan, the husband of my eighteenth great-grandaunt! Our family lived there for 200 years, but not so often in the section pictured here. The castle keep is the fortified tower. The keep was considered one of the most impenetrable parts of the castle. It was used as a refuge of last resort should the rest of the castle fall to the enemy.

Today's verse describes God as a strong tower. David is crying out to the Lord for help as his heart grows faint. This is the prayer of one who is battle weary. He cries out to God as he remembers how He has in the past been a strong tower of defense. David needs God to be his defense against literal enemies. He understands that it is only because of God's love and faithfulness that there is any protection at all (verse 7).

I may not have the same enemies as David. But I too sometimes feel my heart growing faint. Standing up to the world's values can be wearisome. Fighting off temptation and compromise can wear me down. My enemy may be called "discouragement." My enemy may be called "giving up." It could be that I am trying to fight on my own rather than in His strength. He is a strong tower and I can run to Him when my heart feels faint. He promises me His love and faithfulness just as He did to David.

Thank you, Lord, for being my strength today.

Ecclesiastes 7:9

Do not be quickly provoked in your spirit, for anger resides in the lap of fools.

The Accordion

The music of an accordion is such a happy one, reminding me of street performers, dances, and festivals in France. The button board cannot be seen by the player so some buttons have a small depression so the player can navigate by feel. The base-note buttons sound one or more notes in differing octaves. The chord buttons emit a three-note chord when pressed. This button layout can seem confusing. But the one thing each button has in common is that it needs to be pushed to be sounded.

Today's verse is a warning about anger. When someone "pushes our buttons," it can have a predictable result. We can be quickly provoked to anger with the right trigger, especially when there is a history with the one goading us. Certain words, situations, or reminders can rouse us to anger in an instant. Unfortunately, it more often happens with those who are the closest to us. But when we allow anger to settle down and take up residence, we risk becoming a fool.

Anger can sometimes be completely justified. But anger can also turn me into a fool if I let it linger (Ephesians 4:26). And I am to be slow to get to that point of anger if I want to be like Him (Psalm 103:8). If I always react with anger at the mention of someone's name, then anger is residing in my lap! I need God's Spirit to cultivate the same kind of love, compassion, and forgiveness in my heart that the Lord has shown me. That way, pushing my buttons produces something melodious!

Lord, make me slow to anger and quick to forgive.

Romans 5:5

And hope does not put us to shame, because God's love has been poured out into our hearts through the Holy Spirit, who has been given to us.

A Loving Heart

There is something very special about the bond one can have with a horse! That touch, caress, and hug can do something for one's heart as well. The cardiologist Dr. Sandeep Jauhar explained that feelings of love can affect one's heart. This is true whether it be a romantic love or love for children, parents, or even for pets. Those feelings of love can relax and dilate blood vessels and can lower blood pressure.

Today's verse teaches that for the one who has placed their faith in Jesus, God's love has been poured into the heart by His Spirit. Any other love on this earth comes from the outside. But God's love is unique as it reaches to the inside and fills our hearts. His love actually resides on the interior. There is nothing hidden from His love. He knows our deepest thoughts and desires. He understands all of our motivation and fear. Because He lives and loves from our hearts, He knows what makes us mad or makes us cry.

There is no other love as intimate or knowledgeable. How amazing that He could love me, knowing all the junk in there! I can be completely honest and open with Him, as He knows it all anyway. And yet, He still loves me! He does not love me because of who I am but in spite of who I am! As my Creator, He knows that I cannot survive without loving and being loved. When every kind of human love fails, how wonderful to know that His love never will.

Thank you, Lord, for placing Your constant love in my heart.

1 Peter 5:10

And the God of all grace, who called you to his eternal glory in Christ, after you have suffered a little while, will himself restore you and make you strong, firm and steadfast.

Petrified Wood

This piece of petrified wood hardly resembles wood any longer. The inside is as hard as rock. Petrified wood is classed as a fossil and it is formed when a tree falls to the ground and is covered with mud or ash. Rather than decaying, the organic plant material breaks down, forming a void. Over much time, as mineral laden groundwater flows through the inside, the deposits build up, forming rock in that void.

Today's verse is a process that takes much time as well. But the result is a strength every bit as strong as that rock. The Lord allows suffering for a while. He uses it to empty us of all of our own resources, pride, and self-sufficiency. Then when there is a void, He moves in with His strength. Little by little we are filled with those rock-making materials. We no longer resemble ourselves when we are filled with His strength and power.

It is in the middle of those difficult hurting moments that I realize I am weak. Any other time I think I am strong. All it takes is a bit of suffering to realize that I am not. The Lord is so gracious to come to me Himself and personally restore me. He gives me His strength and helps me be strong and steadfast. I may look the same on the outside, but something has changed inside. And it would not have happened had He not allowed the void and emptiness first.

Thank you, Lord, for filling me with Your strength.

2 Corinthians 11:14

And no wonder, for Satan himself masquerades as an angel of light.

Catfishing

These two innocent baby catfish are getting a very bad reputation! Their name is used as a verb to mean scamming others through a fictional online persona. Dating sites unfortunately are the playground of these scammers. The "catfish" posts stolen fake photos. He (or she) describes himself with stories of their background and accomplishments that are too good to be true. He tries to win your sympathy and your love, usually in an effort to extort money. Anyone can fall victim as the one seeking love online is sometimes vulnerable and operating from hope.

Today's verse describes the biggest scammer of all: Satan. He pretends to be an angel of light. It is the old "bait and switch." He reels the unsuspecting in with promises of love and happiness when all he really wants is to destroy (1 Peter 5:8). He is the master of convincing people that they can ignore God, who IS love, and find love their own way. Many victims of catfishing reported that the scammer said all the right things. Satan knows where we are vulnerable and just what to promise.

Satan has been at this scheme of his for centuries. I dare not underestimate him. Yet, God's Word says that when I am submitted to God and resisting Satan, he will flee from me (James 4:7)! I can spot his lies when I know and study God's truth in His Word. The best way to combat a lie is with the truth, and Jesus declares that He Himself is truth (John 14:6). I can unmask Satan and his lies when I am submitted to the One who shows me true love!

Thank you, Lord, that Your truth is all the light I need!

Psalm 33:22

May your unfailing love be with us, Lord, even as we put our hope in you.

Love Letters

What a treasure trove it was when my sister came across love letters written by our parents during World War II! I am now thankful that my mother saved every scrap of paper. These letters are windows into their souls! In the earliest letters the words were a bit stilted, surprisingly on Mom's part. It was my quiet, reserved dad who expressed his love so well! They are now with their beloved Lord, but their love story lasted seventy-one years!

Today's verse describes a love that spans centuries. This love is an unfailing love that not only lasts forever but delivers our souls (Psalm 6:3–4). It is a priceless love (Psalm 36:7), its value surpassing any human attempt at romance. And when we pin our hope on His unfailing love, His eyes are on us (Psalm 33:18)! We are the better for always being mindful of this incredible love (Psalm 26:3). We are told to even meditate on this love (Psalm 48:9). And we do that by immersing ourselves in the words of the greatest love letter ever written, the Bible.

In writing this, I was amazed at all the references to God's love in Scripture! I was reassured of His unfailing love and could feel it wash over me. So often when reading the Bible I get bogged down in the details of study. I get distracted by all the injunctions I find there. I am so sidelined by word studies or cultural references that I forget the main point. Reading His Word is reading His personal love letter to me. His love is behind every list of blessing, every faithful miracle, every promise, and even every warning.

Thank you, Lord, for reassuring me of Your unfailing love!

Ephesians 6:12

For our struggle is not against flesh and blood, but against the rulers, against the authorities, against the powers of this dark world and against the spiritual forces of evil in the heavenly realms.

The Manatee

Who would ever want to harm this gentle creature? The Florida manatee, or sea cow, measures up to thirteen feet and 1,300 pounds. Their slow, lolling nature make this large marine mammal a favorite of tourists. But there are Manatee Zone signs saying "Slow Speed" and "Minimal Wake" in an effort to protect them. Even so, the manatee is classed as "vulnerable." Their greatest threat is human, as they are hunted, drown in fishing nets, face habitat degradation, or collide with fishing boats.

Today's verse reminds us that our greatest enemy is not human. Our biggest threat is spiritual against our souls. We protect ourselves from evil by the different pieces of God's armor: truth, righteousness, the gospel of peace, faith, salvation, and the Word of God (verses 10–19). We can stand firm against evil with the protection He provides. We can stand with confidence as well, knowing that He not only has determined the outcome of this war, but He fights with and for us!

My courage is so nonexistent that I need to enlist my husband when in combat with a spider! There is nothing in me to inspire fear in those dark forces of evil. Yet, the devil will flee from me when I am wholly submitted to God (James 4:7). I can face the dark and stand strong, never with my puny efforts but in the power of His might! Although this is a subject that can illicit fear, God reassures my heart. If God is for me, who can be against me (Romans 8:31)?

Thank you, Lord, that my heart, mind, and soul belong to You.

Philippians 3:8

What is more, I consider everything a loss because of the surpassing worth of knowing Christ Jesus my Lord, for whose sake I have lost all things. I consider them garbage, that I may gain Christ.

Lost Luggage

There was a time when our eldest daughter had the worst luck with lost luggage! For at least three consecutive flights overseas, the airlines lost her suitcase. To be fair, the luggage was delivered to our door in the first few days. But on one occasion, it took weeks, and she was reimbursed for the contents and her trouble. Seeing this pile of lost luggage makes me cringe for their owners. What a hassle!

Today's verse describes a loss that Paul does not consider so important. Paul's background was stellar as a righteous, educated, and privileged pharisee. He was full of religious zeal and entrusted with a mission. He had the admiration and respect of the world in his day. Yet, all that he had gained he considered garbage. The surpassing value of knowing and loving Jesus had given Paul a different perspective. This beautiful and satisfying relationship with Christ made all his past accomplishments seem worthless.

I tend to base my self-worth and importance on past diplomas, accomplishments, and recognition from others. But gaining Christ far outweighs their importance. If renouncing the accolades of men helps me gain Christ, then it is well worth it! My relationship with Him is what makes my life sweet and meaningful. It is no loss to turn my back on the world's idea of value when I can enjoy the surpassing worth of knowing Him. Had I the whole world, it could not compare to having Jesus!

Lord, give me more of You today.

2 Timothy 1:12

That is why I am suffering as I am. Yet this is no cause for shame, because I know whom I have believed, and am convinced that he is able to guard what I have entrusted to him until that day.

Guarding the Queen

Did you know that those guards at Buckingham Palace are actual soldiers in the British army carrying real guns? There are four sentry guards when the Queen is in residence and only two when she is elsewhere. In addition, there are five regiments of foot guards: Grenadier, Coldstream, Scots, Irish, and Welsh. Their uniforms differ subtly but they all have the same charge to guard and protect.

Today's verse is Paul's declaration of faith in God's power to guard what he has entrusted to Him, namely his soul. During a time of discouraging imprisonment, Paul stays confident of God's control. He is suffering but does not feel shame for being in prison. He shares in the sufferings of Christ but is also experiencing Christ's abundant comfort (2 Corinthians1:5). Paul knows that his soul will live on even if he does not survive. God has promised, and He is all-powerful and able to keep His word.

Knowing and being convinced of God's power to guard my soul makes all the difference to how I live. And it will make just as big a difference to how I die. My eternal security rests on His finished work of perfect sacrifice. It does not rest on me, my laundry list of good works, or how I am feeling. My soul is in His powerful hands and nothing and no one can pluck me out of there (John 10:28)! I have no power to guard anything. But He does.

Lord, I trust You to guard my soul!

Proverbs 3:5–6

Trust in the Lord with all your heart and lean not on your own understanding. In all your ways submit to him and he will make your paths straight.

Bison in the Road

We have recently learned on the roads of Yellowstone Park that bison have the undisputed right of way! There was no sign saying so. It was just common sense to stop and make way. With their huge shaggy heads and their gruff snorting, we did not argue! There was no going around them or passing cars to get by them. Everyone just waited until they decided they would clear the road! Whether waiting took five minutes or ninety, there was nothing else to do! It was out of our control.

Today's verse tells us we are to yield or submit to the Lord in each and every way we choose to take. By acknowledging His control, His superior knowledge, and His goodness, we travel a path much less complicated by twists and turns. He makes our paths straight, unencumbered by lengthy unnecessary detours. We reach our destination in good time, or in His time (regardless of the bison in the road!).When we give way to Him rather than insisting on our own plan, we find He had a better idea all along!

Yielding my will to His is so often a struggle. Even knowing that my own understanding is limited, I stubbornly resist. I like being the one who makes the decisions. Trusting Him with all my heart is scary without having some measure of control. But He promises that when I do, He will make my paths straight, choosing the best way. No time will be lost as He has a purpose in every delay.

Thank you, Lord, that I can fully trust Your heart of love for me!

1 John 2:21

I do not write to you because you do not know the truth, but because you do know it and because no lie comes from the truth.

Measuring Tape

We have several measuring tapes around the house. They never seem to be at hand when needed. Instead, they are hiding out in the most inconvenient place in the house. They must change places behind my back. In my Sunday School class, I handed out homemade rulers. One was correct, but the others were off in some small way. When I asked the children to measure the same object, they each came up with different results. The arguments that followed were lively and comical! Before they came to blows I stepped in to explain how the measures they used were different from each other.

Today's verse talks about truth as if it were indeed an absolute and not up for individual interpretation. One can know and discern what is true and what is not true. Just as there was only one ruler with a true standard, so there is objective truth and not contradictory ones, even in the spiritual realm. This way of thinking is so contrary to today's prevailing thought saying that . what is true depends on one's point of view and experience.

"What is truth?" was the question Pilate posed to Jesus (John 18:38). He asked this just after Jesus explained that everyone on the side of truth listens to Him. Jesus proclaimed that He Himself IS truth (John 14:6). I can be confident that hearing His voice is hearing truth. The lies of the Deceiver are designed to restrict and bind me but His truth, found in His Word, sets me free (John 8:32). I am to intentionally set my mind on truth (Philippians4:8). I do not want to waste mental energy on anything less!

Thank you, Lord, that You are truth.

Proverbs 31:25

She is clothed with strength and dignity; she can laugh at the days to come.

The Kookaburra Bird

I only knew about this bird from the children's song growing up. So I was curious to see this Australian bird at the zoo. She was a lot bigger than I imagined, being eighteen inches long. Her beak is four inches long, and with it she can eat chickens, ducklings, and even some small snakes! She is monogamous and she defends her territory. Often, her young will remain with her to help raise the next year's brood. But most surprising is her loud laugh!

Today's verse describes a woman whose qualities raise what seems to be an impossible standard for others! This description of the perfect wife and mother was given by the Queen Mother to her son, King Lemuel. The passage describes a woman of "noble character" fit for royalty (verse 10). After an extensive list of characteristics, the conclusion is that charm and beauty are less important than fearing the Lord (verse 30). Fearing the Lord makes it possible to "laugh at the days to come." There is a light heart even when facing the unknown future.

Of all the qualities listed for this perfect woman, this ability to laugh at the days to come has got to be the most difficult! It is a litmus test of my faith in God and His plan for me. To laugh at the days to come does not mean I do not prepare for them. But it does mean that I can trust Him for the unexpected. I can trust Him for what is around that blind curve. Whatever He allows to happen, He will carry me through it. Whatever the challenge of the days to come, He is enough.

Thank you, Lord, for giving me a light heart.

Jeremiah 32:17

Ah, Sovereign Lord, you have made the heavens and the earth by your great power and outstretched arm. Nothing is too hard for you.

Powerful Arms

This statue in Colmar, France was sculpted by Bartholdi, the same artist who created the Statue of Liberty. It is called, "Les Grands Soutiens du Monde" or "The Great Supports of the World." There are three figures representing three lofty ideas: two arms of justice, one arm of work, and one arm of patriotism. They are depicted walking and supporting the world with their powerful arms. I appreciate the artistic sentiment behind this sculpture. But unfortunately, sometimes those arms get a bit weary and drop.

Today's verse reminds us of God's incredible power and control. How reassuring it is to know that planet Earth has much stronger arms holding it up! The powerful arm of the Sovereign Lord brought about the creation of the heavens and the earth. What is more, His arm is outstretched still! Creation around me attests to His amazing power. The night skies above overwhelm me with His majesty. Nothing is too hard for Him. All He needs to do is to stretch out His arm.

I forget that when I get overwhelmed with my little world. Yet, He is able and willing to again stretch out His arm in my life. All things are possible with God (Mark 10:27). For Him there are no limits of time or space or any other constraint. He established the laws of nature and can just as easily put them aside for His purpose. Those arms not only create but they hold me up when I feel weary. Those are the arms that tenderly carry me when I just can't anymore.

Thank you, Lord, that I can lean on and trust Your powerful arms.

John 4:10

Jesus answered her, "If you knew the gift of God and who it is that asks you for a drink, you would have asked him and he would have given you living water."

Deep Water

D id you know that over 60 percent of the earth is covered by deep water more than a mile in depth? How wonderful it would be to scuba dive and enjoy all the varied colors of the coral and of the fish! Even in the extreme depths far from sunlight there is life found in the cold sweeps and hydrothermal vents. There is a whole other world when one goes deeper!

Today's verse is from the story of the woman at the well. Jesus offers her water that will so satisfy her that she will never thirst again. The woman's response is understandable. She keeps the discussion on a physical rather than spiritual plane. But if she had known who it was that was speaking to her, she would have realized that there was a deeper meaning. He wanted to satisfy her deeper longings and not only her physical need.

My requests and prayers to the Lord often stay on the physical plane. It is understandable to ask Him for a physical healing. He understands when I ask for help with finances or a miracle that would change my circumstances. But He wants me to go deeper with Him. He wants me to recognize and ask Him for what I cannot see or touch or measure. He offers to fill me up with the fullness of Him. He wants me to ask for His peace, His power, and the assurance of His presence. Filling these deeper needs carry me through all the rest!

Thank you, Lord, for giving me what I truly need; more of You.

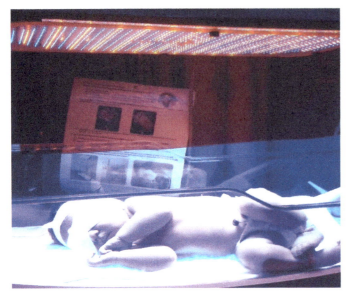

Ephesians 5:8–9

For you were once darkness, but now you are light in the Lord. Live as children of light (for the fruit of the light consists of all goodness, righteousness and truth).

Light Treatment

It was hard to see our newborn granddaughter having to go through light treatment for her jaundice. But the light was necessary to break down the excess bilirubin in her blood. She was surrounded with that light above and below. That special light in the blue and green spectrum changed the bilirubin molecules so that they could be evacuated from her little three-day-old body. What a difference as the yellow tint to her eyes and skin disappeared!

Today's verse encourages believers to live as children of light. Darkness was our past with its evil, unrighteousness, and deceit. But now there is light because of the Lord. His light breaks down and eliminates everything dark in us. Believers can now live a life characterized by goodness, righteousness, and truth. His light gives life (John 1:4). The light He shines on us changes life with its healing and warmth. With His light we can see what is dark and in humility confess it to Him. And we can be a light to others, bringing them to the source.

Although so much darkness surrounds me, the light He sheds will never be overwhelmed by it. I may feel insignificant, but even a small pinpoint of light dispels darkness. He wants me to let His light shine to those who are unwittingly living in the dark. The fruit of His light is what will attract others to Him. Living a life of goodness, righteousness, and truth is living the life He modeled. But it does not happen without the Spirit's gifts of strength and power!

Lord, make me a light today.

1 Thessalonians 5:16–18

Rejoice always, pray continually, give thanks in all circumstances; for this is God's will for you in Christ Jesus.

Bingeing

We used to think of bingeing only in terms of eating and drinking. But of course, bingeing can refer to indulging to excess in any activity. Bingeing on a television series has become a common pastime for some. A "binge racer" is someone who completes an entire season of a television show within a day of its release. While we were living in France, friends would send us a show's entire season. To binge watch was a true temptation, although real life usually interrupted the idea of "indulging to excess."

Today's verses seem to indicate that there is no such thing as excess when it comes to joy, prayer, or thankfulness. All three of these activities can be indulged to our heart's content. In fact, each please the Lord and are part of His desire for the way we live. To always have deep-seated joy would include in the middle of any circumstance, even the negative ones (James 1:2). Being in a continual attitude of prayer means that the lines of communication remain open and intact. And to always give thanks recognizes God's loving control in every circumstance.

I can never rejoice too much. I can never pray more than I should. And the Lord never tires of hearing my grateful praise. Each of these activities can never be indulged too much. He asks me to make them part of my everyday life. He knows how enriching they can be and how they direct my heart toward Him. When I choose joy, when I take time to talk with Him and when I am grateful for every blessing, I can feel His pleasure!

Lord, keep me close to You today.

Psalm 10:4

In his pride the wicked man does not seek him; in all his thoughts there is no room for God.

No Entry

The plumage of the peacock is breathtaking! That gorgeous tail exhibited for the benefit of the peahen measures over five feet! Because of the wing size, the peacock cannot stay airborne for long. Instead he will run, hop, and flutter a bit. The peacock has every reason to be proud with his magnificent tail on display. However, it must be a bit awkward to move around when his big tail fans out! In this image the sign says "no entry." Apparently there is no room for him!

Today's verse is part of a passage describing the wicked. In the thinking and in the pride of the wicked there is no room for any thought of God. He does not seek the Lord, as he feels he has no need of Him. His life is easy and prosperous (verse 5). He lives his life his own way, scorning God's laws. He feels he can get away with it believing God never sees (verse 11). What this man does not realize is that his pride tops the list of sins that are detestable to the Lord (Proverbs 6:16–17).

It is only because of the grace and salvation of Christ that I am not counted among the "wicked." However, that does not mean that I do not struggle with pride. Every time I disobey what God has clearly commanded, my pride is showing in thinking I know better! Pride has crept in when I neglect to seek Him with my whole heart. When there is room for every thought except thoughts of Him, then pride has kept me from realizing His presence.

Lord, fill my mind and heart today with thoughts of You.

Isaiah 26:7

The path of the righteous is level; you, the Upright One, make the way of the righteous smooth.

Zorbing

It looks like a giant hamster ball! In fact, that is one name for the extreme sport of zorbing. The idea is to roll down a hill, enjoying the sensation while being protected. This plastic ball is actually two balls, one inside the other. The "zorber" rolls head over heels being strapped in (or not) and sloshes around when water is added. More control is possible the more level the ground is.

Today's verse describes a path that is level and smooth. It is not that way as a result of our own efforts. It is level and smooth because of what the Lord does for the righteous. Without His intervention, life is full of ups and downs and unwelcome jolts to our progress. On our own, the path we take not only becomes rough and uncomfortable but also takes us in the wrong direction (Isaiah 53:6)! But in living out the righteousness that He gives us through Jesus Christ, we can have a totally different ride!

I wish this verse meant that there would never be any problems in my life. The Lord affirmed that there will be trouble in this world (John 16:33). But in choosing to follow His Word, I at least avoid additional and unnecessary problems of my own making. Sin complicates my life, and disobedience and rebellion make for a very bumpy ride. Thankfully, in His grace the Lord will sometimes smooth over even those rough patches. When He allows the jolts, He brings me through with new dependence on Him.

Lord, thank you that I can trust You to smooth out the road ahead.

He sits enthroned above the circle of the earth and its people are like grasshoppers. He stretches out the heavens like a canopy, and spreads them out like a tent to live in.

Little Grasshopper

Of all the insects I can run into, I am the least threatened by the grasshopper. Perhaps the delight of seeing them jumping in the grass when I was a child has stayed with me. According to the Urban Dictionary, calling someone a "grasshopper" is to refer to someone as a novice, a student, a subordinate, or just ignorant. This use of the word was made popular by the Kung Fu television series in the seventies. "Patience, my little grasshopper."

Today's verse refers to all of mankind as grasshoppers when compared to the God of the universe. God's creativity, His sovereignty and His incomparable power are so far above man's experience and capabilities. We are only small insignificant grasshoppers next to such greatness! If God had not revealed Himself to us, we could never have had any relationship with Him. There are no limits to His knowledge and understanding. When communicating with us I can just imagine Him saying, "Patience, my little grasshopper."

How ludicrous of any "grasshopper" to say there is no God! But even though I love Him and belong to Him, I can act as though He is not there. I get so busy jumping from one thing to the next that the whole day can pass without even a thought of Him. Yes, He sits enthroned above but He is also intimately involved in every detail of my puny, insignificant life! His love and faithfulness are as high as those heavens He spread out. What an amazing thought that He could care for me!

Lord, thank you for loving this grasshopper!

1 Peter 4:12

Dear friends, do not be surprised at the fiery ordeal that has come on you to test you, as though something strange were happening to you.

Roasting Coffee

That small coffee bean goes through quite a long, involved process before it finally makes it into my cup! But toward the end, just before the grinding and the brewing, there is that all-important step of roasting. The green bean is kept moving to avoid burning and turns brown at 400 degrees. At that point, a fragrant oil is released, producing that wonderful aroma and flavor.

Today's verse is an encouragement to believers who are suffering for the name of Christ. Rather than be surprised by the intensity of the heat, we are to see it as normal. Suffering abuse and rejection for Him makes us participants in the suffering He endured for us (verse 13)! The Lord promises special blessing and an evidence of His presence (verse 14). The heat of the trial tests our faith and produces in us a stronger flavor and aroma of testimony. There is no shame in being insulted, rejected, or marginalized. Instead, there can be praise and joy at this privilege!

The hostility I encounter at the name of Jesus Christ is surprising. The reaction seems so unwarranted and sometimes out of character from the person I thought I knew. The name of Jesus is a polarizing one. There may be additional difficulties in my life for proclaiming His name, but there is also additional blessing! The heat of the testing can make my faith stronger. Rather than discourage me, it can make firm my resolve to live for Him. My piddly little problems of being misunderstood do not even compare to what Jesus went through for me!

Thank you, Lord, that You know and You understand.

Nahum 1:7

The Lord is good, a refuge in times of trouble. He cares for those who trust in him.

Sticking My Neck Out

It is obvious how this Eastern Snake-Necked turtle got its name. The neck on this common Australian turtle can be as long as his body! When it feels threatened it can emit a strong musky liquid from the armpits and groin area. Of course, its best protection is its shell. But for this species, to fit that long neck into his carapace he has to bend his head and make it go in sideways. Retreating into his shell may take some extra maneuvering but is worth the protection it gives.

Today's verse talks about the Lord being our refuge in times of trouble. He is good and He cares when we have stuck our necks out too far! The refuge He offers is His presence and is always available. There is no situation that is too difficult for Him, regardless of how vulnerable and exposed we feel. By hiding in Him we can wait out whatever is making us feel threatened. He is our refuge, our fortress, and our hiding place. In His loving and protecting presence, we can patiently wait out any pressure, stress, or assault. It is God who gives perseverance and encouragement (Romans15:5).

I do not know what tomorrow may bring. But I do know that He is already there and He will give me what I need to persevere. At the first sign of trouble, He wants me to hide myself in Him. He cares for me because I trust in Him. He responds to my trust by being exactly what I need when the hard times come. What a comfort that He is good and ready to hide me!

Thank you, Lord, that You care for me.

Romans 13:11

And do this, understanding the present time: The hour has already come for you to wake up from your slumber, because our salvation is nearer now than when we first believed.

Doomsday Clock

The time left on the "doomsday clock" is not very encouraging. This symbolic clock has recently read two minutes to midnight, or two minutes to a global man-made catastrophe! The members of the Bulletin of the Atomic Scientists started the doomsday clock in 1947. Since then, it has read as much as seventeen minutes to midnight (1991). This year marks the third time it has shown two minutes remaining. Nuclear risk and climate change are factors that influence the clock.

Today's verse talks about an hour that has already come; the hour to wake up from spiritual slumber. The night is almost over and the day is about to arrive. This is not a doomsday clock for the believer, but it is something for which we need to be prepared. We are to understand our times, the present time, and the time that is to come. God's Word gives us signs for what is coming. Although there are lots of different ideas about how to interpret them, one thing is sure; our salvation is nearer now than when we first believed!

It is easy for me to be sleepy and to believe that things will always continue as they are. I need to "wake up" and realize that my time is limited. Knowing that Christ's return could happen at any moment changes my priorities and how I live. When I live with this certainty, it makes me want to live a pure life that pleases Him (1 John 3:2–3). I want to live wisely, making the most of every opportunity the Lord offers me (Ephesians 5:15–16).

Lord, wake me up today!

Ephesians 4:4–5

There is one body and one Spirit, just as you were called to one hope when you were called; one Lord, one faith and one baptism.

Singing Stress Away

Have you ever noticed how singing with others can lift a mood? A study was recently done saying 96 percent of those participating in singing groups felt less stress in their lives. Singing releases endorphins and oxytocin, relieving anxiety and stress. And this wonderful effect is amplified in a group. In fact, music vibrations can be felt by each member, moving through bodies simultaneously. When this happens, the heartbeats of each member can even become synchronized!

Today's verse stresses oneness and unity. With all the possible divisions between believers, it is good to be reminded that our hope and faith make us one. When we meet together for corporate worship rather than worshiping on our own, we can sense this unity through song. Singing together brings us together, getting our minds off our differences and turning our thoughts toward the Savior we have in common. Together, we are to hold unswervingly to that "one hope" we profess (Hebrews 10:23). Meeting together and singing together encourages our faith and spurs us on to love and good works (Hebrews 10:25).

Discouragement can so easily overtake me when I give up meeting together. I need to be stimulated and strengthened in my faith. We all need to lift one another up and give one another support. I need that deeper connection that comes from being with people of like mind. Lifting my voice up in song with other believers makes "having the same love, being one in spirit and of one mind" a reality (Philippians 2:2)! Although every tongue and nation will sing with one voice in heaven, I need those moments of "oneness" today.

Thank you, Lord, for those precious moments of unity!

Psalm 14:2

The Lord looks down from heaven on all mankind to see if there are any who understand, any who seek God.

The Elf Owl

I was drawn to the elf owl by its odd name. But rather than having anything to do with elves, the elf description refers to its tiny size. It is the smallest owl in the world, no bigger than a sparrow. Many people in seeing it mistaken this owl as just a young one. And because of his size, he only eats small insects. He is not an aggressive bird and will fly away rather than stay and fight. Perhaps that has something to do with his size as well. The elf owl will play dead when captured until the danger is past. This owl's reputation as being wise is certainly seen in his behavior!

Today's verse equates seeking after God with wisdom and understanding. The fear of the Lord is the beginning of wisdom (Psalm 111:10). Those who are actively seeking the God of the Bible are showing that wisdom. Wisdom is seeing just how tiny we are when compared to His grandeur! Like the owl, our reputation of being wise is seen in our behavior. And wisdom can be evaluated by our righteous and godly living. In contrast, Psalm 14:1 describes the fool as the one who says in his heart that there is no God.

The more I seek Him, the more I am showing wisdom. Seeking after God is always rewarded, as He wants me to find Him. He has promised that those who earnestly seek Him will find Him (Hebrews 11:6). It is worth the effort as He is the One who not only created me but loves me and has only the best in mind for me!

Lord, may I never stop seeking after You.

Psalm 71:18

Even when I am old and gray, do not forsake me, my God, 'til I declare your power to the next generation, your mighty acts to all who are to come.

Taking it Easy

This image has rest and relaxation written all over it! I can imagine that the couple pictured have lived a busy and productive life, maybe with several career changes. Perhaps they have stopped punching a clock. The hard part of raising a family is behind them. They have paid their dues and are now enjoying their "golden years."

Today's verse is looking forward to this stage of life. But rather than thinking about well-deserved rest and relaxation, David still has a "to-do" list in mind. He looks forward to declaring to the next generation all that the Lord has done for him. There is still a story to be told to others of all God's miracles seen in a lifetime! With age, the story becomes longer and richer and more credible.

I know He will never leave me or forsake me (1 Kings 8:57). He has shown Himself faithful to me time and time again! Declaring His power and His greatness is a privilege belonging especially to those of a certain age. In testifying to His faithfulness throughout a long life, others are encouraged to persevere in the faith. In this sense, there is no retirement when it comes to speaking to the next generation of God's greatness! And it is often in looking back over the years that I see more clearly His miraculous hand! I know my children and my grandchildren are watching me. They will never see perfection but my prayer is that they will hear from me praise and testimony to God's power!

Lord, keep me praising You to others.

Matthew 5:16

In the same way, let your light shine before others, that they may see your good deeds and glorify your Father in heaven.

The Magic of Fireflies

Fireflies are so intriguing! When they light up a tree, it is magical and looks like a fairyland. The chemical reaction of these ugly winged beetles produces light but not heat. They glow without wasting any energy. All one hundred percent of their energy goes into making their light. The purpose of their glow is to attract either a mate or their prey. Their light attracts me too, although I do not fit either category!

Today's verse talks about the attractive light of our good deeds. When our kindness to others is done to give honor to the Heavenly Father, we shine as lights. In a dark and selfish world our lives stand out and shine. The purpose of our light is not to attract people to ourselves, but to our Lord. We are to be open about the reasons behind our giving to others. It is not about me. It is about Him.

I often feel that my acts of love and kindness toward others do not make much difference. But even a pinpoint of light in the darkness is noticed. When He is given the recognition He deserves, then my little light has a huge purpose. My focus should not be praise and recognition for myself but for Him! My light is to pierce the darkness and point others to Jesus, who Himself is the Light of the world! And of course, when a group of flickering lights are together (as in the Church) the impact is that much more remarkable and beautiful!

Lord, show me how to shine for You today!

John 3:8

The wind blows wherever it pleases. You hear its sound, but you cannot tell where it comes from or where it is going. So it is with everyone born of the Spirit.

Kite Mishap

I did not see the beginning of this kite mishap, but I can just imagine it! The wind this day was not so terribly strong but it was capricious. The dangling string did nothing to help free it from the tree's clutches and of course climbing the tree proved too difficult. As far as I know, the kite is still there, victim to the wind's change of direction.

Today's verse likens the work of the Spirit to the wind. Man has learned how to harness the power of the wind, but we still cannot control where it is coming from. Man has no say in when it will arrive, how strong it will be or when it will abate. In the same way, we cannot explain the movement of God's Spirit, but we do see the results. We see His presence by the change produced in hearts and lives.

Just as I cannot control the wind, I cannot control God's Spirit. He is a Person, not just a force of nature. I do not have the power to oblige Him to do anything. He is God, and it would be presumptuous of me to think that I could control Him! His power and how He chooses to use it is part of what makes Him God. But I can be assured through His Word that His movements are not capricious, but purposeful and good. No, I do not control Him. What I desire most is that His Spirit controls me.

Lord, may Your Spirit empower and direct me today.

Revelation 3:15

I know your deeds, that you are neither cold nor hot. I wish you were either one or the other!

Hot or Cold?

He is adorable but I am confused. Being that I am not a dog person, I am unsure if this dog is cold, needing the coat, or if he is too warm wearing two coats! My body today is having the same confusion, unable to decide whether it is hot or cold. A flu will do that, making me vacillate between fever and chills.

Today's verse comes from the Lord's reprimand to the church of Laodicea. This is a message of hard truths but He reassures that those He loves He disciplines and rebukes (verse 19). These believers were doing good deeds. But something was wrong. They were not done with any kind of passion. It was as if they were on autopilot, showing kindness and giving to others out of habit or a sense of obligation. However, the Lord sees the heart and the motivation. And like the good works that prove to be wood, hay, and straw rather than gold, silver, and costly stones, there is a marked difference (1 Corinthians 3:12–13).

The difficult question I ask myself is whether I am lukewarm. No one else can know the answer, as it is a matter of the heart. Frankly, the good I may do for someone else may be tainted with thoughts of self aggrandizement or reciprocal expectations. When my thoughts of "I should help" outweigh my thoughts of "I want to help" than perhaps I am being lukewarm. The only way I know to be passionate is to continually connect to that Vine and have that fruit naturally flow from my relationship with Him!

Lord, keep me from being lukewarm today.

1 Peter 4:12

Dear friends, do not be surprised at the fiery ordeal that has come on you to test you, as though something strange were happening to you.

Burnt to a Crisp

We are smiling here but not when we got the news of the fire! Our two cars were burnt to a crisp as the result of a gang coming through, causing trouble. This form of protest in France is concerning but we never thought we would be a target! It was surprising, but the Lord had a plan in all of it. He graciously replaced our cars with two that were newer with better mileage. And He did this through the gifts of His people! Through this test our faith has grown and become more fireproof!

Today's verse tells believers not to be surprised at the hard times we suffer. They are not the exception, but the norm. We are not exempt from difficulties, although sometimes we think we should be. The "fiery ordeal" in this verse is not something that is caused by our own wrong choices. It is an ordeal that comes from living as a believer in an unbelieving world.

It is easy for me to think that I should be shielded from hard times. But I am to view any suffering for Him as a privilege and a joy (verse 13)! And the end result of this story is joy at seeing how Jesus used it for His purposes and His glory! Our faith was strengthened. And the evil intent of this gang was turned around to His praise and glory in our lives. Because of this drama, I am less surprised at opposition and more confident that God will use it!

Lord, keep my faith strong in whatever I face.

Proverbs 16:25

There is a way that appears to be right, but in the end it leads to death.

I Did It My Way

The music of the famous song, "My Way," was based on the French song, "Comme D'Habitude." But the lyrics were written by Paul Anka. After dining with Frank Sinatra and hearing about his unhappiness that things were not going his way, Anka penned the now-famous lyrics. They describe a man facing his own mortality and reflecting on a life done his own way. He questions what man is and what he's got explaining that if he does not have himself, then he has naught.

Today's verse talks about how right and good our way can seem. There is a rebel lurking in all of us, and we would rather question God's way than question our own. But this verse is saying that even though our way may seem right, it can still be wrong. Our subjective stamp of approval does not change the objective truth that certain choices will lead to death. We all need to be taught and led in His way (Psalm 27:11) and led in the way everlasting (Psalm 139:24).

How glad I am that I have more to live this life than the lyrics suggest! I am not on my own. My life has a plan and a purpose, created by the One who created me! It is true that I do not always understand His way and His logic, but I am to walk His way in faith. His way leads me on to level ground instead of the steep inclines of my ill-conceived short cuts (Psalm 143:10)! His way leads me by still, quiet waters instead of the turbulent waters my choices create (Psalm 23:2).

Lord, in looking back on my life, may I be able to say, "I did it YOUR way."

Galatians 5:15

If you bite and devour each other, watch out or you will be destroyed by each other.

Tasmanian Devil

Despite his name, I would hate for the Tasmanian devil to become extinct. His only natural habitat is the Australian island-state of Tasmania. Because of his husky snarl and bad temper, he often has what is called a "devilish expression." Since 2008 he has been on the endangered list. The reason? A cancer called, "devil facial tumor disease," which results in grotesque tumors around the head and mouth. It is thought to be transmitted when they bite each other!

Today's verse teaches that the words from our mouths can inflict pain and even destroy another. Life and death are in the power of the tongue (Proverbs 18:21). So much of what displeases the Lord comes from the mouth, whether it be gossiping, lying, mocking, arguing, criticizing . . . the list goes on. And each of these has such a devastating effect on the one to whom it is directed. What is more, the "tit for tat" reciprocity only escalates the problem until both parties are destroyed.

It is only by His Spirit that I can love and forgive the one who has inadvertently or intentionally hurt me. My memory is long when it comes to hurtful words. But I have definitely taken things a step further when I want to retaliate. There might be a momentary feeling of satisfaction, but the relationship remains tense and broken. Forgiveness is so difficult but without it, the relationship is "endangered" and at risk of extinction. Realizing God's forgiveness for me helps me get a better perspective on the whole mess. And His love and His power are there to make forgiveness and restoration possible. It is just not possible on my own.

Thank you, Lord, that You heal those difficult relationships.

214

Psalm 143:10

Teach me to do your will, for you are my God; may your good Spirit lead me on level ground.

Level Ground

This traveler can see for miles and miles. Because there are no hills, mountains, turns, or trees she can see far ahead. But not only that, she herself can be seen from a distance. I enjoy walking when there are no ups and downs to change my pace. But because of this level ground I would be vulnerable and open to scrutiny.

Today's verse is David's prayer to do what pleases God. He prays that God's Spirit will lead him to level ground. This is the path of righteousness or as some versions say, "the land of uprightness." This level path was walked by Jesus. The rough ground was made level for Him when every valley was raised up and every mountain and hill were made low (Isaiah 40:4). The reason for the level ground was not for ease of walking. It was rather for His glory to be revealed and for all people to see it (verse 5). There was nothing on that level ground to obstruct the view of His glory.

The way I walk is open to scrutiny and like David, I need His Spirit to teach me. People are watching how I walk whether I realize it or not. He is my God and His glory is at stake. When I walk to please Him, He is lifted up and glorified. When I follow what I know He wants, then those watching can be helped to faith. Level ground does not necessarily mean that my way is easy. Far from it. But that level ground does makes me visible.

Lord, lead me to level ground and may nothing obstruct the view of Your glory in my life!

You blind guides! You strain out a gnat but swallow a camel.

Camel on the Menu

This camel looks a little ridiculous and undignified, when really they are magnificent animals! They can carry 200 extra pounds and travel twenty miles a day. Camels can drink forty gallons of water at a time and can eat anything without injuring their mouths. They can close their nostrils against wind and sand, and store energy in their humps in the form of fat. But one thing they never have to worry about, and that is being swallowed whole!

In today's verse the Pharisees are the blind guides that Jesus addresses. One would have to be blind not to see the difference between a gnat and a camel! The Pharisees were all about keeping every detail of the Law, including the tithe on their mint, dill, and cumin. But they were ignoring the larger and more important matters of the law: justice, mercy, and faithfulness. Keeping the details of the Law had become for them a point of pride as details of the Law were visible to others. Justice, mercy, and faithfulness were intangibles and frankly, more difficult to follow.

I am afraid that sometimes I am just as guilty of this in my Christian walk. I tend to use an accepted set of rules as a shortcut to spirituality. I know the right words. I can follow routine. I can look like I have my act together. Outside conformity to a set of rules can mask the real state of my heart. But the Lord knows when my thoughts toward others are harsh instead of merciful. He sees when I excuse myself but no one else. And of course He knows when my heart is unfaithful.

Lord, keep my heart close to Yours.

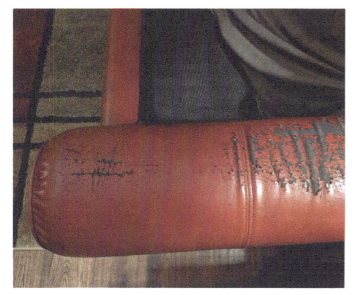

Ephesians 4:3

Make every effort to keep the unity of the Spirit through the bond of peace.

Bonded Leather

I was horrified to pull back my couch cover and see how the bonded leather was "unbonding!" After just two years, the couch was showing signs of this kind of wear. It was my own fault for not researching the meaning of "bonded leather" before buying it. But because the price was hefty and it was from a reputable well-known brand, I made some wrong assumptions. This kind of leather is made up of many small pieces bonded or glued together. Those who sell it admit that it will only hold up three to five years. What a disappointment!

Today's verse talks about a supernatural bond of peace that is the work of the Holy Spirit in believers. Those belonging to Jesus come in all shapes and sizes, different races and cultures, social standings, income and education. We are little pieces bonded together, making a whole. We are part of one body, one Spirit, one hope, one Lord, one faith, one baptism, one God and Father (verses 4–6)! And this peace is something we are to strive to keep.

The Lord knows me. He knows how easily I can nitpick and criticize. I so easily focus on differences rather than recognize what unites me with my brothers and sisters. The Lord has shown me incredible grace, and yet I am slow to show that same grace to others. Our unity is more important than me being right, recognized, or visible. Our unity can be a powerful draw to the world. And oh, how good and pleasant it is when God's people live together in unity (Psalm 133:1)!

Thank you, Lord, that You make possible this bond of peace. Help me to keep it!

1 John 2:21

I do not write to you because you do not know the truth, but because you do know it and because no lie comes from the truth.

The Inchworm

Do not believe everything you read! This little inchworm is not a worm, nor is it exactly an inch long! But the inchworm name is given to thousands of moth species in the Geometridae family when in their caterpillar stage. The family name comes from the Greek "geo" meaning earth, and "metron" meaning measure. However, if you used this little guy to measure, your measurements would surely be off!

Today's verse is clear that one can know what truth is and what truth is not. That must mean that truth can be measured. This verse contradicts the prevailing thought that in the spiritual realm, there is no objective truth. There is "your truth" or there is "my truth" when it comes to spirituality. The famous question of Pilate to Jesus, "What is truth?" (John 18:38) was in response to what Jesus had just said. "Everyone who is of the truth hears My voice." Jesus is the standard of truth as He said of Himself that He is the truth (John 14:6).

In a world where truth changes from one decade to another, what a comfort to know and be sure of objective, unchanging, and eternal truth! The truth of His Word is always a faithful measure. Without it I would be lost! He is my standard of truth. He is the one and only measure of truth. Because of Him I can recognize the lies that can so easily deceive me. And because of Him being truth I can build my life on a sure and unmovable foundation.

Lord, keep me in Your truth.

Hebrews 11:1

Now faith is confidence in what we hope for and assurance about what we do not see.

Seeing Is Believing?

While living in Grenoble, France, we would often have foggy socked-in days. Nestled in the valley with the Alps soaring above, we knew sun was shining on those peaks. We knew because as often as schedule would allow, we would drive up the mountain to see the sun. We would look down on that blanket of fog covering everything and revel in the sun's warmth. But life awaited below, so back down into the fog we would drive, remembering the sun but no longer seeing it.

Today's verse is a very clear definition of the word "faith." It is confidence in our hope and assurance of what is there even though we cannot see it. We cannot see with our physical eyes what we can see with our spiritual ones! Thomas would not believe the Lord had risen until he could actually physically see and touch Him. But we are in that special group that is blessed for believing without seeing (John 20:29)!

Most of the time my spiritual eyes are seeing His beauty, His power, and His grace toward me. But there are days when my spiritual vision seems clouded. Just as the fog blurs the landscape, so my view of spiritual truth can seem blurred. I know He is still there but my perspective has changed. It usually happens when I neglect His Word. It is sure to happen when I am not speaking with Him. And that fog can become quite thick, the longer I doubt or ignore Him. But I am amazed at how quickly that fog can lift when I turn back to Him, His promises, and His whispers of love!

Lord, lift that fog today!

Proverbs 28:1

The wicked flee though no one pursues, but the righteous are as bold as a lion.

Bold as a Lion

It was in the back of the Edinburgh Castle that my cousin found the origin of our family name, Leonardy, belonging to my maternal grandmother. It is a very old name originating in Gascogne, France. The original bearer of this name was thought to be as bold as a lion. So the name meaning, "lion-bold," was given to this individual. Although my grandmother married into this name, she certainly showed courage living to the ripe old age of almost 105!

Today's verse describes the righteous as being as bold as a lion. This is in contrast to the wicked whose guilt makes them fearful. The wicked flee even though they are not being pursued. Knowing in their heart that they are deserving of punishment, they run. In contrast are the righteous or those who are in right standing with God. They are not running and they are not fearful because they are assured of God's forgiveness. This position of righteousness is given through faith in Jesus Christ (Romans 3:22). Being seen as righteous in God's eyes makes us bold and not fearful of punishment, as Christ took on Himself our sins and the wrath they deserve.

My faith does make me bold. I am not being pursued for my wrongdoing. And it is not presumption to take Jesus at His Word that I am "righteous." It is a gift given through His grace (Ephesians 2:8–9). What confidence and boldness He gives in facing any struggle in life or even in death! My eternity has been secured by Him. The question of my guilt has been settled. That makes me bold to approach His throne for all the mercy and grace I need (Hebrews 4:16).

Thank you, Lord, for the boldness You make possible!

Jeremiah 8:7

Even the stork in the sky knows her appointed seasons, and the dove, the swift and the thrush observe the time of their migration. But My people do not know the requirements of the Lord.

On the Move

I am fortunate to have lived in an area of France known for its stork population. I so enjoyed watching them fly past our windows. The cranes around there were almost as big but do not have the same "wow" effect for me. Every year I watched for them to return with the warmer weather. They would spend the winter in Sub-Saharan Africa, something I wished I could do in the middle of those long cold months! And they often returned to the exact same nest.

Today's verse talks about four different kinds of birds but with one thing in common; they all migrate. Their little bird brains know instinctively when it is time to move on so as to avoid the freezing temperatures. Jeremiah mentions these birds as a contrast to the Israelites. The people prided themselves in possessing the Law of God. But they continually turned to their own individual course, rather than following God's way. The Law, instead of being written in their hearts, became a mere code or outward ceremony.

I wish obeying God was as instinctive for me as migration is for the birds. But then it would not mean as much. God wants my obedience to be an intentional choice. Knowing what God expects of me is a good thing. But I do not want to make the same mistake as the Israelites. The point is not how many Bible verses I can recite by heart. He is more interested in how many I obey!

Help me, Lord, to be obedient.

2 Corinthians 4:6

For God, who said, "Let light shine out of darkness," made his light shine in our hearts to give us the light of the knowledge of God's glory displayed in the face of Christ.

Zen

The other day while exploring the tide pools of Cabrillo National Park with my grandsons, I saw an older man sitting cross-legged. He had built three stacks of stones just like the one pictured. His eyes were closed and he looked peaceful. This rock configuration brings to mind the idea of "Zen." This Japanese sect of Mahayana Buddhism asserts that enlightenment can come through meditation and intuition rather than faith.

Today's verse gives us the true source of enlightenment. It is God's light that gives us enlightenment. No matter how long or how well we meditate, our own ideas of truth are subjective and without Him, fall short of His objective truth. It is His light that gives us the knowledge of God's glory in Jesus, His Son. If He had not revealed the truth with His light, we would still be in the dark. And when believers meditate, it is on His truth that we meditate.

In this world full of so many distractions, it takes an effort of the will to turn my mind to spiritual things and meditate on His truth. But what a blessing when I do! There are no loftier thoughts than thoughts of Him. And meditating on His love and all that He has done for me encourages my heart. His light and His Word reveal to me so many worthy subjects of meditation, all of them centered on Him!

Lord, keep me meditating on You and Your truth throughout the day.

Psalm 18:2

The Lord is my rock, my fortress and my deliverer; my God is my rock in whom I take refuge, my shield and the horn of my salvation, my stronghold.

The Chuckwalla

I had never heard of a chuckwalla until it was spotted and photographed by a family member in an arid rocky area of Arizona. They can weigh up to two pounds, measure up to sixteen inches and live as long as twenty-five years! But what is most surprising is the way they escape predators. They dodge into the crevice of a rock and inflate themselves with air! This wedges them in so firmly that it is nearly impossible to remove them!

Today's verse describes our God as a rock. He provides refuge, protection, and the strength of our salvation. When we feel threatened or vulnerable, we can run to the permanence of this Rock. His strength and protection are constant and constantly available. It is a place that is safe when we feel under attack. In the crevice of this rock we not only catch our breath, but are filled with His Spirit in this place of refreshment.

Sometimes it takes a crisis for me to realize that I am far away from my Rock. When life is smooth I can be lulled into thinking that there is no danger. Self-sufficiency begins to subtly influence my thinking. But even when I do sense any kind of threat, I am ashamed to admit that my first reaction is not always to run to my Rock. I need to remember that it is no weakness to run to His strength. He invites me to firmly wedge myself in and enjoy His love and protection! In the crevice of this rock, I will not be moved or removed!

Lord, be my Rock today.

Psalms 90:8

You have set our iniquities before you, our secret sins in the light of your presence.

Soft Candlelight

I love candlelight. I love the way it adds ambiance to a special dinner. One of the reasons I like candlelight so well is that it softens hard realities. I just look better in the low light. One does not see my wrinkles, my blemishes, or the bags under my eyes. All the defects are hidden in the soft flattering light. My husband even looks better!

Today's verse talks about another kind of light; the light of His countenance. This light is brighter and much more revealing. It does not soften anything but brings to light some hard realities. I do not look so good in this light as it exposes the truth. The light of His face exposes all the sins I have ever tried to cover up, even from myself. But those secret sins that no one else knows about are not hidden from Him. His light reveals what I am hiding even from myself.

I may feel more comfortable in low candlelight, but He will have none of it! His light exposes the problem out of love for me, so that it can be confessed and forgiven. I need to agree with God about my secret sin so that He can deal with it. In doing so, I can actually enjoy His light. This same Psalm ends with a prayer, "and let the beauty of the Lord our God be upon us . . ." When I am honest with Him about those secret sins and confess them, I become more beautiful as I reflect His beauty! No more need for candlelight!

Thank you, Lord, for Your beautiful light and the forgiveness You offer.

Psalm 31:7

I will be glad and rejoice in your love, for you saw my affliction and knew the anguish of my soul.

My Hamster

This sweet hamster is called a "dwarf hamster." They are different from the larger more territorial ones as they are social and thrive in pairs. That did not seem like reason enough to call the love of my life my "hamster!" But to my untrained ear, it seemed as if couples on French television were calling each other "hamster." In fact, they were saying, "âme soeur" meaning "soul sister," or loosely translated, "soulmate." But somehow it stuck, and that is our English term of endearment in our marriage!

Today's verse tells us there is someone who knows our soul more than any lover could. The Lord not only sees our physical afflictions but He goes deeper and He knows and understands the anguish of the soul. Not knowing what we should pray, His Spirit intercedes with wordless groans expressing our anguish (Romans 8:26). The Lord sees and understands what we are feeling far better than we understand ourselves. He knows when we are loving Him with all our soul (Deuteronomy 13:3). And in His love He knows when to restore and refresh our souls (Psalm 23:3).

I can trust this lover of my soul. He will never betray my confidences. He will never renege on His promises. What's more, nothing in my soul shocks and dismays Him. After all, He does not love my soul because it is worthy of love. He loves me in spite of myself. God not only shows me love, He IS love. And it is a love that knows all the ugliness inside. How amazing that He could love me! And it is even more amazing that nothing will change that love.

Thank you, Lord, for being the lover of my soul.

1 Peter 4:10

Each of you should use whatever gift you have received to serve others, as faithful stewards of God's grace in its various forms.

Pickleball Ball

Pickleball has become more and more popular, using elements from tennis, badminton and ping-pong. But who knew there could be so many choices of pickleball ball? There are indoor or outdoor ones. The weights and colors can be different. But they all have to have 26–40 round holes. If this ball had no holes, there would be problems in playing the game. Without the holes the ball would not travel in a true line but would fly upward, downward, or sideways.

Today's verse explains that every believer has been given a gift for the service of others. More than a natural talent, these spiritual gifts are supernaturally infused with God's strength (verse 11), and He uses them uniquely for His glory. The gifts come in various forms and God uses them in different ways. But like the pickleball ball, we are imperfect and full of holes. This is no problem for the Lord as He uses even our weaknesses to show His strength (2 Corinthians 12:9). What He looks for is our availability and faithfulness.

I keenly feel my imperfections. Dwelling too much on them can completely block me from any kind of service for Him! But it is those very "holes" that He uses to point us in the right direction. Thankfully, I do not need to be perfect before He can use me. I do not have to have all the answers before I open my mouth. I do not have to have my life completely together before I can help someone else. He uses every weakness and covers it with the strength to serve Him!

Thank you, Lord, for the privilege of serving You.

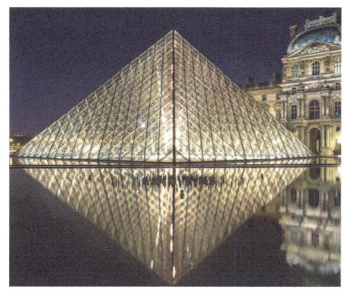

Colossians 3:9–10

Do not lie to each other, since you have taken off your old self with its practices and have put on the new self, which is being renewed in knowledge in the image of its Creator.

Old or New?

I loved living in France and seeing the old next to the new. Side by side, the old looks older and the new looks newer. Pictured here is the beautiful Louvre in Paris, built in the late twelfth century. The pyramid looks much more modern and new, having been built in 1989. For me the contrast is striking! But in fact, the pyramid has started to show signs of aging as well, and the French government has had to do some renovations to keep it looking new.

Today's verse talks about the old and the new for the believer. We have both going on at the same time. Although we are a new creature in Christ (2 Corinthians 5:17), the old self is still hanging around. As long as we live on this earth in the flesh, we will always need the reminder in these verses to "lay aside" or "put off" that old self. And as for our new self, we can count on a continual renewal. Our new spiritual selves are continually being renewed by Christ Himself though His Word.

As I look forward to what lies ahead, I can be confident that my new self is being restored and renewed by Him. Every time I lay aside that old self, I am cooperating with Christ's renewal in me. Every time I choose to obey Him rather than having my own way, He is bringing me closer to His image. Slowly, He is renewing and transforming me to be more like Him!

Thank you, Lord, for Your patient steady work in me!

Philippians 2:1–2

Therefore if you have any encouragement from being united with Christ, if any comfort from his love, if any common sharing in the Spirit, if any tenderness and compassion, then make my joy complete by being like-minded, having the same love, being one in spirit and of one mind.

Flying in Formation

This image of perfect synchronized flying is amazing! These birds must have the same destination in their little bird brains. But more than that, they are flying at the same height and the same speed to get there! No one is jostling for position or lagging behind the others. Their united purpose brings them together and keeps them together.

In today's verse, Paul seems to think that Christians can be united in spirit. Not only that, but he appears to be saying that believers can be in agreement, loving one another and intent on going in the same direction. How does that happen? When there is encouragement. When there is consolation. When there is fellowship and affection for one another. We not only need the love and encouragement of other believers to keep going, but "flying together" brings honor to Christ! It is what signals to the world that we are His disciples (John 13:35).

I am going in the same direction as so many other believers. Like them, my desire is to grow in faith and be more like Jesus. It is a long lifetime purpose. But going it alone is not what the Lord wants. Just as I take notice of these birds flying in perfect harmony, so the world sits up and takes notice of believers that are showing love and unity. Being united and showing love to one another is something supernatural, but He makes it possible!

Thank you, Lord, that I do not have to do this alone!

Ecclesiastes 5:20

They seldom reflect on the days of their life because God keeps them occupied with gladness of heart.

Simple Pleasures

Simple pleasures are the best! How sweet to see the pure joy on the face of this little boy! Squealing with pleasure, he chases those bubbles, and popping them has made his day. Somehow, as we age, it takes a bit more to distract and occupy us. With the weight of worry, the stress of responsibilities and the jaded skepticism that can creep into our thinking, we can miss out on having that glad heart.

Today's verse teaches that God can occupy us with gladness of heart. Rather than negative reflections on the days of our lives, we can experience gladness. Rather than chasing after riches which in the end are meaningless, we can be happy and contented with simple pleasures. The art of being glad and satisfied has very little to do with what we can acquire. All our work can be toiling for the wind (verse 16), or we can be happy in our toil, enjoying its fruits as a gift from God (verse 19). It is a choice we make. The Lord can keep us away from thoughts of always wanting more and instead occupy us with a glad heart.

Which is better, to have little with a glad heart, or to have lots but be frustrated with what I do not have? I find it such a comfort that God cares about the state of my heart. He does not want me occupied with stuff. He offers a light glad heart when I turn from my temporal wants and desires toward what is eternal. And when I do that, I can much more easily enjoy the simple pleasures in this life!

Lord, keep my heart occupied and glad!

Romans 1:16

For I am not ashamed of the gospel, because it is the power of God that brings salvation to everyone who believes . . .

Walking Stick Bug

My niece is a brave soul to put her hand next to this huge walking stick bug there in Costa Rica! It is true that they do not bite, but the idea of it crawling over me does not appeal! There are over three thousand species worldwide, and all differ according to their habitat. Each species has evolved to resemble the plant material in their area. They escape notice so well that they can hide in plain sight and blend in perfectly.

Today's verse is a bold statement of Paul's that is the very opposite of blending in to one's surroundings. Paul wants to be detected. He wants to be noticed and to stand out from the crowd. And believing in the gospel of Christ in the midst of a non believing world will do just that! But there is no shame in standing out for something so powerful. There is no shame in being different from others when it can mean the salvation of a soul. It is worth any discomfort to draw attention to the amazing power of the gospel!

It is a strong inclination of mine to blend in and belong. It is uncomfortable for me to draw the eye or incite the comments of others. Worry over what others think can sometimes nullify my testimony. But rather than the approval of men, my overriding desire is the approbation of the Lord. He scorned the shame to hang naked on a cross for me (Hebrews 12:2). How could I possibly be ashamed of a few odd looks or comments?

Lord, may I scorn shame in any form. Keep me bold with the truth!

Psalm 130:3–4

If You, Lord, kept a record of sins, Lord, who could stand? But with you there is forgiveness so that we can with reverence serve you.

The Abacus

Counting on an abacus looks complicated and time consuming. But in fact, the merchants we saw in Hong Kong and Taiwan seemed to have no trouble at all. Their fingers would fly over the beads faster than a calculator! The Chinese abacus dates back to the second century BC. Variations of it were used as well by the Greeks and Romans in ancient times to keep an accurate record.

Today's verse mentions keeping an account. If the Lord were to keep a record of our sins, the small abacus would not be able to keep up! If He were to treat us according to our sins, we would be crushed. We would not be able to stand or even to lift our head. Thankfully, with His forgiveness, the record is swept clean. Because of His forgiveness, we can serve Him with reverence and a grateful heart. He removes our sins as far as the east is from the west (Psalm 103:12). Because of the loving sacrifice of Christ, He chooses not to remember our sin (Hebrews 10:17).

His undeserved forgiveness is so amazing! There is no other response I can make but to serve Him. He does not forgive and forget my sin so that I can keep sinning. He does it so that I can have the privilege of serving Him. It is in this grateful service that I find purpose and significance in life. He is worthy of all my praise, fear, and obedience. Not only does He forgive me but He allows me to stand in His incredible presence and enjoy Him forever!

Lord, where would I be without Your forgiveness?

Nehemiah 9:17a

They refused to listen and failed to remember the miracles you performed among them. They became stiff-necked and in their rebellion appointed a leader in order to return to their slavery.

Stubborn as a Donkey

When a donkey refuses to budge, it might as well stick out his tongue at you! Donkeys have the reputation of being strong willed and obstinate. But in their donkey brains they are stubborn for a reason. No matter how hard one pulls on a donkey, he will not move if he feels in danger or if he feels he is being overworked. Sometimes a donkey just has to stop and think whether he wants to obey or not. And if not, they will plant their hooves and refuse to move.

Today's verse describes the Israelites as stubborn and stiff-necked. God had made His commandments very clear, but they refused to listen to His voice. They also chose not to remember all His miracles in leading them out of slavery from Egypt. The result was a stubborn conviction that their way was best, even if it meant returning to that slavery! They planted their feet and refused to go on. Perhaps they felt it was just too hard to obey. Thankfully, God did not give up on them (verse 17b). Because He is gracious and compassionate, He forgave them.

It is easy to see their stubbornness, but I tend to gloss over this trait in myself. Any time I refuse to listen to God's voice of conviction, I am at risk of stubbornly returning to sin's slavery. Any time I forget all of what He has done for me, I am likely to stubbornly do what seems best to me.

Thank you, Lord that You do not give up on me. Help me to listen and remember today!

Philippians 4:8

. . . whatever is true, whatever is noble, whatever is right, whatever is pure, whatever is lovely, whatever is admirable—if anything is excellent or praiseworthy—think about such things.

The Thinker

This iconic and very recognizable sculpture sits proudly at the Rodin Museum in Paris. The Thinker was originally only twenty-seven inches tall! In 1881 he was created to sit at the top of an entryway called Gates of Hell. Rodin named him "The Poet," as he represented Dante. But this piece was so well received that he grew figuratively and literally to the size we see today. His deep concentration gives rise to all sorts of ideas as to the subject of his thoughts!

Today's verse encourages the believer to think about a list of things that are excellent or praiseworthy. If we are what we think, then the subject of our thoughts makes an incredible difference to how we live! This list of what we are to think about is sandwiched between two verses on peace (verses 7 & 9). What occupies our thoughts has a direct bearing on experiencing God's peace. And each of these excellent and praiseworthy thoughts can easily describe one Person: Jesus Christ! His Word tells us to fix our thoughts on Jesus (Hebrews 3:1).

How often other thoughts crowd in that are diametrically opposed to this list! The world pushes thoughts at me that are untrue and just ugly. But I can be proactive and intentional about my thoughts! I can control what I read. I can control what I watch. I can control to whom I listen. And the more my mind remains steadfastly on Him, the more I have His peace (Isaiah 26:3). The lyrics from "Be Thou My Vision" are so true: "Thou my best thought by day or by night."

Lord, keep my thoughts on You today.

Psalm 139:9-10

If I rise on the wings of the dawn, if
I settle on the far side of the sea,
even there your hand will guide me,
your right hand will hold me fast.

Zip Lining

I had never tried zip lining until just recently and I was plenty nervous! The staff there was very reassuring but still, that first lunge off the platform made my heart drop all the way to my feet! I had seen others ride the line with no hands, turning and laughing and calling to friends below. I was strangely silent and still, holding on for dear life! Just as I was starting to relax and enjoy it, the ride was over. I wished I could have come to that confident place sooner!

Today's verse is reassurance from someone who is in control of the whole lifelong ride. He holds fast those who belong to Him. Whether we are zip lining, mountain climbing, or living overseas in a strange culture, He promises to guide, direct, and never let go. His love holds us in the palm of His hand and nothing can touch us without His permission (John 10:28). No one can snatch us out of His hand!

When I really grasp this truth, like I did that line, I can more quickly reach that place of confidence and enjoy the ride! I have experienced His faithful care living overseas for more than thirty years. He has carried me through some unbelievable challenges in most every area of life. I do not have to fear what tomorrow may bring, because He has proved Himself faithful and true to His Word. If life seems to be going too fast or I cannot see what is ahead, I can still be confident and relax.

Lord, help me feel Your reassuring hold on me!

1 Kings 19:12

After the earthquake came a fire, but the Lord was not in the fire. And after the fire came a gentle whisper.

Whispers

These meerkats sure seem to be whispering! I have been told that my whispers are too loud. In public, I think I am being discreet when I whisper something in my husband's ear. But he is not the only one to hear me! Some whispers are ones we do not want to hear; things that are shameful if heard aloud. Then there are whispers that surprise! But the best kind of whispers are those sharing sweet secrets or those speaking love!

Today's verse is from the passage where the Lord communicates with Elijah. One would expect the mighty God of the universe to show Himself spectacularly. But God was not in the wind, the earthquake, or the fire. God revealed himself through a gentle whisper. Elijah needed reassurance after being threatened by Jezebel and running for forty days and forty nights. He had been miraculously cared for physically by an angel (verse 7). But Elijah needed something for his soul. What did that whisper say?

What does God whisper to me? He whispers to me through His Word, which is inspired or "God-breathed." He whispers His love and reassurance. He tells me He is in control. He whispers to me throughout my busy day saying, "I am here. I love you. You can count on Me." And He does not mind repeating Himself! His whispers are precious and beautiful. They remind me that I belong to Him. They reassure my soul and keep me going. Oh, how I need to hear Him whisper.

Lord, keep me listening to Your whispered reassurances of love.

Jeremiah 29:11

For I know the plans I have for you," declares the Lord, "plans to prosper you and not to harm you, plans to give you hope and a future.

Wishful Thinking

How can one visit Rome without seeing the famous Trevi Fountain? Sculpted in 1762, this Baroque fountain with its figure of Neptune is touted to be the largest and most famous fountain. And yes, I did the tourist thing of tossing in a coin to guarantee a return. But since the 1954 film, Three Coins in a Fountain, one coin does not suffice. Now it is expected to throw in that second coin to get me a new and exciting romance, and a third coin to lead to marriage. But I couldn't get my husband to hand me more than one coin!!

Today's verse speaks of hope. This is a hope that the Lord gives to us. The word "hope" in Scripture is not just wishful thinking. That is because the object of our hope is something sure. We are to hope in His Word (Psalm 130:5) as well as His unfailing love (Psalm 147:11). Hope like that will never disappoint. But hope in anything else has the potential to disappoint and even make the heart sick (Proverbs 13:12).

How could I live without hope? I am so thankful I do not have to! The Lord has plans for me. He has my future in His powerful and loving hands. He promises blessing for obedience. I cannot possibly know what is ahead but with hope I can be confident that it is all good. It is amazing to me that He loves me enough to plan it all out.

Thank you, Lord, that my hope is in You, and You never disappoint.

1 Peter 5:9

Resist him, standing firm in the faith, because you know that the family of believers throughout the world is undergoing the same kind of sufferings.

The Armadillo

Hello, little armored one! That is what the armadillo's name means in Spanish. Of the twenty-one species, the smallest is the pink fairy at six inches, and the largest is the giant at five feet. However, it is not the size but the number of bands that separates the species. Rather than flee the enemy, this guy quickly digs in the dirt, hunkers down, and trusts the overlapping plates covering his back, legs, and tail to protect him.

Today's verse counsels the believer to resist the devil. Rather than flee, we stand firm in the faith, trusting in our spiritual armor (Ephesians 6:10–18). We can stand our ground (verse 13) by believing truth rather than believing his lies. We can trust in God's righteousness given to us rather than allowing the devil to paralyze us with guilt. We not only stand our ground but take new ground by sharing His gospel of peace. Our unshakable faith and our confidence in His salvation grows when we fill our minds and hearts with His Word.

It is a comfort for me to know that the struggles I have are not unique. Believers all over the world are facing some of the same temptations and tests. And I can have confidence that the Lord has given me everything needed to stand firm in the face of spiritual attack. There is no reason to fear. Christ has already secured the victory for me on that cross. When I am submitted to God, I can resist any of the devil's ploys and he is the one who flees (James 4:7)!

Thank you, Lord, for Your priceless protection!

237

Matthew 20:15

Don't I have the right to do what I want with my own money? Or are you envious because I am generous?

Uneven Slices

Whether it is pizza, cake, or pie, it is important to cut those pieces evenly! Those who get the larger pieces feel special but the one with that skinny piece may feel a bit slighted. If my hostess is the one doing the paying, the cutting, and the serving I certainly cannot say anything. But I may be thinking, "It isn't fair."

Today's verse comes from a parable Jesus told about workers who had come in early in the day. They had made a contract with their employer to work for a certain sum of money. Then at the very last hour of the day a second group begins work and they are paid the same amount. Understandably, the first group was unhappy. It was unfair. The employer reminds these disgruntled workers it is his money and he can be generous if he chooses.

It is not uncommon to have the same thoughts about God. It seems there are times He is generous with someone so much less deserving than ourselves. Perhaps we have worked harder and longer and feel we should be compensated differently. Rather than rejoice at the generous blessings given to another, we grumble that we deserve more. It is just unfair. I am so glad God does not listen to this. If I got what was fair I would be completely lost. The wages of my sin is death (Romans 6:23) and I cannot say I deserve anything else. Eternal life is unfair, as I have not earned it. I am so thankful that He gives me His mercy and not what is fair.

Thank you, Lord, that Your mercy is so much better than fair!

Deuteronomy 6:5

Love the Lord your God with all your heart and with all your soul and with all your strength.

Bufflehead Duck

This duck is remarkable with its beautiful colors! The name of the Bufflehead was derived from "buffalo head" due the male's odd puffy head shape. But what interested me was his feeding habits. He rarely feeds with only his head submerged but instead will completely submerge himself. Many times a whole flock will all surface dive at the same time! This energetic feeder is "all in."

Today's verse describes one who is all in! God's command does not allow for any half measures. He wants a love that is total and complete with no holding back. We are to love Him with ALL our heart, soul, and strength. When Jesus cited this command He added "all your mind" as well (Mark 12:30). This is a commitment like no other. God's commands are to be on our hearts and impressed on the next generation through living them every day in the home (verses 6–9). The love He wants is one that involves our entire being.

It is because He loves me that He wants all of me. But to give the Lord my all is a lifelong challenge. It means trusting Him not to hurt or disappoint. And to completely relinquish all of me to Him also means the giving up of my own control. But He has the right to ask this of me. He so loved, and so proved His love for me by His sacrifice, that it is ludicrous for me to hold back anything! And I find that when I can be "all in" there is a closeness and warmth unlike any human relationship! It is worth the effort!

Lord, may my love for You involve my entire being.

Job 37: 3, 5

He unleashes his lightning beneath the whole heaven and sends it to the ends of the earth. [. . .] God's voice thunders in marvelous ways; he does great things beyond our understanding.

Thunderstorm!

It was quite the show! The storm woke us with peals of rolling thunder and flashes of light that lit up our room at the Mesa Verde National Park. We must have watched it for a good hour, marveling at the force and grandeur of that storm! As it moved overhead, we jumped at the deafening cracks of thunder, and the room even seemed to shake! How thankful we were not to be outside in it. We felt safe and protected.

Today's verse likens thunder to God's mighty voice. The fear that a clap of thunder can evoke is the fear I ought to feel at God's powerful Word. The Law was given to the Israelites in the midst of thunder and lightning. It inspired such fear in the people that they insisted that Moses approach God in their place. It is that fear which leads to obedience and wisdom (Psalm 111:10).

There are times that I lose that sense of fear at God's greatness. But all it takes to remind me is a huge storm that unleashes its fury. God is bigger than the biggest storm. His power transcends everything! I am so thankful that my fear of Him does not include fear of punishment! Jesus took on Himself all the condemnation I deserve. But my fear of Him is one that inspires knee-bending awe of His greatness and power. His thunderous mighty voice reminds me just how small and powerless I am. And His voice is accomplishing so much I do not understand.

Thank you, Lord, that I can always trust Your voice.

Hebrews 10:35

So do not throw away your confidence; it will be richly rewarded.

Thrown Away

Her husband thought he was being helpful. His wife came in late from the baby shower given her. She dutifully emptied the car of all the gift boxes containing all the sweet gifts for their unborn baby. She stacked them in the corner of the garage and went to bed. As usual, she heard the garbage truck come by early the next morning but thought nothing of it. That is until she realized that her helpful husband cleared out the garage that morning. Thinking the boxes were empty, he inadvertently threw away all the gifts!

Today's verse speaks of something that believers are never to throw away: our confidence. This is not a confidence in ourselves. This confidence is the full assurance that faith brings (verse 22). Confidence is ours because of Christ's sacrifice, giving us direct access into God's presence. We have confidence to draw near to God because Christ has sprinkled our hearts clean from a guilty conscience. These believers were facing physical suffering and confiscation of their property. But confidence was still possible in looking forward to what was promised.

It is much easier to doubt and question than to remain confident. When everything seems dark and hopeless, I am tempted to let go. But when I remember His faithfulness, I can regain that confidence. He is faithful to His word and His promises. He wants me to hold unswervingly to this hope I profess (verse 23). With confidence in His love I can persevere, even when circumstances are so negative. He has promised that my confidence placed in Him will be richly rewarded! Already, He is rewarding me with more of Himself.

Lord, keep me confident and holding on.

Psalm 121:2–3

My help comes from the Lord, the Maker of heaven and earth. He will not let your foot slip—he who watches over you will not slumber.

Sleeping Whale

The blowhole of this blue whale can be clearly seen on the top of his head. As a mammal, he needs to periodically surface to fill his huge lungs with air so he can breathe underwater. This means that a whale can never fall fully asleep! Instead, they only allow half of their brain to sleep at a time. The other half of their brain stays awake in order to come up for air when needed.

Today's verse reminds us of how constant God's care is of His own. As the Maker of heaven and earth, He is all-powerful and has no need of sleep. During the contest between God and Baal, Elijah taunted the false prophets when their god did not answer. Maybe he is sleeping and must be awakened (1 Kings 18:27)! The frantic dancing, shouting, and cutting of their bodies did not awaken a god that did not exist. By contrast, our God is a faithful source of help, always attentive to our cry day or night.

What a reassuring thought that He watches over me day or night! There is never a time when I need to get His attention. He is always thinking of me, as His thoughts toward me are more numerous than the grains of sand (Psalm 139:18). His watch over me means that He knows and He cares. Nothing gets past Him. What He allows to happen will be used to strengthen my faith and deepen our love relationship. Whatever I am facing today, I can trust that He knows what He is doing.

Thank you, Lord, for Your faithful watch over me.

Philippians 2:13

. . . for it is God who works in you to will and to act in order to fulfill his good purpose.

The Woodworking Planer

Wood shop in high school was for the boys. Perhaps it was just as well that I stayed away from those power tools and sharp instruments! How the wood got to be so smooth, flat and level remained a mystery, only because I was too disinterested to find out. But when my dad took up woodworking as a hobby, he taught me to appreciate those smooth flawless surfaces and the effort they took to achieve. The planer shaves off those high places in the wood, making the surface level.

Today's verse reveals that God is continually working in us. His goal is to mold our desires and actions to mirror His. He has a purpose for this work, and we can trust that it is a good purpose because He is good. He is working to make us smooth and level by taking out the high places in us. He is opposed to the proud (James 4:6) and will work to flatten those thoughts of superiority and self-sufficiency. The result is something beautiful that He can use!

Having my pride worked on hurts! That blade is shaving off what does not belong. It is humbling to be brought down to the right size. He may use the reprimand of others. He may use a miserable failure and allow me to fall flat on my face! He often uses His Word to convict and point out areas that need flattening. Whatever the case, it is not a comfortable experience. But when it is all over, He gives favor to the one He has humbled.

Oh how I need Your favor today! Lord, keep me smooth and humble.

Psalm 130:5

I wait for the Lord, my whole being waits, and in his word I put my hope.

Watch and Wait

Have you ever seen a cat watch and wait for his prey? The total concentration is surprising as they lay in wait. Every muscle is tensed and the pupils are wide in anticipation. The patient focus of a determined cat is amazing! Our cat, Tiger, used to spend much of his time in the yard crouched in readiness. And often, just before he pounced, his whole back end would quiver in excitement!

Today's verse is a statement of faith and trust of the one who cries out to the Lord for mercy. Faith is most evident when there is waiting involved for a response. And when we wait it is with our whole being, putting our hope in His sure and infallible Word. We wait for the Lord to act more than the wait of the watchmen (verse 6). They guard a sleepy city by watching and peering into the distance as they wait for the morning. Our wait will not last forever. As morning comes for the watchmen ending their shift, so we will eventually see His Word fulfilled!

I have been watching and waiting for a response to a particular prayer request these last twelve years! My morning has come with His incredible answer! I could wait with hope because of His unfailing love and His full redemption (verse 7). But there remain more reasons to watch and wait with unfulfilled promises in my life. I am encouraged, though, to persevere, having seen Him respond! One day there will be no more watching and waiting. One day, there will be no more need to hope as every hope will be realized in His presence!

Lord, thank you that I can wait with hope.

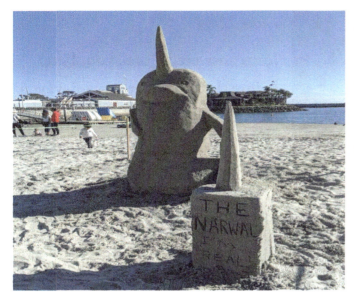

Hebrews 3:13

But encourage one another daily, as long as it is called "Today," so that none of you may be hardened by sin's deceitfulness.

Unicorn of the Sea

It is easy to see why the Narwhal has been called the "Unicorn of the Sea"! For the male, the canine tooth becomes a long tusk, piercing its upper lip. This pale medium-sized whale swims in the Arctic waters and sometimes dies from drowning! They need wide open spaces to breathe. But if they do not leave before the waters freeze over in late autumn, then they can suffocate!

Today's verse says that we can become hardened. Our hearts have the tendency to turn away from God in rebellion and unbelief (verse 12). Like the formation of ice, it can be a slow, insidious process that we do not even realize is happening. Sin is deceitful, pulling us gradually and subtly away from the God we love. Sin is deceitful as it seems so good and right! It can appear sophisticated and desirable. We need encouragement every day in order to resist its attraction. By recognizing sin's empty promises and praying for one another, we can hold on firmly to what we have in Christ (verse 14).

I would like to think that I am immune from sin's attraction. But even though I have known and loved the Savior for a long time, I am not immune. I understand the complications and danger sin can bring to a life. Even so I will always need the example and encouragement from other believers. He is always ready to forgive, but I do not like the distance I feel from the Lord when I give in. I know that if I flirt with sin, my heart will no longer be soft and pliable to Him.

Lord, do not let my heart ever become hardened.

Luke 22:34

Jesus answered, "I tell you, Peter, before the rooster crows today, you will deny three times that you know me."

Wake-up Call

When I see a rooster, I think of denial: denial of sleep! We recently spent some time out in the countryside of the Bas Rhin of Alsace, France. The rolling green hills were beautiful and I even enjoyed the baaing of the sheep next door. But what I did not appreciate were the noisy roosters! It was barely light out before they would start their sleep-denying racket. There was certainly no need for an alarm clock!

Today's verse also associates the rooster with denial. Jesus tells Peter that he will deny Him three times. I am sure Peter was shocked to hear this, especially after confidently declaring his commitment to Jesus. The Lord knew as well that Peter would turn back to Him (verse 32) and because of this experience, he would be able to strengthen his brothers in Christ. But before that could happen, Peter was given the opportunity to declare his love for Jesus three times (John 21:17). The Lord did not need to hear it so much as Peter needed to say it! The guilt from that denial could have destroyed Peter and the chance to serve Him.

God's grace covered that denial as it does for all my repented sin. I am so grateful that Jesus uses imperfect people! If not, where would I be? After failing the Lord, Peter could move on. After David's sin with Bathsheba, he could move on. After being responsible for the death of Christians, Paul could move on. After my sin, I can move on! There is no denying it: His grace is amazing!

Thank you, Lord, for Your constant and surprising grace!

Isaiah 42:8

I am the Lord; that is my name! I will not yield my glory to another or my praise to idols.

Moonlight

O ften when my children were young, we would see a big bright moon in the sky and chant the little ditty, "I see the moon and the moon sees me. God bless the moon and God bless me!" The moon can be so beautiful and it inspires so many romantic scenarios! But what is interesting about the moon is that it has no light of its own. The light that it shines is of course the reflected light from the sun. In fact, the side of the moon that is not facing the sun is always cold and dark.

Today's verse teaches that there is only one source of glory and that is the Lord. We can not claim any glory or praise as originating in ourselves. The Lord does not share His glory. However, He does want us to reflect it! It is our purpose here on earth to shine in this darkness and point others to Him. But it is HIS glory and light that we are reflecting.

Unfortunately just like the moon, when I am not facing the Light I cannot reflect it. I cannot reflect His glory when I claim that glory for myself. The dark side is the part of me that takes credit when it rightfully belongs to His work in me. But I do not want any cold or dark sides to me. I want all of me to shine! I want to give Him the glory for any and all accomplishments. I want Him to have the credit for anything that is good in my life.

Lord, may I reflect Your glory today!

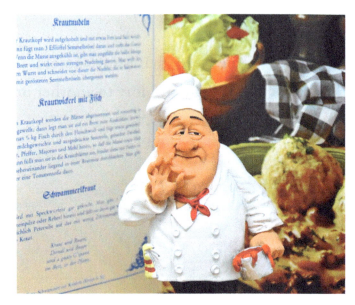

Psalm 119:137–138

You are righteous, Lord, and your laws are right. The statutes you have laid down are righteous; they are fully trustworthy.

Following the Recipe

I love following a good recipe that is tried and true. And if I wanted a German dish to be authentic, I would go to the trouble of translating those instructions (as well as converting the measurements). I would not worry about all the verbs being in the command form. It is a recipe, after all. I do not expect it to say, "Please beat the eggs." Or "Would you mind chopping the nuts." But I am not offended. The directives are there to obtain a good, tasty result!

Today's verse describes God's directives. Sometimes they can seem very blunt. There is no softening what God requires of us. But His commands are always with a good goal. They are always for our good and for our protection. We know that because HE is good. What He commands is fully trustworthy and an expression of His love and care. This is why David could say that they are a joy to the heart and light to the eyes, sweeter than honey, and more precious than gold (Psalm 19:10)!

If God's commandments are really for my good, then why am I always trying to change the recipe? Because that is in fact what I sometimes try to do. I think I know better or that somehow I am an exception to the rule. Maybe I can "sort of" follow the instructions but introduce a variation which makes it easier on me. The result is never as good. His way is always the best, and I am the one who benefits when I carefully follow what He wants.

Lord, thank you for Your love expressed through your commands.

Psalm 119:137–138

As he was scattering the seed, some fell along the path, and the birds came and ate it up.

Canadian Geese

Homeowners in a Tallahassee neighborhood did not share my appreciation for these beautiful birds. That's because they roamed the streets, entering garages and making a nuisance of themselves. And for anyone trying to plant a lawn, they considered the seeds as their personal lunch buffet! But they would only go after the seeds lying on the surface. All it took was a fourth inch of soil to discourage them.

Today's verse is part of the parable of the sower. The seeds sown did not sprout and grow, as they were quickly devoured by birds. Jesus explains that those who hear the Word but do not understand it are prey to the evil one who snatches away what was sown, before it can take root (verse 19). That seed is exposed and vulnerable without the topsoil of understanding. The understanding of His Word keeps the seed safe, rooted, and growing. And this understanding comes from the Son of God, who is true (1 John 5:20). When one quickly gets into God's Word with the understanding He offers, then those birds have no chance to snatch it away!

How vitally important it is that the seed of salvation in me is protected by understanding His Word! The more I read, study, and meditate, the more I am protected from the deception of the evil one. He cannot snatch away what is taking root and growing. And understanding His Word is a lifelong process. I can never close the book and think, there . . . I know it completely. It is the Spirit of His Son who speaks to me and brings to light something new each time I open it.

Thank you, Lord, that You give me Your understanding.

The whole earth is filled with awe at your wonders; where morning dawns, where evening fades, you call forth songs of joy.

Aurora Borealis

These light shows are eerie and breathtaking! I have seen them in the countryside of Vermont and from the airplane window flying over Iceland. These bright dancing lights are most often pale green and pink, although they have also lit the skies in shades of red, yellow, blue, and violet. They can take the form of clouds, patches, arcs, and shooting rays. But what I find most impressive are the rippling curtains they sometimes form! I understand that they can be explained away as gaseous particles from the earth colliding with charged particles from the sun. But that does not lessen the awe I feel when seeing this creative wonder of our God.

Today's verse tells us that the whole earth is filled with awe at His wonders. From the mountains He has formed to the stilling of the roaring seas, He answers us with His awesome and righteous deeds (verses 5–7). And because we see His incredible creative power in nature, we have hope. He not only stills the roaring waves but also stills the turmoil of nations (verse 7). He stills the turmoil in our hearts as well, calling forth "songs of joy" where there were none.

Seeing the light of the Aurora Borealis or the beautiful light of a sunset reminds me that Jesus is Light as well (John 8:12). His light dispels the darkness and gloom that can gather in my heart when I'm faced with an impossible situation. His power has no limits. He can heal my heart when I'm overwhelmed with crushing emotion. He can bring back the joy when I turn to Him and trust His power.

Thank you, Lord, that for You nothing is impossible.

Romans 8:31b–32

If God is for us, who can be against us? He who did not spare his own Son, but gave him up for us all, how will he not also, along with him, graciously give us all things?

Underdog

There does not seem to be much question as to who would win in this face off between boxer and chihuahua! We often like to cheer the underdog or the one who seems to be facing insurmountable odds. There is something about the weaker one carrying the victory that encourages us to hope and to greater effort in our own circumstances.

Today's verse encourages the heart of every underdog. God sees our predicament. He understands that we are limited and often powerless to stand firm in our faith. We are mocked and maligned, misunderstood and marginalized. We may feel like we are in a weaker position being in the minority. But we are on the winning side and that changes everything!

God is for His own. He has sacrificed His dearest Son to have this relationship with me. No one can snatch me out of His hand (John 10:28). No one can separate me from His love (Romans 8:38–39). No one. He has won the victory for me (1 Corinthians 15:57) and I can hold my head up! I may feel outnumbered and insignificant, but with God on my side, suddenly the playing field changes.

Lord, how could I live this life without You being for me? Thank you that I do not have to!

2 Corinthians 4:8–9

We are hard pressed on every side, but not crushed; perplexed, but not in despair; persecuted, but not abandoned; struck down, but not destroyed.

Pizza Dough

I t all seems a bit complicated. After punching down the rising pizza dough and kneading it, the dough is further manhandled by throwing it up in the air! It looks like an art designed to impress the onlooker. But in fact, this process of spinning it in the air creates the round shape and allows just enough airflow for easier handling. With this method, the dough retains more moisture making the crust softer.

In today's verse, Paul is recounting some of the hardships he and Timothy had faced. At the beginning of the chapter and at the end, he says, "We do not lose heart." It would have been completely understandable if they had! Paul had been shipwrecked, beaten, stoned, and imprisoned for his faith. Being perplexed, he perhaps did not always understand the "why" behind what was happening. Yet he remained confident that the pulling and stretching was producing something of value, forming the likeness of Jesus in him (verse 10).

When I am faced with hard times, I often feel perplexed. I usually cannot explain why the Lord allows certain difficulties in my life. But He promises that all the pulling and stretching will be producing a "weight of glory" one day (verse 17). All that is painful or devastating is only a "light affliction" compared to what lies ahead. I can be confident that even when I'm panicked and confused, He is in control and His control is good. How good of Him to reassure me!

Thank you, Lord, that You use it all. Help me not to lose heart.

1 Corinthians 10:12

So, if you think you are standing firm, be careful that you don't fall.

The Woodpecker

I had never seen a woodpecker until living in France. There was one who frequently visited our yard, and with his red markings he was easy to spot. There was one fruit tree that he especially liked to peck for insects. I was always happy to see him, not realizing what he was doing to that tree. One night we had a huge windstorm and with an impressive crack, that tree came down, snapping at exactly the very place that woodpecker had been working! I feel differently about woodpeckers now. I missed that mirabelle plum tree!

Today's verse is a loving warning. After describing the failures of the Israelites in the wilderness, Paul cautions that falling is a real possibility. We can think that we are standing firm while at the same time being slowly weakened by compromise. Like the small attacks made by the beak of a woodpecker, our resolve can slowly erode, leaving us vulnerable. A strong wind of temptation can come along and knock us flat. We fall to the ground and we no longer bear fruit.

No one wakes up in the morning and decides to give in to temptation. Being drawn away from Him is usually a slow sneaky process. And it can come from something normally beautiful or agreeable. The next verse is such a comforting promise. God will not allow me to be tempted beyond what I can bear. He provides a way out. I have a choice. That enticement to sin is never so strong that with His help I cannot resist!

Don't let me fall, Lord. Keep me firmly standing and bearing fruit.

Psalms 85:8

I will listen to what God the Lord says; he promises peace to his people, his faithful servants—but let them not turn to folly.

Conch Shell

My first inclination when seeing a conch shell is to put it to my ear. I enjoy hearing that whooshing sound resembling the sound of ocean waves. Some say that the sound is just one's own blood rushing in the brain with every heartbeat. Others believe that ocean sound is just the surrounding sound resonating within the shell. In either case, the shell would have to be vacant before I would let it anywhere near my ear!

Today's verse talks about hearing something else; what God has to say. It begins with a statement of intention: "I will." There are a myriad of sounds out there clamoring to be heard. But listening to the Lord through His Word is worth the effort and discipline. He speaks peace to those who belong to Him. So many times I have come to Him in prayer, totally agitated and stressed. He speaks peace. He calms me down, and listening intently, I hear reminders of His love and control in my circumstances. I get in that troubled state usually because I have not been listening to Him in the first place!

Not only do I hear Him speak peace, but listening to Him keeps me from folly or from doing something foolish. If I am honest with myself, I realize I am quite capable of doing all kinds of foolish things with impeccable rationale! Listening to Him daily through His Word is the best way to avoid my own folly. And I so need the peace and calm He offers.

Lord, keep me listening to You today.

Revelation 19:11

I saw heaven standing open and there before me was a white horse, whose rider is called Faithful and True. With justice he judges and wages war.

The Westbury White Horse

This huge white horse has been standing on this hill outside Westbury in Wiltshire, England since at least 1742. It can be seen for miles as it measures 180 feet tall and 170 feet wide. It was originally done in chalk and needed constant restoration but has been covered over with concrete since 1950. Folklore says that when the nearby church clock strikes midnight, the horse goes down to the spring below to drink!

Today's verse mentions a white horse seen by John as part of God's revelation. But more important than the white horse is its unique rider, He who is Faithful and True. This is the King of Kings and the Lord of Lords (verse 16) and He bursts on the scene as a mighty unstoppable warrior, bringing judgment and justice. Following Him are the armies of heaven, also riding white horses and dressed in white linen. What an incredible sight, which signals the beginning of a thousand years of Christ's rule on earth! He is Faithful and True to fulfill every outstanding prophecy about His coming kingdom!

I could not love Him or worship Him if He were not absolutely faithful and true to His Word. But He is. The word of the Lord is right and true. He is faithful in all He does (Psalm 33:4). He will defeat evil. He will bring righteousness and justice. He will reward faithful service and right living. I can stand firm knowing He is faithful and true. Others may renege on their word, and even loved ones may break promises. But I can always count on Him.

Thank you, Lord, that I can rely on your faithfulness even today.

Do not be wise in your own eyes; fear the Lord and shun evil.

The Wombat

The wombat is one strange marsupial. This burrowing animal from Australia carries its young in a pouch facing backward so as not to get dirt in the young one's eyes! Their backside is covered with a thick hide impervious to the claws of predators. When chased, they will dive into their tunnel with their rump sticking out and stay that way until their predator gives up! They are said to have the largest brain of any marsupial. Maybe that is why a group of them is called a "wisdom."

Today's verse is one of many that warn us not to consider ourselves wise. This is a danger as it can lead to the conviction that we know better. This brand of pride considers rules as being for other people to follow and not applying to us. Those who see evil as good, dark as light, and bitter as sweet are the same people who are "wise in their own eyes and clever in their own sight" (Isaiah 5:21).

It is easy for me to think that wisdom comes from my own schooling or perceived mental prowess. But God's Word makes clear that the source of wisdom is the Lord. I demonstrate wisdom when I am humble enough to follow and obey Him in every area of my life. But the minute I consider myself wise is the same minute I risk becoming foolish (Proverbs 26:12). To become or remain wise is simply the by-product of humble, dependent obedience to my Creator. It is in living life God's way that there is any possibility of becoming wise.

Thank you, Lord, that right relationship with You makes me wise. Keep me humble, submissive, and close to You today.

Hebrews 13:5

Keep your lives free from the love of money and be content with what you have, because God has said, "Never will I leave you; never will I forsake you."

The Bench Seat

The classic cars are great for one very personal reason; they often have that bench-style seat! Instead of being separated from my honey by bucket seats, I can snuggle up close. I have heard it said that one can see how long a couple has been married by the distance the wife puts between herself and the driver. Of course, the driver has not moved. But the wife would sometimes inch her way toward the door a little more each year!

In today's verse, Jesus promises never to leave us or abandon us. He does not move. His love remains constant. It is because of the promise of His presence and care that we can be free of money worries. Rather than loving money, we love Him. Rather than looking for contentment elsewhere, we find it in His love.

There are times I feel very far from the Lord. I know He is there but I do not sense His presence. Without even being aware, I find I have inched toward that door. It has happened through my own neglect of His Word. Or I have simply let drop my conversations with Him. He has not moved. I have. Inching away from Him leads to feeling discontented, and I start looking out the car window at all the things I think I should have. Because He has not moved, the solution is simple. Through His Word and through our conversations I come back to where He is. He waits for me and He promises to be there.

Thank you, Lord, that You never move!

Ephesians 2:4-5

But because of his great love for us, God, who is rich in mercy, made us alive with Christ even when we were dead in transgressions – it is by grace you have been saved.

Hummingbird Drama

All the windows and doors were opened and this little guy got confused. Poor little thing tried to find his way out but was totally disoriented. In his fright he repeatedly flew into the skylight, knocking himself to the floor. My husband carefully transported what looked to be a dead hummingbird to some shade in the backyard. The story ends well as the bird eventually revived and flew away!

Today's verse tells us that we are made alive with Christ. And unlike the hummingbird, we were truly dead. Our sin kept us from having a relationship with our Creator. There was not a thing we could do to make ourselves alive. Christ, because of His incredible love and mercy, decided to do for us what we could never do for ourselves. He showed His grace by making us spiritually alive to Him. There is no true life without that spiritual awakening that He gives.

I felt so bad for the confused hummingbird going toward that skylight that could not save. In the same way, man thinks he can find some sort of light, joy, and peace within himself and apart from his Creator. Satan masquerades as an angel of light (II Cor. 11:14) and is thrilled when man misses the true Source. The Light of God's presence will not deceive or disappoint me. He makes me alive to Himself, to love and enjoy Him. I am forever thankful that in His grace He took the initiative! Because of His great love and His rich mercy, He has made me alive!

Thank you Lord, for Your undeserved favor toward me!

Ecclesiastes 4:6

Better one handful with tranquility than two handfuls with toil and chasing after the wind.

Storm Chasers

Why would anyone chase a storm? To risk everything and knowingly put oneself in the path of danger seems insane! Storm chasers include locals with cell phone cameras, news crews, researchers, photographers, university field trips, and van loads of storm tour groups! Whether they are motivated by adventure or science, those who drive hundreds if not thousands of miles to chase a storm are passionate! I can understand the thrill and the awe of nature, but my sense of self-preservation is too strong to join them. After all, it is just chasing after wind.

Solomon in Ecclesiastes often repeats the phrase, "chasing after the wind." Today's verse notes just one of the activities he lists as futile. Chasing after more and more wealth may fill two hands rather than just one, but it does not give us peace. The more we have, the more we seem to want. There is always more to acquire with the promise of peace, security, and satisfaction. But when we arrive, we find that the promise was false.

Just as one cannot catch wind, one cannot find meaning in the material world. We were created with "eternity in our hearts" (Ecclesiastes 3:11). Everything else is not only temporal but in the end, unsatisfying. Having more handfuls does not insure having peace. More often than not, having more creates its own worries and headaches and robs us of peace! Some of the most contented and peaceful people I know have surprisingly little in their hands. But how easily I forget that fact. The truth is, I want heart peace more than any material benefit that exists.

Thank you, Lord, for the peace and rest I have in You.

Psalm 62:11–12

One thing God has spoken, two things I have heard: "Power belongs to you, God, and with you, Lord, is unfailing love"; and, "You reward everyone according to what they have done."

The Serval

This cat is all ears! The serval is a wild African cat believed to be the ancient ancestor of the cheetah. Their ears are the largest of any cat. They live in tall grass and are not as likely to see their small prey. So their ears are huge to hear what they cannot see. The ears of a serval are so sensitive they can recognize sounds made by animals moving in their underground tunnels! But it was for their grace and strength that the ancient Egyptians worshiped them.

Today's verse was written by David, a very wealthy and powerful king. His ears were attuned to God's Word. Rather than trust in his own strength and riches, David acknowledges that only God has real power. David had been listening to many things God had spoken to him personally, but these two truths kept him in an attitude of trust. Not only does God have all the power, but He uses it to fight for and protect those He loves.

I need to be listening for these same truths. Unwittingly, I put God in a box with my thinking, forgetting just how formidable He is. I need to remember that He is all-powerful and nothing escapes His perfect justice. But how thankful I am that His power is coupled with His love! His sacrificial love has made a way for me to escape the punishment my sins deserve. Nothing and no one can prevail against me or separate me from this incredible love (Romans 8:38–39).

Lord, help me hear Your reassurances of power and love today!

Psalm 36:5

Your love, Lord, reaches to the heavens, your faithfulness to the skies.

Solar Eclipse

How eerie to see the sun completely covered by the moon today! The total solar eclipse was oohed and awed by many along its trajectory. Those not in its path still had the opportunity to see the partially covered sun with their special glasses. For many of a certain age, it may very well be their last opportunity to experience the celestial show as the next one does not occur until 2024. It was odd to see crowds of people clapping and cheering as the sky became completely darkened. The return of the sun did not get the same response. As nature's spectacle came to an end, I do not think there were many that doubted that the sun would reappear.

Today's verse is a wonderful reassurance about something that is warm and full of life-giving energy and it is something that can never be eclipsed. God's love can never be darkened. Nothing can thwart or obstruct His faithful love for His own. His love reaches to the heavens and there are no shifting shadows that can change it (James 1:17). He is faithful!

Whenever I feel that He has abandoned me, it can seem very dark. When my doubts obscure His love there is only one solution: I need to turn back again to His love letter to me. There I am reminded of His faithfulness. His love has not changed. His love and compassion are renewed every morning (Lamentations 3:22–23). Though I may not see the light of His love, it is still there. He lifts my head to see His faithfulness reaching to the skies!

Thank you, Lord, that regardless of my feelings, Your love for me never fails!

Proverbs 12:16

Fools show their annoyance at once, but the prudent overlook an insult.

Sticky

There is nothing that annoys more quickly than stepping on a piece of gum. It stubbornly sticks to the shoe and resists most efforts at cleaning. There is lots of advice out there on how to remove that nasty gum, including ice cubes, WD-40 motor oil, peanut butter, and freezing the shoe in a plastic bag. But those methods do not help when I am out and about. I end up walking on that foot gingerly, smelling like mint until I can get back home!

Today's verse reminds me of how insults can stick like gum to the shoe. We remember every harsh or unkind word. The more publicly it is uttered, the more it sticks to our memories. But showing annoyance at the time it is said puts us at a disadvantage. We are seen as "foolish" when we show that the insult of another annoys us. However, we are viewed as prudent when we can immediately overlook that insult. When we can manage to overlook it, it will not stick to us. Not only will others not remember it, but we ourselves have a better chance of forgetting it as well.

It is such a wonderful quality to be able to shrug off an insult. It is even "to one's glory" to overlook an offense (Proverbs 19:11). We are viewed as the better person for taking this high road. But quite frankly, I find it very difficult to do. It helps me to look to the model of Jesus who was insulted, reviled, mocked, and misunderstood. Yet, He did not reply in kind or hold a grudge. He responded with an offer of forgiveness. It did not stick!

Lord, give me the wisdom and prudence to overlook insults.

Psalm 126:5

Those who sow with tears will reap with songs of joy.

The Sea Turtle

My grandson was entranced with this sea turtle off the coast of Hawaii! His family had specifically risen early and gone to where they were known to congregate. But rather than going out to it, this gentle reptile came up close and personal! If it had been on land it probably would have been a female nesting. When laying her eggs, the female sea turtle will shed large sticky tears that wash off excess salt from their bodies and prevent sand in the eyes.

Today's verse mentions tears that can be a prelude to songs of joy. Being filled with joy can follow a time of long, arduous preparation and waiting. The Lord fulfilled His promise to the Israelites to bring them back from captivity and restore their health. Other nations took note and God was glorified! After many tears, their mouths were even filled with laughter (verse 2)! Despite the weeping and waiting they could say, "The Lord has done great things for us" (verse 3)!

The Lord has given me a similar promise. In His presence is fullness of joy (Psalm 16:11) and one day that joy will be overflowing! All tears will be wiped away from my eyes (Revelation 21:4). All the waiting and longing and disappointment will come to an end. The new song He has put in my mouth (Psalm 40:3) will continue on into heaven. It is my firm hope and conviction that I will be trading in my tears for astonished and eternal joy! I look forward to the time when the sowing will be over. But even here and now in the midst of tears I can say, "The Lord has done great things" for me!

Lord, I praise You for a future without tears.

Matthew 16:18

And I tell you that you are Peter, and on this rock I will build my church, and the gates of Hades will not overcome it.

Thor's Well

On the Oregon Coast at Cape Perpetua, the Pacific gives visitors quite a show with the moving waters of Thor's Well. Over the years it is thought that the waves carved out a sea cave where later the roof collapsed. The resulting bowl-shaped hole looks as if it is continually draining and refilling. At high tide the water fills it from the bottom. Then it bubbles or sprays out the top, the cycle repeating itself. This strange phenomenon is also called "Gate to Hell" although it is not thought to be particularly dangerous.

Today's verse encourages the believer that despite enemies and opposition, the gates of Hell (Hades, or realm of the dead) will not overcome the Church Jesus has established. That is because Jesus Himself builds it and it is built on the confession of Peter. He avowed that Jesus is the Messiah, the Son of the Living God (verse 16). The Church is built on this fundamental truth, the identity of Jesus being its cornerstone (Acts 4:11).

The Gate to Hell is a busy place with churning water that seems to fill and drain constantly. And there will always be plenty of activity and evil directed at bringing down the Church. Sometimes, I can be discouraged reading of Christians martyred for their faith in Jesus. I can feel dispirited to see very public Christian workers fall into sin. But this wonderful truth reassures me that nothing and no one can thwart God's plan. The Church is His Bride and He loves her. I am part of that body and I can be confident that evil will not win.

Thank you, Lord, for Your promise of victory!

2 Corinthians 12:9

But he said to me, "My grace is sufficient for you, for my power is made perfect in weakness." Therefore I will boast all the more gladly about my weaknesses so that Christ's power may rest on me.

The Silverback Gorilla

The silverback gorilla is the strongest and most experienced male leader of his "troop." He is the one who decides where the others will travel, forage, and sleep. He is responsible for the safety of the group. When challenged by interlopers, he will beat his chest, scream, bare his teeth, and charge, sometimes shaking a branch broken off from a tree! What an amazing show of strength!

Today's verse talks about a different source of strength that empowers the believer to accomplish more than what was thought possible. It seems so paradoxical, but to experience His power and strength, we admit and even boast about our weaknesses! There is no "show of strength" on our part. For the believer, all the power and strength has Christ as its source. It is through our weakness that God has the opportunity to manifest His strength. And when this happens He gets all the praise, glory, and recognition.

My pride keeps me from admitting to weakness. No one wants to appear weak. But the more I admit to my weaknesses and my limitations, the more He can and does use me when I turn to Him. When I admit to my weakness, something amazing happens. He lovingly takes that weakness and transforms it into something strong. How good He is to provide Himself that very strength He asks of me!

Lord, make me strong today.

Isaiah 28:16

So this is what the Sovereign Lord says: "See, I lay a stone in Zion, a tested stone, a precious cornerstone for a sure foundation; the one who relies on it will never be stricken with panic."

The "Great Rock"

This strange structure sits on an even stranger landscape: Burren, on the west coast of Ireland. The name, Burren, means "great rock." Dry limestone rock covers this flat barren area, making it resemble a moonscape. This structure is called Poulnabrone, a portal tomb that has stood the test of time. Originally covered with soil, it served as a collective burial site as well as a territorial marker. All that remains today is its "stone skeleton."

Today's verse describes the only true and firm foundation. The people were deluding themselves thinking that they could mock God's words, live how they pleased, and not be touched by calamity. They were taking refuge in lies and falsehoods (verses 15 & 17). They relied on themselves and their own righteousness and justice rather than the foundation of God's truth. But the "stone" on which we are to build our lives is a tested precious cornerstone. That cornerstone is Jesus Christ (Ephesians2:20) and the one who trusts in Him will never be put to shame (1 Peter 2:6).

My whole life is like a building that is based on the Rock. Jesus is not just an afterthought, but the cornerstone from which everything else is fitted. He is my point of reference for all truth. Relying on my own rationale or reasoning is like building on sand (Matthew 7:24–27). When the storms of life whirl around me, I want to be remain stable. I will not panic at whatever life throws at me because I am founded on His unshakeable and eternal truth.

Lord, keep me stable today.

Isaiah 41:10

So do not fear, for I am with you; do not be dismayed, for I am your God. I will strengthen you and help you; I will uphold you with my righteous right hand.

The Sea Otter

The little furry face of the sea otter looks too cute to be related to the weasel. The otter is made for the water and spends most of his time there. His feet are webbed, his fur is water repellent and his nostrils and ears close up in the water. Despite their fur being the thickest of any animal, they often float on the surface, even falling asleep in this position. They look so calm and peaceful, without a care in the world.

Today's verse is a wonderful promise of support for God's chosen ones. Those He has redeemed for all eternity need have no fear of sinking in the water of this world's troubles. He gives strength and help. He upholds us with His powerful and righteous hand. Regardless of how deep that water is, we have no cause for fear. His steady love and power will hold us up and keep our head above water.

Moving through hard times, I need to hear this. There are times I feel as if I am sinking, but I am not. He has never let me down. And I know He has a plan and purpose for those difficulties. But I feel dismay and fear even so. I paddle as if my life depended on it. I panic and swallow water when I could be trusting Him and floating on the surface. He is holding me up from underneath where I cannot see, and I can relax in His control!

Thank you, Lord, for Your strength and support!

Romans 8:2

. . . because through Christ Jesus the law of the Spirit who gives life has set you free from the law of sin and death.

Revolving Door

Although fancier, this resembles very closely the revolving door at my French grocery store. There seems to be plenty of room to maneuver, that is until a couple of carts and people are added! Rather than roll into someone or bang the sides, I have on occasion taken one turn too many! The "revolving door" is used in idiomatic expressions to mean that one can end up inadvertently where one started.

Today's verse reassures the believer that through His Spirit, God has set us free from the law of sin and death. Sin no longer has power and authority over the believer. Where once we were in bondage to repeat over and over the same sin, through Him we can break that cycle. Of course, temptation is still a struggle. But the believer has His promise that the temptation will never be more than we can bear, and He will provide a way out of it without us sinning (1 Corinthians 10:13). There is choice, and there is power available to do the right thing.

It does seem that I am sometimes covering the same ground over and over. When my patience is again being tested, I am glad when there is no one near to hear my knee-jerk reaction! In my own power I am destined to a life of repeating the same mistakes. But when I stop and look to Him and His power, there is a different outcome. I can respond to testing and trials in a way that pleases Him. When through dependence on Him I do it right, I absolutely feel free, and I feel His pleasure!

Thank you, Lord, for Your life-changing Spirit!

Matthew 5:6

Blessed are those who hunger and thirst for righteousness, for they will be filled.

S'mores

Warm weather is the season for this yummy treat! Summer campfires are the perfect cooking method for the "s'more." That wonderful combination of cookie and chocolate held together by the gooey roasted marshmallow has long been a favorite. This mouthwatering concoction is attributed to the Girl Scouts of the USA. The recipe was first published in 1927 by troop leader Loretta Scott Crew. To quote her, "Though it tastes like 'some more,' one is really enough!"

In today's verse, there is no thinking about wanting some more! Those that hunger and thirst for righteousness will be filled and satisfied. With His righteousness we do not pine for something more. There is no feeling of missing out on something better. A righteous life is the best kind of life. Doing the right thing, following His way, and experiencing right standing with our Creator gives a sense of well-being that is complete. No other kind of life can be quite as full or satisfying!

My problem is that I hunger and thirst for other things, good things, that give only temporary satisfaction. But of course, I hunger and thirst for those things or experiences all over again. However, I do not want my life to be characterized by wanting more. I desperately want to experience that contentment and satisfaction He offers. If I make the Lord the object of my longing, He will satisfy me. He never intends for me to have an appetite that is insatiable. That I should always pine for more must grieve His heart as He has promised life to the full (John 10:10). The abundance He offers gives a deeper satisfaction to my soul!

Thank you, Lord, that You fill my longings with Yourself.

Psalm 84:2

My soul yearns, even faints for the courts of the Lord; my heart and my flesh cry out for the living God.

Stork Sightings

How fun to be back in the land of the storks! Here on the French/German border I see them daily on my walks and they always take my breath away, soaring above my head or foraging in the fields. There are lots of beliefs and legends surrounding this magnificent bird. In ancient Egypt, a stork was used as a hieroglyph for the "Ba" or "soul." And in Germany, storks have long been protected because of the belief that their souls were human!

Today's verse describes a soul that yearns and even faints for the presence of the Lord. The soul of man is created to have intimate relationship with his Creator. The courts of the Lord are a lovely place (verse 1). Being in His courts for even just one day is better than a thousand days anywhere else (verse 10)! We are told to "dwell" in His house as a sparrow and swallow would nest in her home (verse 3). This is not just a Sunday church experience, but a daily closeness with Him. Those who dwell in His house are happy and blessed, praising Him for His goodness (verse 4).

I know I am far from His house or presence when I am dissatisfied and negative. When I am feeling far away from my Creator, there is a lack of joy, and praising Him is not a natural impulse. When I have had enough of my own company, I feel my soul being drawn again to His wonderful and lovely presence. I yearn for those soft sweet whispers of love and reassurance.

Thank you, Lord, that You always welcome me back to Your presence!

1 Corinthians 15:51–52

Listen, I tell you a mystery: We will not all sleep, but we will all be changed—in a flash, in the twinkling of an eye, at the last trumpet. For the trumpet will sound, the dead will be raised imperishable, and we will be changed.

The Closing Bell

When that bell peals its piercing note and the sound of it drifts away, all the frantic activity comes to an abrupt halt. Everything stops. At least until the next day, there are no more opportunities for trade on the New York Stock Exchange. Everyone carefully listens for it as the timing can change priorities for those traders on the floor.

In today's verse is the sound, not of a bell but of a trumpet. It is the last trumpet and signals a stop as well to all frantic activity. It is a sound that will signal the end of all time as we know it. This trumpet announces the resurrection, and it will be heard all over the world. What a day it will be when that trumpet is blown! At that very moment, new incorruptible bodies are given to those believers who have already died. And bodies are changed for those believers still living. What a victory over death that will be!

Reading about this future event affects me TODAY. Knowing this truth helps me stay steadfast, immoveable, and prioritizing my service to Him (verse 58). Looking toward the resurrection and eternity convinces me that my work for the Lord is never futile or in vain. I want to be listening for and anticipating this sound. It closes the opportunity to serve Him here on earth. But look what it opens! An eternity of rest and reward with the Lover of my soul!

Thank you, Lord, for the change that is coming!

2 Corinthians 2:15

For we are to God the pleasing aroma of Christ among those who are being saved and those who are perishing. To the one we are an aroma that brings death; to the other, an aroma that brings life. And who is equal to such a task?

The Ring-tailed Lemur

These sweet-looking lemurs are known for their black and white striped tails, and they apparently enjoy sunbathing! Originally from Madagascar, they have powerful scent glands. They use their distinctive odor to communicate and to dominate. The lemurs will mark their territory by their scent, but they will also try to "outstink" each other during mating season! They do this by rubbing their smelly secretions all over their tails and waving them in the air to establish dominance.

Today's verse speaks of differing reactions to our "smell" or influence. To those God is calling to Himself, we have a pleasing aroma. These are people in our lives who seem to be open and friendly. They know of our relationship with Jesus and continue their contact with us. We can and do pray that the Lord is continuing to draw them to Himself and that He will use our fragrance. But there is another group that is in the process of rejecting the Savior, and we stink to them. We can be as friendly as possible, but they are continually offended by our stench!

I am a people pleaser and it bothers me when I am rejected because of my faith in the Lord. Yet, I understand that the claims of Jesus do have a polarizing effect on people. The lines are drawn and there is no middle ground when it comes to saving faith in Christ. I am just thankful that for those God is drawing to Himself, I can be a pleasing aroma.

Lord, keep me faithful to You.

Psalm 3:3

But you, Lord, are a shield around me, my glory, the One who lifts my head high.

Texting

I hurt just looking at him! This hunched-over position while texting can have some serious consequences. With the head weighing 10–12 pounds, bending over our phones increases the force, pulling on those neck muscles and joints. Not only can our poor posture lead to headaches and spine problems, but some researchers have even made a connection with depression! The idea is that the relationship between mind and body can run both ways. We slump over because we are sad, or we are sad because we slump over!

Today's verse tells us that the Lord's presence in our lives is a protective shield. He looks out for His own. Nothing and no one can snatch us out of His hand (John 10:28). And as believers, He is our glory. Our lives are to progressively reflect His glory as He creates Christ's character in us (2 Corinthians 3:18). But in addition to all of this, He lifts our heads! And not just a little bit. He lifts our heads high! We no longer hang our heads in shame and disgrace. We do not have to look down in humiliation and guilt. It is because of His love and forgiveness that our heads are lifted high! What an amazing thought!

When He lifts my head, I have the advantage of seeing more of His wonders in my life! With the perspective that comes with grace and forgiveness, I can see just how much He has blessed me! Like Mary in her song, I can say that I am blessed, "for the Mighty One has done great things for me—holy is his name" (Luke 1:49).

Lord, lift my head high with the assurance of Your love.

Deuteronomy 31:8

The Lord himself goes before you and will be with you; he will never leave you nor forsake you. Do not be afraid; do not be discouraged.

The Quokka

This seemingly sweet quokka looks as if he is smiling. He is the smallest member of the "big foot" family that includes the kangaroo and wallaby. They look so cuddly with their teddy bear ears and their doe-like eyes. But in fact, they can be quite vicious when using their sharp claws. This adorable looking animal is not so adorable when the mother pushes her baby out of her pouch. She does this to escape her predator when chased!

Today's verse is a promise that the Lord will never abandon His own. What a comforting truth that the Lord our God will go with us! He not only is with us but He goes before us and leads the way. Because He will never leave us nor forsake us, we are not fearful or discouraged. There is never a question of being abandoned by God. These words were spoken by Moses to the Israelites (verse 6) and then repeated to Joshua and the Israelites (verse 8). Moses' leadership was coming to an end and he did not want them to feel abandoned.

It is during the hard discouraging times that the Lord wants to reassure me of His loving presence and control. Looking at my unclear future causes anxious fearful thoughts to fill me. Looking at my daunting circumstances brings discouragement. But looking to Him brings me hope. He is right there in front of me, clearing the way through the mess. The promise that He will never leave me nor abandon me helps calm me down.

Lord, help me remember that You are there and working on my behalf.

Psalm 65:10

You drench its furrows and level its ridges; you soften it with showers and bless its crops.

After the Rains

With the recent rains, our local hills are green and beautiful. And the wildflowers have put on quite a show this year. But not everything that grows is welcome! I knew that if I did not attack our hill soon, the weeds would be much more difficult to clear. The warm, drier weather will soon arrive and that ground will harden and be unforgiving. But for now, the ground is soft and easily gives up the roots of those nasty weeds.

Today's verse describes the rains and what they do for the land. This psalm describes God's abundant blessings on this earth including His forgiveness when we're overwhelmed with sin (verse 3). There was special blessing for those who God brought near to live in His courts (verse 4). His blessings are sometimes depicted as rain on thirsty ground. And when we realize that what is good in our lives comes from Him (James 1:17), it can soften our hearts with gratitude. Soft hearts not only soak up His blessings but also hear and obey His voice. But we can harden our hearts as well when we ignore His voice (Hebrews 4:7).

I want the soil of my heart to be soft. I want the weeds of sin and the roots of bitterness to be easily removed. When I stubbornly choose to ignore His convicting voice, I can almost feel my heart hardening. I belong to Him, and so I can expect Him to correct and reprimand me. When my heart is soft and I respond with humility, the experience does not have to last very long and is a lot less painful. He is waiting to love on me with His forgiveness!

Lord, keep my heart soft toward You.

1 Corinthians 15:55

Where, O death, is your victory?

Where, O death, is your sting?

The Scorpion

I hope I am never stung by this disgusting creature! The Indian red scorpion is said to have the most lethal sting. One could die if not treated within seventy-two hours of being stung. They are quite hardy and can live up to a year without food or water. Because they are very sensitive to light, they stay hidden during the day and only come out at night. One good thing about them is that they can glow in the dark!

Today's verse describes death as a "sting." Death will no longer have the victory when the mortal is changed into immortality (verse 54) and the perishable becomes imperishable. Death seems to have the victory for now, but in fact, Christ's empty grave means that death has been swallowed up in victory! The venom of that heartrending grief is no longer lethal as we look to the life to come. We share in Christ's victory over death. We have hope that death is not the end as we look to the One who conquered and defeated death forever!

The news is disturbing, as I hear of senseless and violent death. I can feel overwhelmed with news of terminal cancer in friends and loved ones. Yet, as much as I grieve, I can grieve with hope, knowing that for the believer, He has promised that the very best is ahead of me. Because of what Christ did on the cross, death and evil do not win. No despair can erase this truth. No tragedy nullifies my hope. Because of Christ's power in me, I do not have to live with guilt or be fearful of death.

Thank you, Lord, that death does not have to sting.

Hebrews 11:13

All these people were still living by faith when they died. They did not receive the things promised; they only saw them and welcomed them from a distance, admitting that they were foreigners and strangers on earth.

Caribou

Caribou seem to always be on the move. They are called the "Nomads of the North" for good reason. The caribou lay claim to the longest terrestrial migration on the planet! Some of these beautiful animals, also called reindeer, travel up to 2,737 miles per year! Different factors affect the timing of their movements, but the migrations in general follow the seasons. Perhaps the reason the caribou have survived tough conditions for so many years is the fact that they keep moving.

Today's verse is in a chapter that lists the great men and women of faith. What is true of all of them is that they were looking for a country of their own. They were not comfortable where they were. In a sense, they were nomads. Rather than becoming too comfortable where they were, they were longing for a better country, a heavenly one. Therefore God is not ashamed to be called their God.

As a believer my citizenship is in heaven (Philippians3:20), and I am not to feel too comfortable in whatever country I live. I am not home yet. But there are times when I am so steeped in this world and its values that I forget that this is not my home. Of course I want to live comfortably here, but I can become too complacent and forget to have that eternal perspective. By living like a stranger or foreigner here, I can keep my eyes on my forever home!

Lord, keep me looking forward to my true home.

Proverbs 4:26–27

Give careful thought to the paths for your feet and be steadfast in all your ways. Do not turn to the right or the left; keep your foot from evil.

Walking the Line

It was 1956 when famous country singer Johnny Cash sat backstage and wrote the song "I Walk the Line." As a newlywed, he wrote it as a pledge to his wife. The lyrics are all about personal responsibility and avoiding temptation. I love the fact that he commits himself by promising that for her, he would walk the line. This expression has long been used to mean behaving or abiding by moral standards. Or in other words, walking the straight and narrow.

Today's verse tells us to think carefully about where and how we walk through life. We do not walk close to the edge, courting disaster as the thoughtless might. Rather than wondering just how far one can go in a particular behavior before it becomes sin, we need to walk with a healthy fear of falling. We need to stay away from that tempting edge. We do not turn to the left or to the right. We stay right in the middle and away from temptation. In other words, we walk the line. Walking on a dangerous edge gives no room for error. One moment of inattention or one small misstep can mean disaster.

When I am walking the line, I feel His pleasure. Walking in obedience to His commands is how I show my love for Him (2 John 1:6). And His commands make the path smooth, straight, and manageable. It is when I veer left or right and start to compromise on His standards that life becomes more difficult. Thankfully, He offers His forgiveness and helps me get back on track.

Lord, help me love You by walking the line today.

Exodus 15:13

In your unfailing love you will lead the people you have redeemed. In your strength you will guide them to your holy dwelling.

The North Star

For centuries the North Star, or Polaris, has been helping travelers get their bearings. Whether traversing a dry uncharted desert or sailing through waters without a horizon in sight, the North Star has kept travelers from losing themselves. Because it is located nearly at the north celestial pole, it marks the way due north. It is bright but only the fiftieth brightest star above us. The North Star is famous for holding nearly still while the entire northern sky turns around it.

Today's verse reminds us of the fact that the God of this universe is willing to lead and guide His people. He shows us the way because of His amazing unfailing love. He uses His incredible strength to lift us up out of the deep slimy pit of mud and mire and to set our feet back on firm solid ground (Psalm 40:2). His love for us never falters, even when we ignore His leading and fall away. We may step out of His will, but we never step out of His care. His correction and instruction light the way back to His presence (Proverbs 6:23).

What a precious thought that He cares enough to see every wayward step. He does not want me to go through life unclear and confused about my direction. He has redeemed me and I am His. Even when I am not looking up for His direction, His love will never fail me. In my pride I may think I have it all together, when in fact I may be inadvertently putting distance between us. But His guidance keeps me warm and close.

Lord, keep me looking to You for each step.

Isaiah 43:19

See, I am doing a new thing! Now it springs up; do you not perceive it? I am making a way in the wilderness and streams in the wasteland.

Looking Through the Kaleidoscope

This beautiful image was taken through an iPhone lens fitted to the eye hole of a kaleidoscope. I used to look through them as a child, fascinated with the different colors, shapes, and patterns. The kaleidoscope was originally invented in 1815 as part of a scientific experiment on light polarization before becoming a popular toy. It is amazing how those mirrors inside can change loose pieces of glass, beads, and pebbles into amazing vibrant patterns!

Today's verse is an encouragement to look at life differently. Rather than focus exclusively on the past and what God has done, we are to rotate that kaleidoscope and see the new image the Lord wants to produce. We can miss the new thing He wants to create in our lives. To us it may not look like much. Our lives can seem like random bits and pieces. Our lives can even resemble a wilderness or wasteland. But He has a purpose and is creating a new and exciting pattern!

He makes a way. The Lord is a master at taking the broken pieces of my life and fashioning them into something beautiful. Sometimes, all I see are the ups and downs of the past. So often I miss seeing how they are fitting together. I do not always see the new thing He is creating. But He is faithful to His promise to work *all things* for the good of those who love Him (Romans 8:28). He is continually creating His character in me.

Thank you, Lord, that You use each detail to produce something beautiful!

Psalm 40:3

He put a new song in my mouth, a hymn of praise to our God. Many will see and fear the Lord and put their trust in him.

The Mockingbird

Growing up, we had many mockingbirds in our suburban yard, much to the chagrin of our cat! He would slink across the yard, hoping to avoid the swoop and attack of these territorial birds! I have always loved their singing although my parents were not too thrilled to be awakened early by their loud song. These birds are not too original as they mimic the songs of other species. One mockingbird in Massachusetts was recorded singing thirty-six songs from other birds!

Today's verse describes a song that is an original. It is a new song of praise to the Lord. It resembles no other but is a tribute to what the Lord has done in an individual life. There is no need to mimic other songs as personal experiences make up the lyrics. The Lord Himself has put this song into the mouth of the psalmist.

As a believer, I too have a new song! My song stands out from the others. It sounds different and distinctive and it is full of praise for what God has done for me. It tells a personal story of His love and faithfulness. Unfortunately, there are some discordant notes and minor chords included that depict the hard times. But it always ends on a high note as I look forward to an eternity with Him. If I sing it loud enough and often enough, others hear and are challenged to trust Him!

Lord, keep me singing Your song today!

Psalm 42:5

Why, my soul, are you downcast? Why so disturbed within me? Put your hope in God, for I will yet praise him, my Savior and my God.

Teddy Bears

The teddy bear got its name from President Theodore Roosevelt as a result of a bear hunting trip in 1902. A political cartoon followed that event and inspired the creation of the first teddy bear. Originally made to look similar to a real bear, it has evolved to be a comforting presence for many children. In fact, a program called "Teddy Bear Cops" was created to distribute teddy bears to children in the midst of crisis. It was found that the teddy bear would calm them down.

In today's verse, David is speaking to his own soul in an attempt to calm down from the despair he feels. He had plenty of reason to have a soul disturbed within him. He was under constant attack from his enemies. Rather than focusing on his circumstances or giving in to despair, the psalmist reminds himself of the hope he has in God. Because of that hope, he could look forward to a future where praise for God would come again to his lips.

It is true that God's promises tend to calm me down. I can get so worked up and panicky in the middle of a problem. I need the quieting influence of God's voice through His Word. He reminds me that He is in control. He reassures me of His presence. He upholds me with declarations of His love. He calms and quiets me much like the teddy bear does for the child. A calm and quiet spirit is not natural in the middle of crisis. Thankfully, I have someone who does the supernatural for me.

Thank you, Lord, for Your calming presence.

Romans 12:11

Never be lacking in zeal, but keep your spiritual fervor, serving the Lord.

Turkish coffee

It is a careful multistep process to make an authentic cup of Turkish coffee. If there are not at least a few grounds in the bottom of the cup, I would be suspicious! The coffee is very finely ground, preferably in a brass grinder. The cezve or metal long-handled pot can be brass or copper. But just as important as the equipment is the process of boiling the coffee twice, building a foam, and allowing the powder to settle before serving. All I know is that the resulting caffeine high can last me the entire day!

Would that spiritual energy could be found in a simple drink! Today's verse encourages believers to be zealous in their service to the Lord. We are to keep our spiritual fervor so as to persevere and not give up when the hard times come. We are to keep fueled, tanked up, or aflame, not burning out. That enthusiasm we started with needs to continue pushing us forward.

How do I keep to that level of zeal? When I do not see results from my service, I lose my enthusiasm. When I do not see that it makes much difference, I can easily lose heart. There is only one way to be refueled and rediscover that joy and motivation to serve Him. And that is by the Spirit's filling (Ephesians 5:18). His filling gives me strength to keep on keeping on! His power provides that excitement and motivation to advance His agenda today. His filling even helps me to face a mundane routine. I do not need to fill up with coffee. I need to fill up with His Spirit!

Thank you, Lord, for being the source of my zeal and fervor.

Psalm 142:1–2

I cry aloud to the Lord, I lift up my voice to the Lord for mercy. I pour out before him my complaint; before him I tell my trouble.

Squeaky Wheel

I am not so sure that the "squeaky wheel gets the grease" at my grocery store. Too many times I have inadvertently pulled out a cart with that annoying noise. A poem titled "The Kicker" first used this saying in 1870. This American proverb affirms that the one who complains the loudest attracts the most attention and service. The Chinese have a similar saying: "The crying baby gets the milk."

In today's verse, David cries aloud to the Lord for mercy. He lifts up his voice, pouring out his complaint and telling Him about all his troubles. He is complaining to the Lord, and not in some quiet whispering voice. He is loud and noisy about it. This entire psalm is a cry of complaint about his enemies. God does not reproach him for this open and honest prayer.

Out of His grace and mercy God hears the cries of His children. But the "squeaky wheel" idea does not work with Him. I do not manipulate Him with the emotion and fervor I add to my prayers. His will and plan are already determined. However, pouring out my complaints to Him is such a release. I can unburden my heart as He understands and He can take it. He would much rather I complain to Him rather than murmur and complain to those around me (Philippians 2:14–15). Often, even before my prayer finishes, He changes that complaint into praise for what He will do!

Thank you, Lord, for listening to my complaint.

Psalm 18:38

I crushed them so that they could not rise; they fell beneath my feet.

Secretary Bird

Do not let this stately bird with beautiful eyelashes fool you! The secretary bird is an accomplished hunter who corners its prey in the tall grass of southern Africa. From a standing position they will use five times their body weight (an average of 8.9 pounds) to kick and stomp on a snake. More than just stunning the snake, they jump, kick, and stomp on it until the neck or back is snapped. As I am not a fan of snakes, I do not feel too sorry for them. But the whole process seems a bit ruthless.

Today's verse seems a bit ruthless as well. David is describing what happened in battle when the Lord delivered him from his enemies. It was kill or be killed, and David recognizes that it was God who armed him with strength (verse 39). Instead of taking credit, David praises and exalts God for avenging him and saving him from his enemies (verses 46–48).

The image of victory in battle seems far removed from my everyday life. Yet, each time I succeed in resisting temptation, it is a victory. Each time I do the right thing when it would have been so much easier to compromise, it is another battle won! I am in a continual battle against forces that I cannot see (Ephesians 6:12). Ruthlessness is called for with an enemy that wants to destroy me. I dare not underestimate him. And as with David, there is no victory without God's strength. He graciously gives me His armor along with His strength and mighty power.

Thank you, Lord, that in You there is victory!

Psalm 73:25

Whom have I in heaven but you? And earth has nothing I desire besides you.

Rabbit Trails

We have all experienced the chagrin of having to return from a "rabbit trail" while in a group discussion! Veering off the topic is easy to do when a story or explanation is interjected that goes nowhere. These mazes of unrelated detail can derail a conversation and be totally frustrating for someone trying to guide a discussion. These side trips may be interesting but can easily confuse, as they add no light or clarity and lead nowhere.

Today's verse could be thought of as a purpose statement to a life. With a focus like this, there are not as likely to be too many distractions or rabbit trails. Asaph declares that God holds him with his right hand (verse 23), guides him, and will take him one day to glory (verse 24). He describes God as the strength of his heart (verse 26). His relationship with God is so intimate and fulfilling that nothing in heaven or earth can compare!

My deepest desire is to have a relationship with the Lord that is just that focused! Too easily, I get distracted by pretty baubles. Wonderful relationships and exciting experiences make life rich, but can also draw my attention away from the One who is blessing me! I do not want to be so diverted by good gifts that I forget the Giver. Chasing after what the world values is a true rabbit trail leading nowhere. Of course, I desire lots of things that are truly good. But above all else, I want to desire Him. He is the only one who reaches deep within me and fills me with His love!

Lord, keep me close to You today.

John 13:10

Jesus answered, "Those who have had a bath need only to wash their feet; their whole body is clean. And you are clean, though not every one of you."

Plane Tree Bark

I love seeing ornamental plane trees lining the roads in France. They grow quite tall and quickly, providing welcome shade. They are especially used in urban areas as they do so well in the dirty air. The plane tree is impervious to the smog as their bark routinely peels off. The dirty bark is exfoliated and in its place, the inner shades of white, gray, green, and yellow show through.

Today's verse talks about ridding ourselves of dirt. Jesus is washing the disciples' feet, a custom normally relegated to the servants. He uses this image to teach, not only about the humility He expects of believers, but also about keeping our hearts cleansed of sin. With the exception of Judas, the disciples had already bathed in His complete forgiveness. But journeying through daily life, feet pick up the dirt of wrong choices, bad habits, and failures to withstand temptation. It is a daily exercise to agree with Him in confession and allow Him to wash our feet.

Agreeing with the Lord about my wrong thoughts or behavior is not always easy or comfortable. But there is a wonderful sense of renewal when I can stop being defensive and own up to it. Yes, He has already bathed me in complete forgiveness. Every sin I have done, past, present, and future has been paid for on that cross. I am under no condemnation for my sin (Romans 8:1). But when I allow my feet to remain dirty, I am the one who misses out on blessing and closeness with my Lord.

Lord, keep me clean and close to You today.

Psalm 119:116

Sustain me, my God, according to your promise, and I will live; do not let my hopes be dashed.

Plenty of Fish

The phrase, "there are plenty of fish in the sea" is often used to console those who have loved and lost. The idea is that there are plenty of potential mates still to be discovered out there. There is even an online dating service called "Plenty of Fish," with 40 million fish in its waters. The problem comes from those "predators" who raise hopes in others, only to dash them. One predator in particular decided to dine and dash, leaving his online date stuck with the bill!

Today's verse is found in the longest psalm extolling the joys of knowing and following God's law. The author prays that God would sustain him. He acknowledges that true meaningful life is found in following God's ways. He can pray for God's sustaining power with hope as it is a prayer calling on the Lord's promises. When God makes a promise, He will always be true to His word. Hope placed here will not be dashed.

If I were to place all my hope exclusively in human love, my hopes would sometimes be dashed. No one can love me the way the Lord does. Placing my hope in His promise to never leave me is a hope that will never be disappointed. He sustains me when I am feeling weak. He upholds me when I am discouraged. His peace has kept me close to Him. No other relationship can be this consistent. His love will never let me down. I can always count on Him because His word means something!

Thank you, Lord, that with You my hope is never disappointed.

Psalm 34:5

Those who look to him are radiant; their faces are never covered with shame.

Shamefaced!

C an dogs feel shame or guilt? Looking at this image one would think so. But a number of studies have found that dogs do not feel or display guilt. I am positive that a number of dog owners would disagree. However, scientists believe it is too complex a reaction and it is just not how their brains work. What seems to be a guilty look happens with scolding or questioning from an angry owner. The dog is simply reacting to the owner's behavior, tone of voice, and gestures.

Today's verse describes a face that is not covered with shame. In fact, there is radiance in place of shame. When looking to a righteous, perfect God, it would be natural to feel shame for our sin. One's first reaction would be to cover one's face in the blinding light of His holiness! But for those who fear the Lord and belong to Him, there is no more shame. In His grace, He has paid for all our sin and guilt with the sacrifice of His Son. No one who trusts in Him will be condemned or held guilty (verse 22).

Because He has erased my sin and shame, I can look to Him and be radiant! No longer will I blush for my past sins. He has removed my sin and guilt as far as the east is from the west (Psalm 103:12)! He has said that my sin He will remember no more (Hebrews 10:17). Any shame felt with my memories is not from Him. I am in Christ (Romans 8:1) and no longer condemned. The Lord not only took away my sin, but the shame of it all as well.

Thank you, Lord, that my face can be radiant with Your forgiveness!

Psalm 119:164–165

Seven times a day I praise you for your righteous laws. Great peace have they who love your law, and nothing can make them stumble.

Seven

There is something about the number seven. Gamblers consider it a lucky number. The television character George Costanza thought "Seven" a beautiful first name. Many ancient cultures had seven gods. In Scripture, the number seven has special significance. Creation, with the Sabbath, took seven days. Solomon's temple took seven years to build. The walls of Jericho came down after seven days of marching. Revelation records seven stars, lamp stands, churches, seals, trumpets, and bowls. Seven is thought to be the number of perfection or completion.

In today's verse David does not use the number seven literally. There are other times he prayed three times a day (Psalm 55:17). And David writes that His praise shall continually be in his mouth (Psalm 34:1). He uses the number seven here to express a desire to worship the Lord perfectly, or completely. In turning toward a holy and righteous God, David is showing a special care in his devotion. His praise is specific: for God's law. He recognizes the stability His law gives to life. David praises God for the great peace that comes from being obedient. He knew the difference. He experienced first hand the agony and awful consequences of breaking God's law.

What a beautiful and worthy subject of praise! God's law gives stability and direction to my life. It keeps me from stumbling. Following His law gives me heart peace instead of guilt and confusion. Seven times a day is only the beginning of my praise and worship!

Lord, may I continually praise You today! You are worthy!

Isaiah 53:6

We all, like sheep, have gone astray, each of us has turned to our own way; and the Lord has laid on him the iniquity of us all.

Sheepish

What was that racket? My husband was in the middle of his shower when he heard some strange noises! It sounded as if someone was rearranging the furniture, but there was also loud bleating, shouting, and running footsteps. How bizarre to see this sheep in the living room knocking into things with a crazed look in his eyes! He had run in from our rural French street into the open doors, with his handlers in hot pursuit! It took three of them to hold him down and get him under control!

What a perfect way to illustrate the truth of today's verse! This sheep was not where he was supposed to be. He had certainly gone his own way, ignoring his keepers and the other sheep. His headlong movements could have hurt him and it took some pretty drastic measures to correct him. I am sure he was none too happy to be bound with that rope. And we are just like that sheep. We turn our back on the Shepherd, thinking we know better.

How loving and gracious God is to take on Himself the punishment of my silly rebellion! Jesus paid the ultimate price of my sin, giving me peace with God (verse 5). And as a forgiven "sheep," I have the enormous privilege of following my Shepherd. His way is so much better than my own. He does not lead by prodding me from behind. He goes before me, showing the way and confronting for me the unknown.

Thank you, Lord, for turning me back to You and Your way.

2 Corinthians 4:8–9

We are hard pressed on every side, but not crushed; perplexed, but not in despair; persecuted, but not abandoned; struck down, but not destroyed.

Sea Glass

I feel as if I have found treasure when I see that gleaming colorful piece of glass nestled in the sand! The beaches of California are especially good for their discovery. In their original form, I would not look at them twice. After all, they are just shards of glass bottles or tableware. But after years and years of being broken up and tumbled by the waves, they lose their rough edges and become smooth. Gone is the normal sheen of glass as it is replaced by a frosty appearance, worthy of being art or jewelry!

Today's verse describes the life of Paul. He was persecuted, thrown in jail, shipwrecked, and beaten. Through all of this he was never crushed, in despair, abandoned, or destroyed. He calls his experiences "light momentary troubles" (verse 17). He does not lose heart, because he believes they are achieving for him "an eternal glory." Rather than focusing on what he is going through, he sees what God is producing in him.

Whoever said that life was easy has not lived very long! Being a follower of Christ does not guarantee me a smooth ride. I am tossed around and pounded by the waves just as much as everyone else. My sure hope is that He is producing something meaningful and beautiful through all the negative. Knowing He is in control and that His control is good keeps me from despair. There will be no punishing pounding waves in heaven. All my rough edges will be gone and I will be complete!

Thank you, Lord, that I can trust what You are doing in my life.

Psalm 119:131–132

I open my mouth and pant, longing for your commands. Turn to me and have mercy on me, as you always do to those who love your name.

Panting Dogs

I will admit it. I am not a "dog person." Hopefully I am not offending any dog lovers, but cats are my animal of choice. One of the many reasons I prefer cats is that they do not normally hang out their tongues and pant. I do not enjoy dog slobber or doggy breath either! But seeing their tongues hanging out is not especially an endearing quality. Of course, God in His wisdom and creativity designed the dog to pant in order to cool down. Except through their paw pads, a dog will not sweat through their skin and so they need to pant. The circulating air enters their bodies and cools them down.

Today's verse speaks of panting for God's commands! It is a surprising sentiment as one does not normally embrace laws and commands with such enthusiasm. One tends to balk against any restrictions on one's freedom. Rather than seeing them as something negative, the author embraces them, knowing that wisdom and blessing come from obedience. He pants for them. They are as important as the air one breathes as they make true life possible.

I love the image of the deer panting for water (Psalm 42:1). In just the same way, I want my soul to pant for God. He is the source of all that nourishes and satisfies me. If I am panting and longing for that intimacy with God, then my attitude toward His commands will be just as enthusiastic! By following His commands I stay close to Him and our relationship grows deeper and deeper.

Lord, thank you for the closeness You give when I follow Your way.

But I have calmed and quieted myself, I am like a weaned child with its mother; like a weaned child I am content.

Screaming Baby

We had a young family with three children over for dinner. Everything was calm, quiet, and smooth. Then something changed. The two-month-old baby decided she was hungry and wanted her mother. The noise emitting from her mouth put all of our teeth on edge! Gone were my impressions of a relaxed "chill" baby. She wanted to nurse and she wanted to now! Her mother could not move fast enough!

Today's verse describes contentment. One would think that the picture of contentment would be the nursing baby as he is immediately calmed and quiet. But true contentment is the older child. He stays close to his mother but he is not worried or agitated. He knows from experience that his mother is there and aware. He is peaceful and calm knowing she will meet his need. His need does not overwhelm him and he can patiently wait. Instead of noise there is trust.

This definition of contentment recognizes needs and wants and even desires. Regardless of my circumstances, there is no way I can live life without them. There is so much more I want in my life and those desires may not be wrong at all. Contentment is not the absence of desires but a desire for His presence and love overriding them all. At the end of the day, my contentment is not found in changed circumstances but in a Person. I can calm and quiet myself too, knowing He is there.

Lord, help me to live that contentment today.

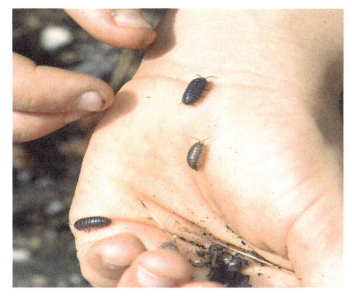

Psalm 17:7

Show me the wonders of your great love, you who save by your right hand those who take refuge in you from their foes.

Pill Bugs

I thought I was just sweeping up dirt on my patio. But when the dirt started fleeing the pile, I knew differently! The pill bug is the common name for a variety of wood lice called, "Armadillidium vulgare." As a child I liked calling them "roly-polies," as they would roll up into a ball when I mishandled them. Their shells look like armor but it is because of their segmented bodies that they can roll up into a ball to protect themselves.

Today's verse is a cry for help as David's enemies had tracked him down, surrounded him, and were trying to destroy him. He calls out to the Lord, recognizing that God's powerful right hand is his best protection. As David had already experienced when confronting Goliath, he could not trust in the armor offered him (1 Samuel 17:38–39). His trust was in the power and love of God. That was his refuge from where God would demonstrate His power to save. God answered his prayer for protection and vindication!

Rolling up into a ball at the first sign of trouble is my natural inclination. When going through something difficult I tend to go quiet, push people away, and isolate myself. But the Lord wants to be my refuge in time of trouble (Psalm 59:16). He never intends for me to go it alone. I need to run to Him to show me the wonders of His great love and to reassure me. His refuge is strong like a rock but as soft as the underside of a bird's wings.

Thank you, Lord, for being my sure and constant refuge.

Psalm 42:8

By day the Lord directs his love, at night his song is with me—a prayer to the God of my life.

Nightingale

The nightingale is not much to look at, being a plain and uninteresting brown. He is shy and likes to hide in dense thickets and bushes. But he has been the subject of songs, fairy tales, operas, books, and poetry over the centuries. His song is exceptional for its variety, range, and power. While the female is strangely quiet, the male regales his listeners with whistles, trills and gurgles. Although he sings during the day, his song is especially noticeable at night without any other noises to distract.

Today's verse describes another song that occurs during the night. This song can be just as beautiful and there is only an audience of One. This song is a prayer of gratitude and praise to the Lord. Without audible notes, it rises up within our souls to be heard by our Creator. Because He loves us, He listens intently to our impromptu concert, and we feel His pleasure. There are no other noises or distractions in those dark quiet hours.

All day long I feel His love directed toward me. I am aware of His presence throughout the day. But in the mundane tasks, the hurried schedule, and all the distractions, I forget to respond with praise. But at night, when the house is finally quiet I can turn my thoughts to Him. Instead of being frustrated at being awake, I can use those moments to compose a song only He will hear. Regardless of words or notes, He is honored by the melody of praise in my heart.

Thank you, Lord, for putting a song in my heart tonight!

1 John 4:10

This is love: not that we loved God, but that he loved us and sent his Son as an atoning sacrifice for our sins.

Mountain Lion Attack

I cannot imagine the horror a mother felt when seeing her seven-year-old son pinned to the ground by a mountain lion! Her son was playing in the yard of their home on Vancouver Island in British Columbia when she heard the commotion. Like any loving mother, she rushed out to save him, throwing herself on the lion. She vainly tried to pry open the jaws clamped firmly on her son's arm. Thankfully, her screams for help caused the young, famished lion to run. Because of her willingness to sacrifice herself, her son emerged needing only some stitches on his arm and head.

Today's verse speaks of another sacrifice also motivated by love. God loved us so much that He gave His Son to die in our place (John 3:16). There is no greater love than this: to lay down one's life for another (John 15:13), and that is what the Lord did for us. Jesus not only paid the price for sin by enduring physical pain but also the pain of separation from the Father. He did for us what we could not do for ourselves. What an incredible price He paid to demonstrate His love!

When I think of the cost of His sacrifice, I am humbled and overwhelmed that He could love me this much! God so loved me that He gave. He gave to save me from certain and eternal death. He gave in order to begin a love relationship that will last into all eternity. He gave, not because I deserve Him but because of His amazing grace!

Lord, thank you for reminding me of Your incredible love, especially today.

2 Corinthians 10:12

We do not dare to classify or compare ourselves with some who commend themselves. When they measure themselves by themselves and compare themselves with themselves, they are not wise.

People Watching

One of the best things about living in Europe is enjoying all the outdoor cafes. And one of the best things about sitting outside is people watching! Ordering and eating is almost secondary to that all-important activity. It is an art to do it discreetly, but we all do it! And as long as one does not make eye contact, it is all perfectly acceptable. Part of the fun is guessing the nationality of a tourist by how they are dressed. Not only am I noticing fashion but I find myself wondering about the social standing of a passerby.

Today's verse addresses those who compare themselves to themselves. Paul is admonishing those who are looking only on the surface of things (verse 7). He did not fit their ideas of a dynamic speaker or an impressive presence. Paul is teaching that boasting has no place in the life of a believer. And boasting is what can so easily happen when we compare ourselves to those like ourselves. Rather than looking for approval by commending oneself, we are to seek God's approval.

Comparing myself to other believers can sometimes lead to complacency and smugness. Perhaps I am not struggling with some of the same issues as a "weaker brother" in Christ. But God knows my heart and how much work still needs to be done! Being well viewed is never the point. True wisdom is comparing myself to Jesus Himself and asking the Lord to make me more like Him!

Keep me focused on You, Lord.

Romans 12:2

Do not conform to the pattern of this world, but be transformed by the renewing of your mind. Then you will be able to test and approve what God's will is—his good, pleasing and perfect will.

Maverick

This horse seems to have a mind of his own! Without a rider or other horses nearby, he walks alone. Perhaps he is a maverick who enjoys his independence. The meaning of the word "maverick" has changed from its original meaning of being an unbranded animal separated from the herd. Now the word has come to mean a person who is unconventional and an independent thinker. Depending on the context, a maverick can denote something negative or positive.

Today's verse encourages the believer to resist conforming to the world's way of thinking. Rather than following the latest ideas or fads, the Christ follower is to think differently. His goal is to find and follow what God wants. It is always something good, pleasing and perfect. With a mind renewed by God's Word, we can evaluate and test our thinking to know when we are following what He wants. His plans are perfect. He wants only what is good for us. And as our Creator, He knows better than anyone else what will in the long run be pleasing.

I am sometimes confused as to what God wants in a particular situation. I know that trusting my own desires and emotions can be deceiving. Sometimes the Lord gives me exactly what I want, but not until I submit all of it to Him first! Being a "living sacrifice" is all about that submission (verse 1). But often I find that His plan is a whole lot better than mine!

Lord, change my thinking to want only what You want.

Jeremiah 31:3

The Lord appeared to us in the past saying, "I have loved you with an everlasting love; I have drawn you with unfailing kindness."

Message in a Bottle

The idea of putting an important message in a bottle is nothing new. There are records of it being done as far back as 310 BC! But the story of a British WWI soldier sending a message in 1914 was especially touching. It did not discuss enemy movements, nor a shipwreck story, nor was it an experiment to test the movements of the currents. It was a love note addressed to his wife. This soldier died two days later and although the wife had since died by the time it was discovered in 1999, his daughter at the age of eighty-six was thrilled to have it!

Today's verse describes the Lord's love for us as everlasting. Much more dependable than a floating bottle, He has written His message of love in the Bible that dates back centuries. It is a timeless message of a love that is kind and unconditional. The everlasting nature of His love draws the receptive and searching heart. But unfortunately, too many walk by that message, never stopping to investigate. He has been faithful to communicate His love clearly, but the message is not always received. Or the message is misheard to be, "I will love you if . . ."

His love for me changes how I look at myself. I am important enough for Him to actually write down how He feels about me! Of course my husband's love and my family's love is important. But nothing is as wide, long, high, or deep as His love (Ephesians 3:18). It is always kind. It will never fail. And He loves me in spite of who I am!

Thank you, Lord, for Your everlasting love for me.

Luke 19:10

For the Son of Man came to seek and to save the lost.

Lost Sock

Do you ever wonder where that wayward sock went? It is one of those unsolved mysteries in life. There is a child's bright pink sock hanging out in the bushes in a public area near my daughter's house. Each time I pass it I wonder how on earth it got there. But inevitably, socks go missing with disturbing regularity with enough washes. And I will admit to throwing out that single sock after enough time has passed. Of course, not long after, the missing sock will innocently show up!

Today's verse is an answer to criticism Jesus was facing for being a guest in the house of a sinner, Zacchaeus. Jesus went out of his way to greet him and invite Himself over to his home. Zacchaeus welcomed Him gladly and experienced God's salvation that very day. This tax collector and cheater of his people knew he was lost and he was ready to be found. Those criticizing Jesus were also lost but they stayed that way. They did not think they needed finding.

How incredible that the Lord takes the initiative! He actively seeks me as I am too lost to find the way to Him on my own. He loves me enough to go out of His way and extract me from the mess of my own making. He left heaven to come after me! I am no longer confused and lost, fearful or panicked. I am found now and I am His. I know where I am and to whom I belong. What security that is!

"I once was lost but now am found." Thank you, Lord, for seeking and finding me.

What has been will be again, what has been done will be done again; there is nothing new under the sun.

Merry-Go-Round

The merry-go-round is always a safe bet. I enjoy the ride, as there are no heart-stopping descents or speeds that take my breath away! The movement is gentle, the music is appealing, and the views of folks enjoying themselves all make the ride pleasant. But of course, after a little bit the sameness starts to get to me. When the novelty begins to wear off, I begin looking at my watch.

Today's verse recognizes that there can be a sameness to our days that can make life a challenge. The same view may present itself again and again. The same experience with only a few variations can have us thinking, "déjà vu." There is the feeling of "been there, done that." What has been done before will be done again. And life can feel like it is going around in circles.

Thankfully, I can view life differently when the Lord is involved. There may be "nothing new under the sun," but the One who gives purpose to my life is above the sun! I do not always understand His purpose, but it is a comfort to know that there is one! I can take heart in the thought that He had plans for this day even before I was born. I can face the routine and sameness of each day because there just may arise a new opportunity to serve Him, if I am looking for it! My relationship with Christ can make each day different. My communion and conversation with Him can be fresh and new each morning. I am climbing off that merry-go-round.

Thank you, Lord, for making life full and meaningful!

Jeremiah 32:17

Ah, Sovereign Lord, you have made the heavens and the earth by your great power and outstretched arm. Nothing is too hard for you.

Molehills

I can easily make a mountain out of a molehill. This expression is as old as the hills and has been around since the sixteenth century. That loose soil thrown up by a small burrowing mole is pretty insignificant when compared to the height and stability of a mountain. To make a big deal out of something small is to make too much of what is really a minor issue. Yet I find it easy to do. The Finnish have a similar saying: "to turn a fly into a bull." The Germans express this idea by saying, "to make an elephant out of a fly."

Today's verse corrects my perspective on those molehills. The Lord is the God of all mankind, and nothing is too hard for Him. His power and might are obvious when looking at the heavens and the earth. Everything is small when compared to His great power. Nothing is too hard for Him to accomplish when He can speak into being an entire universe!

So why do my obstacles seem insurmountable? I see His power in creation. I see His power in the miracles He has done for great men of faith in the Bible. I know He can do anything He wants. But does He want to help me? Will He outstretch His arm for me? He already has. He has outstretched two arms on that cross and used His power to save my soul. And the same power that raised Christ from the dead works in my favor. I can trust Him to tackle any problem I face.

Thank you, Lord, that nothing is too hard for You!

Hebrews 6:12

We do not want you to become lazy, but to imitate those who through faith and patience inherit what has been promised.

Like Father Like Son

What a great rite-of-passage moment this was years ago for our son! I, of course, was totally excluded from such a masculine activity. Our son would certainly not have learned the right technique from me! Imitating others is something we do naturally, and it certainly is easier to learn by watching someone else than by reading printed instructions. Whether it is cutting a candy bar on a plate with knife and fork, or taking on the habits of the father, imitating others is done almost without thought.

Today's verse encourages us to make that effort and not to become lazy in our Christian walk. God recompenses our love and work for Him, and He has given us examples to imitate. There is quite a choice presented in the great "faith chapter" of Hebrews 11. So many of these heroes of the faith did not even receive the things promised (Hebrews 11:13). Yet they patiently stood firm, seeing them at a great distance with eyes of faith. They were able to endure unthinkable hardships because of their patience and faith.

I need to surround myself with others who exemplify faith and patience. Seeing the perseverance of others spurs me on to persevere myself. Watching another's patience shown through trial encourages me to believe that I can show patience as well. And I want to be that example for others to imitate, especially for my family.

Lord, may I be diligent and persevere in my faith until the very end!

Matthew 5:6

Blessed are those who hunger and thirst for righteousness, for they will be filled.

In or Out?

W hat this cat is doing looks very familiar. Our Tiger does the same thing. He stands at the door waiting to go out. Then, when he is out, not two minutes go by before he is back at the door waiting to come in! And before I know it, he is waiting to go out once again. He never seems happy about where he is! There is a store in France called "Un Jour Ailleurs," meaning "One Day Elsewhere." That store name sums up the problem of cats always wanting to be elsewhere! But I can identify with Tiger.

Today's verse promises happiness and satisfaction. But the condition is that I long for the right things! The one whose desire is to live a life in right standing with God can find contentment. He has already given us everything that is needed to live a godly life (2 Peter 1:3). He does not frustrate our desire to live for Him. He will enable and equip us. And He gives immense satisfaction in our service for Him. When we hunger and thirst after a righteous life, He will make that life worth living!

It is so easy for me to think that a change of place will change my level of contentment. Can I really be happy and complete regardless of whether I am in or out, here or there? God says, "Yes!" He offers to satisfy the desires of my heart when I make living for Him my delight. My contentment and satisfaction will never come from style of life or location or material goods. It all comes from my relationship with Him.

Lord, may hungering and thirsting for You bring me blessing today.

Psalm 103:17

But from everlasting to everlasting the Lord's love is with those who fear Him, and His righteousness with their children's children.

Locks of Love

There is something about Paris that inspires grand gestures of love. Couples have been putting locks on the Pont de L'Archeveche to commemorate their love. What a wonderful way to symbolize the permanence of a relationship! However, a section of this old bridge built in 1828 has buckled and fallen under the weight of these locks. The city has now ordered that all the locks come down for safety reasons.

Today's verse is a promise of a love that never ends. Unlike the best-intentioned human love, God's love for His own does not fail or falter. His love is everlasting because He chose us in love to be His before the creation of the world (Ephesians 1:4). He proved His love by dying for us while we were still rebellious sinners (Romans 5:8). He did not wait for our response. He loved us first and to the utmost! The symbol of His love is more than a lock on a bridge. The symbol of His love is that infamous cross. It reminds me of what He went through to establish a relationship with me! It locked up securely and forever the love we can now share.

There is no way to tear down or nullify what He has done to establish this love. It will continue into eternity! I feel God's love most keenly when I am considering His power and greatness. The fear, awe, and respect that His holy character inspires makes me even more appreciative of this incredible love. I am humbled and grateful that He, being so vast and powerful, could love someone like me!

Thank you, Lord, for Your amazing love!

Ephesians 4:17

So I tell you this, and insist on it in the Lord, that you must no longer live as the Gentiles do in the futility of their thinking.

In a Rut

Whether walking in the countryside or on paths in the vineyards, it can be so much easier to walk in the ruts. One does not have to think quite so much, as the way is already in place. There is less need to look down or to think about where to place that next step. The thinking of elderly people who suffer from Alzheimer's or severe dementia often follows comfortable and familiar ruts. Perhaps the strain of thinking is lessened when following a familiar thought pattern. When the subject is sweet and light one does not mind it so much. It is when the "thinking rut" is painful or false that life becomes so difficult for the caretaker.

Today's verse tells us to live or walk differently from Gentiles, or nonbelievers. Their minds are futile because their understanding is darkened. They are separated from the life of God because they are following ruts of thinking that lead away from Him. Without realizing it, they are following a well-worn path that many others have forged before them. It takes less conscious thought to follow the rut, even though their way becomes progressively darker and further from God.

In contrast, those who belong to the Lord are walking differently. If I am walking by faith then it will require conscious thought and careful stepping. I do not want to blindly follow the rut before me. A new and more exciting path is forged with His guidance! With a new way of thinking, I can climb out of that rut and walk in a way that pleases Him!

Thank you, Lord, that walking by faith keeps me out of those ruts!

Isaiah 59:8

The way of peace they do not know; there is no justice in their paths. They have turned them into crooked roads; no one who walks along them will know peace.

Lawn Bowling

I have a friend who enjoys lawn bowling, and I was interested to learn that the balls they use are "biased." There is no way they can roll in a straight line as they are weighted. The ball is deliberately lopsided so that it always curves toward the flat side as it slows down. Without taking this into account, it would be doubly difficult to roll the closest to that white ball (or jack), which is the point of the game.

Today's verse talks about a road that is crooked. There is no way to walk straight along this path. And because the going is crooked there is no justice or peace. This is a picture of the path of wickedness rather than the path of righteousness. By ignoring God's laws and always doing the wrong thing, there is no peace with God or each other. But just as that lawn bowling ball can look normal, so too we can be unaware of the crooked way we are walking.

My path can only be straight as I submit to His way of doing things (Proverbs 3:6). When He leads along straight paths, my steps will not be hampered and I will not stumble (Proverbs 4:12). I am sure it is the more difficult path, however. He has never promised that it would be easy. But when I make the effort to walk with integrity, I can enjoy peace with Him and have the best chance at peace with my neighbor. It is worth the effort.

Lord, keep me walking Your way.

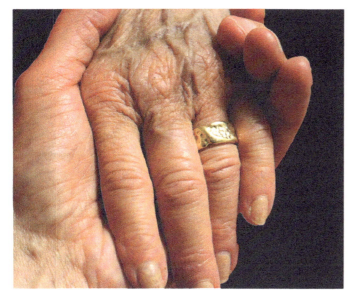

Isaiah 41:13

For I am the Lord your God who takes hold of your right hand and says to you, Do not fear; I will help you.

Holding Hands

They died holding hands. After sixty-two years of marriage, a couple fell ill at the same time and were placed in a nursing home. The staff pushed their beds together, as he wanted to hold her hand. Hand-holding began their life together and ended it. He died while still grasping her hand. She held on to life and his hand for another ninety minutes before dying as well. How beautiful is this expression of love! Holding hands can give courage, help, and support.

Today's verse is a beautiful assurance of God's power and control. The hand of God is a place of salvation, refuge, and protection. It is also a hand of healing and deliverance. By taking our hand He assures us of His help. His hand takes our right hand but not our left. That is because the right hand is the one in Scripture that is used in battle. He hold us by the right hand so that we allow Him to fight our battles!

I need Him to do the fighting. My hands are weak and my grip is loose with discouragement on that "sword of the Spirit," which is God's Word (Ephesians 6:17). But He promises His help. He takes hold of my right hand and infuses me with strength and courage. His help means that my enemies will be "as nothing" (verses 11–12). That impossible relationship that looms so large is no problem for Him. He is in the business of righting wrongs and changing hearts. He has my back and has promised to always be with me (Psalm 73:23).

Thank you, Lord, for the warmth and comfort of Your hand holding mine.

1 John 4:18

There is no fear in love. But perfect love drives out fear because fear has to do with punishment. The one who fears is not made perfect in love.

Flying High

My grandson is flying high but his Nana has her heart in her throat while watching this scene! There is absolute confidence here and no shred of fear. My son-in-law is not about to let my little guy drop. His arms are strong and he is ready to catch him no matter what. My grandson has absolute confidence and trust, not only in his daddy's strength but also in his love. I can just hear him calling out to go higher!

Today's verse describes a love that is unique in that it is perfect and complete. Its perfection comes from the fact that it drives out any fear. We know we are experiencing this kind of love when we are not struggling with a fear of punishment. God's Son took care of the punishment we deserve with His death on the cross. Because He took our place we can be confident in this love He has for us (verse 16). For those who have placed their faith in Christ's sacrifice, the punishment for our sin has already taken place. Fear is gone and we can have security in a perfect love!

Because there is no fear involved in this love, my service for Him comes from a sincere motivation. There is no coercion. Fear does not obligate me. A sense of guilt and shame have no place in this love relationship. He has paid the price of my sin and guilt forever! There is no doubt that He loves me and will catch me no matter what! I am free to love Him completely with all of my being!

Thank you Lord, for Your perfect love.

Galatians 2:21

I do not set aside the grace of God, for if righteousness could be gained through the law, Christ died for nothing!

Gift Horse

I know one is "never to look a gift horse in the mouth," but the temptation is too strong with this smile!! This old expression was first a Latin proverb attributed to St. Jerome in the early fifth century. It referred to the practice of looking into the horse's mouth to determine its age. Nothing seems so wrong about that except that to do so in front of the giver of the horse is not well viewed! It has come to mean being suspicious or critical of something received at no cost.

In today's verse, Paul does not set aside or diminish the importance of God's grace. It is by God's unmerited favor that we are declared righteous. We cannot be justified by the works of the law but only by faith in His sacrifice for sin (verse 16). But there is something innate in our humanness that disdains what is freely given. We want to feel that we had a part in meriting salvation. We feel we need to work, sacrifice, or do something. But as Paul says, if that were so, then there was no reason for Christ to sacrifice Himself.

The offer of His salvation came at no cost to me but the cost to Himself was enormous! There is nothing left to do but respond in joyful surrender. What heartache He must feel when I set aside His grace and start to think that I am really something or deserve anything! But when I understand how far-reaching His grace is to have taken hold of me, I am overwhelmed with gratitude.

Thank you, Lord, for Your sweet amazing grace.

Psalm 55:22

Cast your cares on the Lord and he will sustain you; he will never let the righteous be shaken.

Fly Casting

It looks complicated. I cannot imagine the skill and dexterity it must take to fly cast correctly. If it were me, I would have that line wrapped around me and everyone else! Fortunately, there are lessons, classes, and online video instruction available. Among the basic principles is the idea that every casting stroke is a smooth acceleration followed by an abrupt stop. The better the "stop" the better the transfer of energy and the more efficient the cast.

Today's verse describes a different kind of cast. The form is not so important but we do want to get those cares and worries as far away as possible from us! The Lord invites us to cast all our care on to Him. When we do, He will strengthen and sustain us. Casting all our cares on to Him means an abrupt stop to those worrying thoughts and imaginings. Leaving them with Him means that we can stand firm in our faith, regardless of the shaky ground. He will never let the righteous, or those in right standing with Him, be shaken.

What a beautiful promise to claim when it seems like my world is falling apart! He is there, waiting and willing to takes those cares off my shoulders. It is through prayer that I do the casting (Philippians 4:6). I do not need to carry them. Those worries do not have to weigh me down. He invites me to give them all to Him. No, He asks me to stop and throw them on Him! And what sweet relief comes when I do!

Lord, keep me casting every one of my worries and cares on to You.

Isaiah 53:5

But he was pierced for our transgressions, he was crushed for our iniquities; the punishment that brought us peace was on him, and by his wounds we are healed.

Lightning Rod

What a spectacular sight when this happens! But in fact, the Eiffel Tower is struck by lightning about ten times a year. It happened again just recently on May 30th at 2:00 a.m. Around that time, France experienced a few days with record rainfall and lots of storms throughout the country. Those same storms kept us stuck in an airport for three days trying to fly in! The tower has lightning rods at the top, so it attracts the lightning and protects quite a large space around it. The Parisians are safer with that large hunk of metal absorbing the electricity.

Today's verse reminded me of a lightning rod or conductor. The cross absorbed all of God's wrath against sin. Jesus, who was sinless, took the punishment on Himself that was rightfully ours to bear. He was pierced, crushed, and wounded, all in our place. Because of His sacrifice, He was able to absorb all of God's righteous anger against sin. To talk about God's wrath is not a comfortable topic. Yet, without realizing God's hatred against all wrongdoing, we do not understand how deep is His grace in taking our place!

I am guilty of sometimes treating sin lightly. I have an amazing ability to minimize its seriousness, at least when it comes to me! My sin is never as serious as someone else's! But when I examine my heart in the light of God's holiness I become overwhelmed. When I realize the pain and agony He suffered, then I understand how unworthy I am to have His mercy and grace poured out on me!

I am forever grateful to You Lord, for taking my place.

Psalm 103:5

. . . who satisfies your desires with good things so that your youth is renewed like the eagle's.

Forever Young

This image communicates such a contrast between young and old, vibrant and struggling. However, for a sixty-plus-year-old man from the Netherlands, old was not how he saw himself. In his head and spirit, if not in his body, he was still young. On a job application he put his age down as forty-nine. When he was called on it, he explained that this was how he felt inside!

Today's verse is a call to praise the Lord for all His benefits. David then lists several, ending with this amazing declaration. God satisfies our desires so that even our youth is renewed like the eagle's! There is satisfaction in remembering each of the good things that are already ours. He forgives, He heals. He redeems, and He crowns us with His love and compassion (verses 3–4). Those intangible benefits provide a satisfaction that constantly renews the spirit.

If I did not know His love and compassion, I would feel prematurely old. And realizing all His good gifts is a lift and renewal to my spirit! Focusing on His benefits means there is no longer an energy drain fussing about what I do not have or pining away for what I wish I had. I am freed from discontent when I hand over my desires to Him. He knows what I really want. He knows what it is I truly need. He only gives to me what is good. I want to relinquish every desire to Him and not be dragged down from the heights where I can be soaring! Remembering His benefits is the best way I know to feel young!

Thank you, Lord, that You satisfy and renew me.

Psalm 119:49–50

Remember your word to your servant, for you have given me hope. My comfort in my suffering is this: your promise preserves my life.

Kintsugi

This bowl went from broken to beautiful! The art of golden joinery is the definition of the Japanese word "kintsugi." Fragmented and broken pottery or ceramics are repaired in this process by filling the holes and cracks with a resin mixed with gold, silver, or platinum. What used to be broken pieces thought to be worthless become a thing of beauty! The very brokenness makes the item become more precious and valuable!

Today's verse is a comfort and reassurance when going through suffering. There is hope. The author of this psalm was experiencing ridicule (verse 51). There was intense pressure from the wicked, and perhaps he felt himself cracking from it. He vows to stay faithful to the Lord through it all. In the night he reminds himself of who God is (verse 55) and he resolves to stay the course. Through all the pain he remains hopeful because of God's promises.

It is hope that brings me through the darkest times of my life. I can feel forgotten, rotten and dead inside just like David did when he described himself as "broken pottery" (Psalm 31:12). But then, there are the promises of God. Whatever feels broken He can repair. More than that, He transforms my very brokenness into something useful and a thing of beauty. Nothing is too hard for Him or beyond the skill of His capable hands. He works in the good where everything went bad. Stupid decisions, utter failures, and feelings of shame at having let Him down—these are a pattern that He redeems and makes beautiful! This is my hope.

Thank you, Lord, that Your promises give me hope.

1 Samuel 2:9

He will guard the feet of his faithful servants, but the wicked will be silenced in the place of darkness. "It is not by strength that one prevails . . ."

Elephant Feet

One would think that it would take a serious problem to bring down the mighty elephant. But in fact, the single most important ailment of the captive elephant is the foot-related problem. With limited movement, their soles and nails do not naturally wear down and need constant cutting back. If abscesses, nail infection and arthritis are not guarded against, any of these seemingly inconsequential problems could bring him down.

Today's verse is part of a song by Hannah. She is leaving Samuel, her precious son, at the temple to serve as she had promised. Surprisingly, her heart is exalting in the Lord instead of melting in sorrow at the separation! Hannah is affirming the truth of the sovereignty of God. She understands that God will protect her little boy. He will be keeping the feet of His godly ones, protecting their comings and goings. It is not the strong and mighty ones that will prevail.

It is a tremendous comfort to know that the Lord sees every step, making firm the steps of those who delight in Him (Psalm 37:23). I can even walk through the "valley of the shadow of death" (Psalm 23:4) without fear, knowing He is right there beside me. As His own, I walk in His light, prevailing through His strength. Whatever I may face today, this truth will not change and I can be confident in His loving sovereignty.

Thank you, Lord, for Your intimate knowledge and care for me.

1 Peter 4:12

Dear friends, do not be surprised at the fiery ordeal that has come on you to test you, as though something strange were happening to you.

Hot Air Balloon

What a thrill it must be to quietly glide through the air without the noise of engines! The views from the hot air balloon must be amazing. But there is no gliding above the earth without heating the air that fills the hot air balloon. The burners use gas jets fueled by propane cylinders. The pilot's job is to fire a steady flame from the burner to climb and maintain altitude.

In today's verse, Peter anticipates that the believers will be surprised at the fiery trials they will face. He points out that there is something behind the intense crisis they encounter. The Lord uses every difficulty to test our faith and make us stronger. However, this "fiery ordeal" is not something caused by our own wrong choices. It is an ordeal that comes from living as a believer in a non believing world. Rather than reacting with surprise, we are to respond with joy (verse 13) being confident that blessing and future glory are ours (verse 14). That fiery trial allows us to fly higher and maintain our altitude!

Wouldn't it be wonderful to peacefully glide through life without difficulties? But I need that flame to make me stronger. With each problem my faith can grow. With each difficulty I can see Him work and draw closer to Him. Each time I respond as I should He takes me a little higher and gives me a more expansive view! Of course, I wish the process were not so uncomfortable. But I can trust Him to know what He is doing. I can trust that He knows how to grow my faith.

Lord, may I reach new heights today!

Psalm 46:1–2a

God is our refuge and strength, an ever-present help in trouble. Therefore, we will not fear . . .

Emotional Support Animal

Y ou see them more and more. The "emotional support animal" is often a dog but can really be any animal. They are allowed anywhere the public is but only with a doctor's prescription. They differ from service animals as there is no special training to do any work or task. All that is required is that the animal provide a calming effect for the owner suffering from mental, emotional, or psychiatric disabilities. Their very presence is meant to bring comfort.

The truth of today's verse brings a comfort far greater than any animal can give. God Himself is our refuge and strength. Regardless of the trouble faced, He is there to help. His very presence is the source of protection, strength, and comfort. Realizing His presence keeps us from giving in to fear. He is bigger and more powerful than any challenge.

When tragedy strikes someone close, I often do not know what to say. But it is not what I say that brings comfort but the fact that I show up. My presence is what counts. The person in crisis draws strength just from me being there. How much more true is this principle with God's presence! Burrowing my head in an animal's fur can only console me so much. Even crying on the shoulder of a friend or family member is important but does not go deep enough. But when it is my Heavenly Father there, He can and does touch my soul with His loving presence. He reassures me of His love and control. He gives me hope.

Thank you, Lord, that when troubles loom large, You are there.

Psalm 20:7–8

Some trust in chariots and some in horses, but we trust in the name of the Lord our God. They are brought to their knees and fall, but we rise up and stand firm.

Domino Effect

The art of domino toppling has become a serious competition in much of the world! The term, "domino effect" refers to the chain reaction of their fall. If there is too much space between the dominoes then of course, the chain is broken. A domino show is most impressive when different colors are used and a mosaic is produced, or when there are three dimensional stacks. According to Guinness World Records, a German group holds two records: the most mini dominoes toppled and the most dominoes toppled in a spiral in 2013. The name of this group is interesting: "Sinners Domino Entertainment!"

Today's verse speaks of those who fall and those who stand. The one who puts their trust in their own strength will one day be brought to their knees. Their fall is inevitable. The one who puts their trust and confidence in the name and power of the Lord God is the one who ends up on their feet. That person can rise up and stand firm as they draw on a strength that is not their own, but His!

Just as in the domino effect, correct spacing is important. I can be influenced by the thinking of the world. I can easily align myself with everyone around me, thinking that I can be self-sufficient because of what I own. When I begin trusting in myself more than the Lord, I am too close to those falling and I end up falling too! My prayer is to stand close enough to others to influence them for the Lord, but with enough space not to be knocked down!

Lord, may my trust in You keep me standing firm.

Proverbs 14:15

The simple believe anything, but the prudent give thought to their steps.

Coyote or Dog?

It is not uncommon to hear of coyote sightings in our area. We have low-lying hills nearby where they can roam. They look so much like dogs and their paw prints are similar too. But one can always discern which prints belong to which animal. The dog will go through an open field, stopping to investigate trees, shrubs, or logs. But the coyote will walk in a straight line, all business. He knows where he is going and what to do when he gets there.

Today's verse describes someone who is prudent. He will be thoughtful about where he steps. The prudent is not likely to follow some new untested theory or fad. Behavior that is prudent is characterized by doing what is right, just, and fair (Proverbs 1:3). The simple however, will believe and follow anything. The simple person is not thinking but takes the lazy and easy way, following what everyone else is doing. The simple person is believing without question, without fact-checking, and without scrutiny. Their steps and the path they take can lead to danger (Proverbs 22:3).

Giving thought to my next step makes me slow down. I want to walk with purpose and not aimlessly in circles. I am easily distracted by the trees, shrubs, and logs along my path. But I need to remember the purpose of my walk. The path I have chosen is to please and serve the Lord. That next step is with Him in mind. He has promised to direct me (Proverbs 3:5–6) and I do not want to run ahead of Him! I need His wisdom for every decision as He alone knows what is ahead.

Lord, please guide my steps today.

Ephesians 4:29

Do not let any unwholesome talk come out of your mouths, but only what is helpful for building others up according to their needs, that it may benefit those who listen.

Scrabble Words

It was all over the news! The Official Scrabble Players Dictionary has come out with a new edition for a new generation, adding 300 words. They have added "OK" as well as other two-letter words including "ew." The dictionary has about 100,000 words but for North American tournament play, a supplement is added. This addition allows for 90,000 more words that are "not sanitized to protect children and sensitive players." Really, that many?

Today's verse raises the standard for what comes out of our mouths. If children need to be protected from what comes out of my mouth, then perhaps I need to stop and think about what I am about to say. I may not know if someone is sensitive. The better part of wisdom is to treat everyone as sensitive and watch my words. The standards of Scripture are high. If what I am saying is unwholesome and not helpful, it is better left unsaid.

I can still hear my mother's voice. "If you can't say anything nice about a person, then say nothing at all." The problem is that my need to say it often overrides that caution. Gossip, lying, criticism, swearing, and so much more come from my mouth and displease my Lord. Like James 3:5 says, such a little member of my body does such huge damage. But thankfully, the Holy Spirit offers His control. His power changes my words from unwholesome to wholesome. His control changes my words to be helpful and a benefit.

Lord, I need Your help to control my mouth today.

Psalm 98:5–6

Make music to the Lord with the harp, with the harp and the sound of singing, with trumpets and the blast of the ram's horn—shout for joy before the Lord, the King.

Alpine Horns

These long alpine horns are quite impressive. The longer they are, the more difficult they are to play as there are no finger buttons or piston valves. It can only produce simple sounds by vibrating lips at the mouthpiece. I tried blowing on one once and the resulting blast was anything but musical! The alpine horn in the pasture was used to call in the cows, calm them down for milking and quiet them down for the night. And like the ram's horn, it was used in times past as an important signaling device, calling men to war. The ram's horn was an important part of many battles, including the famous Battle of Jericho.

Today's verse is a celebration of joy, announcing God's salvation and righteousness. This music is celebrating God's love and faithfulness. These sounds together are jubilant and loud, including blasts and shouting! This new song will be sung when the Lord comes to judge the earth. All the earth is making this music! These instruments are accompanied by rivers clapping and mountains singing! It will not only be a new song but a new sound; announcing the coming of righteousness and justice.

The only way I can participate in this celebration of coming justice is by being forgiven and receiving God's grace. I do not anticipate that future day with fear and trembling. That is because I am His own and I have His righteousness through faith in Christ's sacrifice. I can look forward with joyful anticipation to the day when my King will establish justice and right all wrongs!

Lord, keep me focused on what is coming!

Colossians 2:19

They have lost connection with the head, from whom the whole body, supported and held together by its ligaments and sinews, grows as God causes it to grow.

Coxswain Rowing

As I look out the window at Buzzard's Bay, Massachusetts, I see the rowing teams practicing from the nearby private academy. The only one who seems to know where the boat is going is the coxswain who sits in the stern facing the bow. This member of the team does not row but his role is crucial. It is only with his specific calls that the rowers can make any progress. He is responsible for steering the boat and for coordinating the power and rhythm of the rowers. Without him, there is no unity.

Today's verse speaks of the Church as a body with a head. That head is Christ (Colossians 1:18). If we lose our connection with Him, we have lost the ability to work together. We each have a role to play as members of this body, and there is no growth without Him. He is the One who directs and leads. He is the One who steers us in the right direction. He has the same call for all of us and that is to glorify Him.

There is a temptation to think I am really something! I may think I know a better way to move forward. But with this attitude I lose connection with the Lord and I lose connection with other members. That is because it is Christ who holds us together. He sees where I am going but asks me to operate, not by sight but by faith in Him. When I am listening for His calls, I find unity with other believers doing the same thing!

Thank you, Lord, for the progress You make possible!

1 Peter 3:15

But in your hearts revere Christ as Lord. Always be prepared to give an answer to everyone who asks you to give the reason for the hope that you have. But do this with gentleness and respect.

Clams

Sometimes, even in death, a clam will not open up! The advice is to refrain from eating any clam that does not open during the steaming process. That adductor muscle is awfully strong, holding the two shell halves together. This is how they protect themselves from their predators: the fish, eel, snail or starfish. The expression, "to clam up" comes from the idea of a clam shutting down at the approach of danger.

Today's verse encourages the believer to open up to others about the hope that is in them. Part of revering Christ as Lord is being willing and prepared to answer questions from others about our faith. Rather than "clamming up," we are to be vulnerable and transparent with people who are interested. There is always the danger of being misunderstood or even rejected. But as long as communication is done with gentleness and respect for the listener, then God is glorified.

When I speak to others of Christ, there is always the potential to encounter hostility, even with those who ask. Dealing with hostile reactions requires His wisdom which is pure, peaceable, and gentle (James 3:17). I am told to "speak the truth in love" (Ephesians 4:15). I am also told to bless others when I am reviled and mocked (1 Corinthians 4:12). But what I do not want to do is clam up, just because I may be ridiculed. I want to be bold, to declare out loud the very best thing that has ever happened to me . . . His love and salvation!

Lord, help me to be open about my faith today!

Psalm 63:3–4

Because Your love is better than life, my lips will glorify you. I will praise you as long as I live and in your name I will lift up my hands.

Art or French Fries?

I recently attended a painting workshop where the goal was to express praise to God through art. There were no rules or grand expectations. There was just some Christian music playing and some Psalms read. The facilitator gave a title to our work: "Adoration." I tried not to look over at my neighbor's work. I tried to focus on what I was feeling toward the One who created me. But my praise came out looking like french fries! I guess I should not quit my day job just yet!!

Today's verse expresses praise to God in a different way. David used his lips in word and in song to glorify God's name. He lifted up his hands in praise to God's incredible love that he calls "better than life." This psalm was written when he was in the desert of Judah, on the run from his enemies. His praise to God is that much sweeter being in the midst of a "dry and weary land" (verse 1).

My praise to Him may not be of a professional quality. My painting is maybe good enough for the back closet wall! I love singing, but my song may even be a little off key. I lift my hands now, but someday my arms may be too weak. But He sees the heart's expression. Praise to Him is always welcomed. Whatever I do or say can be done in His name and to His glory (Colossians 3:17). Praising Him for His love and power is about the most important thing I can accomplish today!

Keep me praising You today, Lord!

Ephesians 1:3

Praise be to the God and Father of our Lord Jesus Christ, who has blessed us in the heavenly realms with every spiritual blessing in Christ.

Bless You

Our cat, Tiger, would sometimes have a sneezing fit and would always look very surprised when it happened. I never felt obligated to say the words, "bless you." After all, I figured it was usually the cat making everyone else sneeze. There are many ideas on the origins of blessing people after a sneeze. Some believed the sneeze had to do with evil spirits leaving the body. Others felt it was the soul momentarily escaping the body. My favorite is the belief that the heart temporarily stopped during a sneeze!

Today's verse declares that the source of every spiritual blessing is Jesus Christ. He has blessed every believer with unmerited favor and goodness. The blessings He gives are not always tangible but spiritual. And because that is true, these blessings are eternal. They include His choosing us, adopting us, redeeming us, and forgiving us (verses 4–7). He has blessed us by sealing us with His Holy Spirit and has promised us an inheritance (verses 13–14). These blessings are not seen with our physical eyes but they are more real than things that are!

I need to be reminded of His blessings, especially when I see nonbelievers seemingly prosper around me. Like David, I can feel discouraged and tempted to be envious (Psalm 37:1–2). But their success is temporary and my inheritance is eternal! Spiritual blessings are the ones that matter. And the blessing of being His very own outweighs anything else. I can live this life with faith and love because they spring from the hope stored up for me in heaven (Colossians 1:5)!

Lord, open the eyes of my heart to see Your blessings today.

James 4:15

Instead you ought to say, "If it is the Lord's will, we will live and do this or that."

Checkmate

My grandsons had no idea where each chess piece should be placed to begin or even continue a game! Their Nana sure could not help, but they had fun anyway, confidently moving the pieces around according to some unseen vision in their little heads! The strategy of chess escapes me but I do know enough to recognize that "check" is not what one wants to hear, and "checkmate" even less, signaling that the game is over.

Today's verse talks about making plans for the future. Of course it is important in reaching any goal to carefully plan a strategy. A building is not begun without considering the estimated cost (Luke 14:28). But this passage is speaking to the arrogance of making plans without thought to the plans the Lord may have. We do not know what tomorrow will hold or whether we will have life and breath to carry out our future plans (verse 14). The unexpected can always "check" or even "checkmate" our progress.

When I make plans I want to always recognize that the Lord may have something different in mind. Recognizing this keeps me humble and it keeps me in an attitude of submission. Recognizing His control also keeps me asking and listening to Him. As wonderful as I think my plan is, I do not want to miss out on something better! He knows what tomorrow holds. He knows what health issues I may be facing later or what financial challenge lay ahead. Being overconfident about my plans is seen as "boasting" in the Lord's eyes (verse 16). There may be a change of plan but through it all I can trust Him.

Lord, keep me following Your plan.

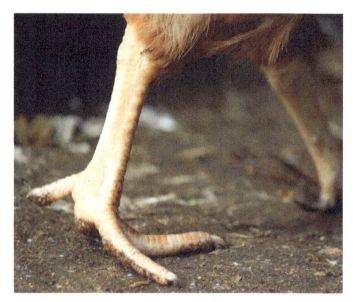

He makes my feet like the feet of a deer. He causes me to stand on the heights.

Chicken Feet

I have loved our excursions in the Alps of Haute-Savoie, France. One time we have even surprised a herd of ibex mountain goats. But we have never come across a brood of chickens on those heights! Even though some breeds have an extra toe, none could grip, climb, and keep their balance on a mountainous terrain. The feet of deer and mountain goats are sure-footed and allow them to scale the heights.

Today's verse comes from David's song of praise for God's deliverance from Saul. He begins it saying, "I love You Lord, my strength." He describes God as His shield, rock, fortress, and stronghold. David recognizes that it is God giving him strength to stand on the heights of victory over his enemies (verse 32). His feet are as sure-footed as the deer, and David even thanks God that his ankles do not give way (verse 36). It is God who helps Him and makes him great.

When I look down at my feet, I see chicken's feet! Without His help and strength, I am unsure and wobbly. When the path is level I can do pretty well on my own. The problem is that life is seldom smooth. My path is strewn with pits and obstacles. My enemies are often the unseen ones of doubt, discouragement, fear, and frustration. They trip me up. I need God's help and strength every day. When He answers my cry, He infuses strength in my soul to face the hard times. He not only gets me through but He gives me victory! How incredible to stand on the heights and enjoy the view of His faithfulness!

Lord, make my feet like the deer today.

Psalm 18:29

With your help I can advance against a troop; with my God I can scale a wall.

Hitting the Wall

The Great Wall of China comes to mind as the best example of an impressive wall. Not only does it run 13,000 miles in its entirety, but sections of the wall have been around since the 7th century! It was built to prevent attack from barbarian nomads but in fact it has been scaled many times. Perhaps its most important role is a psychological one, serving as a barrier between Chinese culture and the rest of the world. My husband had the privilege of jogging on the top of this wall while visiting the country with his Chinese mother.

Today's verse speaks of a wall that is scaled with the power God gives. For David, the troops and wall were literal. The context of this psalm is praise to God for his deliverance from King Saul. He calls God his fortress, his rock, and his shield. But not only is God his protector but He also empowers him to advance and attack! A wall that looks insurmountable is no barrier with God's power!

There are walls in my life that certainly look insurmountable. I do not have a king chasing after me, but my walls could be psychological. Whatever seems impossible to face, impossible to finish, or impossible to forget can be my wall. But I have the same power that David had. God's Spirit lives within me, giving me the ability to fight through and succeed. He is my force. He is not going to allow me to hit the wall, but to jump over it!

There is nothing too hard for You, Lord. Help me to remember that today.

Isaiah 40:11

He tends his flock like a shepherd: He gathers the lambs in his arms and carries them close to his heart; he gently leads those that have young.

Bummer Lamb

This sweet lamb could very well be what is called in agricultural terms a "bummer lamb." These are lambs that need special attention and care, having been rejected by their mothers. If the shepherd does not intervene, the lamb will die. Some shepherds go so far as to bring the lamb into their home and raise him there until strong enough to join the rest of the flock.

Today's verse is such a beautiful depiction of the Lord. This tender picture is sandwiched between two verses describing God's power: His ruling power and His creative power. How amazing it is that His tenderness can coexist with that incredible power! The Lord is our Shepherd and cares about each of His sheep individually. He carries them when they feel weak, not under His arm or even on His back, but close to His heart. Our Shepherd leads and guides His sheep but does it oh so gently for the ewes with their young ones.

In a world that can sometimes seem so cold and harsh, it is this quality of His love that I so appreciate. I especially need His tenderness when I am sore from beating myself up. I need His tenderness when I feel hurt and rejected. His gentleness is like a balm for my soul. Close to my Shepherd's heart I feel warm and cherished. His arms hold me up when I just can't anymore. There is a time for His rod and staff. But there is a time for His tenderness. And He knows exactly what I need.

Thank you, Lord, for Your gentle care today.

Numbers 23:19

God is not human, that he should lie, not a human being that he should change his mind. Does he speak and then not act? Does he promise and not fulfill?

Flip Flops

I would never have thought to use flip flops as a table centerpiece! Thankfully, the flip flops were new and not used! Living in this beach culture, I see this footwear in most any social setting imaginable. Our local mall has a store exclusively dedicated to selling flip flops. But the name of this footwear also calls to mind the idea of changing one's mind or position. In presidential elections, flip-flopping seems to be common on both sides of the political aisle!

Today's verse reassures us that God will not flip flop. He is not like us but always says what He means. He never says He will do something and not come through. When He speaks, He acts. When He makes a promise, it will happen. He can back His word with the power to do it. Being all knowing, God would never say that He was unaware of the extenuating or changing circumstances. No matter how many promises God has made, they are "Yes" in Christ (2 Corinthians 1:20a).

Living in a world of broken promises, it is sometimes hard for me to really take the Lord at His word. Too many times it is easier to doubt than to believe that He means what He says. He says He loves me. He says He will care for me and cause all things to work for good. He does not disappoint. I cannot think of even one time that He has proved Himself unfaithful. Yet, I still hesitate to live like I really believe it!

Give me grace Lord, to trust You more.

For this reason I kneel before the Father, from whom every family in heaven and on earth derives its name.

Chinese Stamps

The Chinese characters that make up my name define me as a forest, as successful and intelligent, and as a precious rare gem! My husband had this Chinese stamp made for me during our tour of China at the start of our marriage. It seemed appropriate as I was marrying into a family giving me a Chinese mother-in-law. I am not sure how accurate it is or why a forest has anything to do with me. But it is fun to think about the meaning of our names.

Today's verse points out a commonality in all of our names. Because God is the Father who created each and every family and its members, we all derive our name from Him. God is "Jehovah-Ab," the Lord our Father (Isaiah 64:8). We are all the work of His hands. But to become a child of God, redeemed and inhabited by his Spirit, takes a step of faith and repentance (John 1:12–13). At that point there is no separation but only unity as His family. Whether those already in heaven or those on earth, His children are part of one family. There is no more Jew or Gentile, slave or free, or even male or female (Galatians 3:28).

Only the God of the universe could succeed in making such diverse people one family. But because He can and does, I have brothers and sisters not only worldwide but across time! That strong desire to belong is completely satisfied. Every time I worship with others so different than myself, I get a small inkling of this incredible truth! And like Paul, I kneel before the Father in gratitude!

Thank you, Lord, for making me part of Your family!

Romans 3:23–24

For all have sinned and fall short of the glory of God, and all are justified freely by his grace through the redemption that came by Christ Jesus.

Cherry Picking

Two cherry-laden trees sat untouched halfway through my vineyard walk. Every day I would check on their progress. Today the cherries were not only at their peak but some were even rotting on the branches. It seemed the most natural thing to do to help myself to a few handfuls. The sweet juice dripped all over my fingers, staining them red and purple. Although I was sure the owner would not mind, I couldn't shake the feeling that I could be caught "red-handed," as technically I had taken something not belonging to me!

Today's verse explains that we are all red-handed. "Sin had left a crimson stain" on our hands as we are all guilty of breaking God's perfect law. There is no way to remove that stain on our own. But thankfully, one pair of hands are not red but nail-scarred. Because of His amazing grace we are justified or declared righteous through what Christ did on that cross. He sacrificed Himself freely out of love for us and not because we deserved it.

I want clean hands and a pure heart. It is only then that I can really enjoy Him as I receive blessing and vindication from Him (Psalm 24:3–5). But there is no cleansing without the humility to admit my guilt and come clean with the Lord. Rather than hiding my hands behind my back, He invites me to discover grace and forgiveness. He is faithful and just to always forgive and give me a clean start (1 John 1:9).

Thank you, Lord, that I can always come clean with You.

1 Peter 4:16

However, if you suffer as a Christian, do not be ashamed, but praise God that you bear that name.

Barbie Doll's Last Name

Who would have thought it, that the Barbie doll has a last name! Apparently, Barbie herself recently tweeted out the big revelation. She and her two sisters wished everyone a Happy Siblings Day from the Roberts sisters. According to novels published by Random House in the sixties, Barbie's full name is Barbara Millicent Roberts. The Ken doll's full name is Kenneth Carson. I, for one, will sleep better tonight having that mystery cleared up for me.

Today's verse talks about proudly bearing a name. It is a name that is above all other names. But it is also a name that could provoke hostility from others. Being a Christ follower carries the risk of being scorned, mocked, and even persecuted. But there is special blessing promised for those who are insulted because of the name of Christ (verse 14). How polarizing the name of Jesus is! The names of other religious leaders do not get the same reaction.

I bear the name of Jesus when I live like He did. I bear the name of Jesus when I speak of Him to others. And I bear His name when I exemplify His character through His Spirit. Bearing His name identifies me as belonging to Him. Even if it draws negative attention, I am not to be ashamed. Suffering for His name is a privilege. I wonder if I am identified so closely with Christ that people see a difference in me. I hope so. I pray so.

Thank you, Lord, for the privilege of bearing Your name.

Psalm 77:11–12

I will remember the deeds of the Lord; yes, I will remember your miracles of long ago. I will consider your works and meditate on all your mighty deeds.

A Squirrel and His Nut

I am not the only one who forgets where I have put things! The University of Richmond did a study and found that squirrels fail to recover up to 74 percent of the nuts they bury! Even so, they do have a strategy. They do what's called "spatial chunking," sorting their nuts by size, type, and taste and then burying them in groups. Even more surprising are the gray squirrels who frequently dig up and then rebury the same nut, a behavior perhaps to refresh their memories!

Today's verse comes from a psalm of Asaph, King David's music director. In his depression he is wondering if God is going to keep His promises. He wonders if God's love for him has vanished (verse 8). He doubts and wonders but then he answers his own questions with these two verses. He resolves to remember all of what the Lord has done in the past for him and his people. He replaces his troubling thoughts with memories of God's miracles and mighty deeds.

I have seen the Lord do so many miracles in my life! He has provided and proved Himself faithful. But those memories are so often buried. I easily forget when I am struggling with a new difficulty. I need to go back and dig it up to refresh my memory of His faithfulness! Thoughts of His "mighty deeds" in the past restore my confidence and trust in Him! Not only my memories do this but the testimony of others do too! He has done it in the past and He will do it again!

Thank you, Lord, for Your incredible faithfulness.

Isaiah 43:25

I, even I am he who blots out your transgressions, for my own sake, and remembers your sins no more.

Checkers

The game of checkers has been around a lot longer than most of us would think! Checkers is thought to be the oldest game in the world, dating back over 4,000 years! According to inscriptions found in the temple of Thebes, Egyptian kings took time out from overseeing the construction of the pyramids to play checkers! Lots of famous people have since had a fondness for the game including past presidents, noted scientists, and popular sport heroes. Whoever the player may be, however, it is certain that they have a "checkered past."

Today's verse is a wonderful reassurance for all of us who regret those black squares that mark our past. No one is immune from having that checkered past, as all have sinned and fallen short (Romans 3:23). But the Lord has promised a forgiveness and pardon that is complete. He blots out every sin and chooses to not remember them. He no longer holds against us all our failures and disobedience. Jesus took on Himself the punishment for each of those sins.

I would love to be able to "remember my sins no longer." But the memories remain. And Satan loves to whisper in my ears his accusations. Thankfully, God's Word is full of reassurances of unconditional love and complete pardon. The Lord graciously softens and blurs memories of past failures. If guilty memories occasionally do reappear, He is there to build me back up. If nothing else, those memories remind me that I am not perfect, but His forgiveness is! Remembering a checkered past, I can also remember that His grace is greater than all my sin!

Thank you, Lord, for wiping out and forgetting my sin forever!

Luke 15:10

In the same way, I tell you, there is rejoicing in the presence of the angels of God over one sinner who repents.

Birthdays in Heaven

Today my mother celebrates her birthday in heaven for the first time. But I am not so sure that she is having a party. I imagine that if everyone there is daily celebrating birthdays, eternal life would be one big continual party! If that were the case, the cake would be delicious but with no calories. The gifts would need no exchanging. And there would be no letdown the following day! I cannot imagine a cake big enough to hold all the candles as each century is added!

Today's verse describes a time of rejoicing in heaven. It is not for the first birthday but for the second: the spiritual one when one is born again. There is rejoicing, and somehow the angels even get into the act. When even just one sinner repents and comes to Jesus for salvation, there is celebration and joy! The noise of it would echo down those streets of gold. This verse follows the parables of the lost coin and the lost sheep that were found. Following this verse is the parable of the lost son whose return was celebrated with a party. In each case there was enthusiastic joy and celebration!

Her joy is complete. Mine, not so much. She is enjoying her reward, whatever form it takes. But I can recapture some of my joy when reminding myself of where she is and what she is experiencing today. There are no more tears, pain, or suffering, and she is surrounded with incredible beauty and splendor. She is enjoying "face to face" the Love of her life; her Savior.

Thank you, Lord, for what You have prepared for all who love You.

James 1:22

Do not merely listen to the Word, and so deceive yourselves. Do what it says.

A Panda-Sized Meal

Who does not enjoy watching these cute cuddly looking pandas! They can look especially adorable when romping around playing. But more likely, they are seen doing what they spend the majority of their day doing: eating! They eat 30–45 pounds of bamboo per day. Their back molars are very strong for tearing this fibrous plant. And they even have a sixth digit for holding those long stalks. But because the bamboo is low in nutrition and pandas digest a very low percentage of what they eat, they must consume huge quantities. They are constantly eating.

Today's verse talks about two ways one can feed on God's Word. One can merely listen to it and be deceived into thinking that is sufficient. Or one can not only listen to God's Word but actually apply it and put it into practice. In obeying God's Word, there is change, growth, and good spiritual health. However, merely listening is much easier to do. There can be momentary feel-good reactions to a poetic passage or a challenging story of faith. But it is when we respond to His commands with submission and obedience that we truly grow.

I can get quite prideful about how well I know Scripture. I can recite verses with the best of them. But large quantities of head knowledge is not what makes for true heart change. It is only in doing what God's Word says that I can grow and become what He wants me to be. It really is not how much I know or how much I listen to that makes a difference. The difference lies in how much I do what it says!

Lord, don't let me be deceived. Show me where I need to obey.

Isaiah 50:10

Who among you fears the Lord and obeys the word of his servant? Let the one who walks in the dark who has no light, trust in the name of the Lord and rely on their God.

Beyond the Storm

With all the technology at our fingertips, we are often forewarned of a storm on its way. Other times a storm will descend suddenly with little or no warning at all. With our many road trips, we are sometimes stuck with no option except to go through its path. But I am not too concerned when I can see the skies clearing ahead. Just the thought of the storm being temporary helps me calm down and get through it.

Today's verse talks about walking in the dark with no light at all. There is no vision of clear skies ahead. This happens for even those who fear and obey the Lord. When those confusing dark times come, we are to trust in His name and who He is. We are to rely on God rather than our senses or our intelligence. Walking by faith has nothing to do with what we can see ahead that reassures us (2 Corinthians 5:7). We are given no "light at the end of the tunnel" on which to focus.

I cannot see that patch of blue ahead. But I can remain calm in the middle of a storm. Trusting and relying on the Creator of that storm keeps me serene. He is trustworthy and He is in control. I have no reason to be fearful for what the future might hold. And the only light I really need in that darkness is the heart conviction of how good and gracious He is.

Thank you, Lord, for Your reassuring presence even in the dark.

Luke 16:17

It is easier for heaven and earth to disappear than for the least stroke of a pen to drop out of the Law.

Banished Words

Every year since 1976, Lake Superior State University has issued a list of banished words. These words are nominated from around the world. They include pet peeves from everyday speech. But they also come from news, education, and advertising, among other fields. The 2019 list includes: yeet, collusion, ghosting, and accoutrements. Their list is comprised of words that are misused, overused, or useless!

Today's verse speaks of the permanence of God's Word. In contrast to the falling out of favor and banishment of words, the Word of God stands forever (Psalm 119:89). It would be easier for all of heaven and earth to disappear than for even one little part of His law to be null and void. What God says stands for all eternity. There are no mistakes and there is never a need for revision. His Word is always relevant throughout the centuries. Because His words are inspired by His Spirit, they communicate unchangeable truth. The standards of the Law are not changed by popular opinion or a nominating committee!

How convicting and comforting His Word can be! It is convicting because it exposes my heart and motives (Hebrews 4:12). And His law shows me how woefully I measure up. Thankfully, Jesus Christ kept the Law and perfectly fulfilled it. His righteousness is mine through faith in His work and sacrifice (Romans 3:22). But His eternal Word is also comforting. It is truth that never changes, and it strengthens my faith (Romans 10:17). His Word reminds me of His love and faithfulness. His Word gives me an unshakable hope that is an anchor for my soul.

Thank you, Lord, that Your Word is forever and worthy of trust.

Luke 6:27–28

But to you who are listening I say: Love your enemies, do good to those who hate you, bless those who curse you, pray for those who mistreat you.

Blessed Thistle

Being that this flower is surrounded by sharp pointy leaves and considered a bitter herb, how is this plant blessed? As pretty as the flower is, the plant is a "blessing" for its medicinal properties. Blessed thistle contains tannins which might help with diarrhea, coughs, and inflammation. It was used to treat bubonic plague during the Middle Ages and as a tonic for monks.

In today's verse, Jesus is speaking specifically to all "who are listening." He was addressing a large crowd, including His disciples. But as in any audience, there are those who are tracking and those who are distracted. These words are for those whose intention is to be a blessing. Being a blessing to enemies who curse, hate, and mistreat you is done by showing love in two ways; doing good for them and praying for them. Those willing to obey will experience great reward (verse 35). And they will be recognizable as His children, being kind to the ungrateful and wicked, just as He is.

Being a blessing to enemies is not usually something very high on my to-do list! I have a hard enough time being a blessing to those who love me! But doing good to my enemies and praying for them is modeled by Jesus and He asks the same of me. I cannot expect any accolades or return from obeying. But there will be great reward one day for this hard thing He asks of me. And behaving as one of His children brings glory and recognition to Him (verse 35)!

Thank you, Lord, that in being a blessing to enemies, I too am blessed!

You provide a broad path for my feet, so that my ankles do not give way.

A Dangerous Path

This is not a path that I would willingly take! In all our hiking adventures in France and Switzerland, we have never chosen a path quite so precarious. We have enjoyed some breathtaking views, but always at a safe distance from the edge. To walk along such a narrow path seems to invite disaster. The vertigo, the tension, and the possibility of a lethal misstep would override any pleasure in the view.

Today's verse comes from a psalm of David praising God for his deliverance from enemies. David affirms that he has kept God's ways (verse 21) and that God's way is perfect (verse 30). The path God gave David to walk was a broad path where his footing could be sure. Despite the attacks from enemies, David praises God for giving him strength and making his way perfect (verse 32). God has enabled David to stand on the heights like the deer (verse 33). This is a path of righteousness that is not only broad but spacious (verse 19). On this broad path, he has a clear view of God's faithfulness.

I have a choice about what kind of path to take through life. The path of righteousness is thought to be the more difficult, arduous one. There are restrictions there that bring out the rebel in me. But in fact, the path of righteousness is the one most sure. There, my steps are not hampered and I can even run without stumbling (Proverbs 4:11–12)! Guilt and sin can narrow my path making it uncomfortable. But in following His perfect way, I can look up and enjoy the view of His hand and His faithfulness.

Lord, keep me following Your perfect way today.

James 1:5

If any of you lacks wisdom, you should ask God, who gives generously to all without finding fault, and it will be given to you.

Ask!

I can ask a search engine anything. Apparently, there are no questions too stupid that it will not answer. In fact, when asking something very obvious that everyone should know, it does not make fun of me or roll its eyes! I get no attitude from it. Imagine it saying, "What? You don't know that?" or "I answered that yesterday! Can't you remember anything?" In the privacy of my own home I can ask it anything without fear of disdain for my stupidity!

Today's verse encourages the believer to ask for wisdom from the Lord. He does not reprimand us for not knowing. There is no exasperation on His part. He is patient and understanding. But we do not receive this wisdom until two things happen: we recognize our lack and we humble ourselves enough to ask Him.

Asking questions can be humbling. It is difficult to put aside my pride and admit not knowing. My motto is often, "Fake it 'til you make it." How often I have continued a phone conversation despite not knowing which Kathy or Jim is on the line! My pride prevents me from asking for a last name. No one likes to admit not knowing. But better than a search engine that is not infallible and only gives the facts, God is available to answer any question. His answers help me live my life with skill and godliness. God invites me to approach Him with faith, anywhere and anytime for help with any area. He is the limitless and infallible source of every answer I need!

Help me Lord, to turn to You today for every answer!

Hebrews 13:8

Jesus Christ is the same yesterday and today and forever.

Yesterday Today and Tomorrow Plant

If you do not like a particular color of this flower, all that is needed is to wait a day! The flowers on the Yesterday Today and Tomorrow plant are unique in that they change color. They first bloom as a purple or violet. The next day, that same bloom becomes a pale lavender. The following day, its color changes to white!

In a world where everything seems to be in a constant state of change, it is comforting to know that our Savior does not change. Today's verse teaches that Jesus is the same yesterday, today, and forever. These flowers may experience changes that are beautiful, but Jesus is perfectly beautiful and needs no improvement! Everything that we need to know about the Lord is revealed in His Word. He does not change nor does His revelation. His message transcends time and is always current. The God in the Old Testament is the same God as in the New. His faithfulness and power shown then is the same faithfulness and power He shows today.

I need Him to be constant and not capricious. I need Him to be faithful to His Word and unchangeable. What was proven true in times past continues to be true today and will be true tomorrow. He is perfect, and perfection has no need of change. There is no reason for me to worry that a promise will no longer be valid. His compassion is daily renewed because He will always be faithful to who He is and to His Word (Lamentations 3:23). He never changes and I can build my life on this rock-hard solid truth!

Thank you, Lord, that You do not change and I can always count on You.

Hebrews 10:36

You need to persevere so that when you have done the will of God, you will receive what he has promised.

Grits

My impression of grits is that it is bland and heavy. But in fact, this ground-corn dish, popular in the Southern States, has many mouthwatering variations. I have enjoyed them with shrimp and with cheese as a main dish. More often, grits are considered a breakfast side dish. In any case, the word "grit" has another meaning, associated with the idea of courage, resolve, and strength of will.

Today's verse also alludes to "strength of will" but curiously, not our own. Believers are encouraged to continue living out God's will. These early Christians endured "great conflict full of suffering" (verse 32). When they were not being persecuted themselves, they were standing side by side with those who were. They were publicly humiliated and insulted, even suffering the indignities of prison and confiscation of property.

It takes perseverance to follow God's desires ahead of my own. We mistakenly believe that the goal of life is the pursuit of happiness. But God's will is much grander than my own little life. He is about building His Kingdom and I am privileged to participate in something that is eternal. My confidence and obedience will one day be richly rewarded. Knowing that helps me persevere in doing His will. I enjoy His blessings now, but they pale in comparison to all He has prepared for me! I frankly do not always understand His will. It is often at odds with my own selfish desires or what I believe are "my rights." But I do know that whatever it takes, He is worth following!

Thank you, Lord, for giving me what it takes to persevere.

345

2 Corinthians 7:9

Yet now I am happy, not because you were made sorry, but because your sorrow led you to repentance. For you became sorrowful as God intended . . .

The Sorry Game

I grew up with this board game and although it has gone through some revisions, it is still enjoyed today. The idea was to get around the board first, usually by impeding the progress of others. As the youngest in my family I often felt put upon and would relish my revenge by landing on an opponent and sending them home. That most feared "sorry card" allowed a player to go directly to any occupied space and knock them off. The expected "sorry" spoken would of course sound hollow and insincere. I was never really sorry!

Today's verse talks about being sorry. Sorrow for sin is something that God intended us to feel. Sorrow is even called "godly sorrow" when it leads to repentance. And of course, this repentance is heartfelt and not just lip service. God sees into our hearts and responds with forgiveness and cleansing when we come clean with Him. Trying to ignoring that sorrow and shame can be destructive, as it can linger on, even for a lifetime. His forgiveness and grace allows us to lift our head again.

Being sorry is not enough if it does not lead me to fall on my knees and repent. It is in repenting that I can turn my back on that sin. That second step is where I find not only His forgiveness but a new start. If I am only sorry I will probably be sorry again over the same thing. He wants to give me victory over sin. He lifts that burden of sorrow and makes my heart light again!

Thank you, Lord, for erasing my sorrow.

Colossians 1:11

. . . being strengthened with all power according to his glorious might so that you may have great endurance and patience.

Willow Leaves

Patience is a virtue that Johann Wolfgang von Goethe likened to the willow leaf. This seventeenth-century German writer and statesman said, "A leaf that is destined to grow large is full of grooves and wrinkles at the start. Now if one has no patience and wants it smooth offhand like a willow leaf, there is trouble ahead." These leaves are shiny, thin, and 2–4 inches long. But of course, they do not start off so large and smooth. It will take lots of sunshine, water, and time to get to this stage.

Today's verse is an encouragement. That elusive quality of patience is something that comes not from ourselves, but from His power. The believer is strengthened with power from His glorious might to have great endurance and patience. It is not something we can naturally muster up on our own. Over time, He develops it in us as we become more like Him. It is part of the work He does in us (Philippians 1:6). And more often than not, this quality of patience grows out of living through difficulties.

In the space of three days, I had ample opportunity to show patience. After experiencing jet lag, toilet emergencies, roof leaks, and a power outage, it was almost comical . . . almost. My leaves are still not so large and smooth. There are still plenty of rough edges! But God's reassurance of His control calmed me down. I am thankful that being in His Word has encouraged me and helped me stay in that place of quiet confidence (Romans 15:4). Things may fall apart around me, but I don't want to fall apart too!

Lord, thank you for Your strength and patience!

1 Corinthians 10:13

No temptation has overtaken you except what is common to mankind. And God is faithful; he will not let you be tempted beyond what you can bear. But when you are tempted, he will also provide a way out so that you can endure it.

Unique

Having visited the pottery factories in Poland has given me a true appreciation for their products. It was fascinating to see each artist bent over their work, hand painting or stamping their pieces with intense concentration. Each piece is signed by the artist as well as stamped with the Polish word for "unique." It is true that each piece is unique. But all the pottery went through the same process of being fired in the kiln.

Today's verse recognizes that each believer faces the same kinds of trials and tests. The details may vary. The timing and even the intensity may differ. But there is a commonality to all the trials God allows us to face. They are never intended to weaken us but to strengthen our faith. In each trial we see God's hand and His faithfulness. And we have His promise that it will never be unbearable.

What I am facing is never unique. Somewhere, someone in the world has faced nearly the same thing. Knowing that helps me to not feel so alone. Not only can I draw strength from others, but I can be encouraged knowing what Christ faced. He experienced every kind of temptation and yet did not sin (Hebrews 4:15). And because He Himself suffered when tempted, He is there to help. He Himself is my "way out." Depending on His strength and help makes all the difference.

Thank you, Lord, that I do not need to do this alone.

James 1:3–4

. . . because you know that the testing of your faith produces perseverance. Let perseverance finish its work so that you may be mature and complete, not lacking anything.

My Roses

I am thinking that my roses need some fertilizer. They bloomed for this spectacular show and then decided to quit. Probably, the soil needs to be replenished with nutrients. In my area the soil is especially dry and full of clay and in need of some help. But we all know how fertilizer is made from animal matter or vegetable matter, at least the organic variety. Rotting vegetables from a compost pile is not too appetizing. And the bat and bird guano is just a discreet way of saying something else!

The Bible is full of references to plant growth and fruit to picture our spiritual journey. Today's verse explains that we become mature in our faith by developing perseverance. It all sounds wonderful until we realize that the only way we develop that lovely flowering perseverance is through some stinky trials. The hard times drive us to our knees and cause us to cry out to Him for help. When we see God work, our faith grows. The next time we find ourselves in the middle of hard times and heartache, we are more likely to stay strong and healthy.

I wish there was a less painful way to grow and bloom. But the beauty and color is more vibrant when born of hardship. It is a comfort to me to know that a horrible circumstance that has nothing to recommend it can be used by Him. He does not waste that stinky situation. In His hands it serves to develop something beautiful in me!

Thank you, Lord, for using it all to grow my faith!

Hebrews 11:6

And without faith it is impossible to please God, because anyone who comes to him must believe that he exists and that he rewards those who earnestly seek him.

My Hero

Having married a "Kent," I have had my share of Superman jokes. When naming our children, there was no question but that we would avoid the name Clark or Lois! But in fact, my husband is my hero if one counts admiration and respect! He does not fly through the air and right all wrongs, but he is certainly a hero for putting up with me!

Today's verse comes from a chapter referred to as a list of "heroes of the faith." These verses describe ordinary men and women who demonstrated tremendous faith in persevering, even when a promise was not fulfilled in their lifetime. The criteria was not the recognition or accolades of men. In fact, the world was not even worthy of them (verse 38). But they are heroes because they never gave up their faith even while facing death. Because of their faith, "God was not ashamed to be called their God" (verse 16).

There are many religious systems that require some kind of faith. The idea of faith and spirituality is normally well received. It is not until I refer to the object of my faith that I face opposition. My faith is in a Person. Not in my religion. Not in my church. And certainly not in my own efforts. My faith in God and His Son, Jesus, exhibits itself in coming to Him repeatedly and earnestly seeking Him. He rewards me by revealing Himself to me more and more. And when I take Him at His word, believe His promises, and obey Him, I feel His pleasure.

"My faith has found a resting place," and He is worthy.

II Peter 3:18

But grow in the grace and knowledge of our Lord and Savior Jesus Christ. To him be glory both now and forever! Amen.

Hot House Orchid

This gorgeous flower needs pampering! When transplanting the orchid out of its tropical habitat, it will need special conditions to grow and flourish. The artificially heated greenhouse will provide an environment that will make this delicate plant happy and stable. In that hot house will be other vulnerable plants not hardy enough to grow under natural conditions. The phrase, "hot house flower" also describes a person who is fragile and vulnerable.

Today's verse talks about what is needed for the believer to grow in his faith: grace and knowledge. There is not a Christ-follower alive that does not need these special conditions to grow. Being exposed to the harsh world-environment can choke out what God wants to produce in us. His grace or unmerited favor and the knowledge of Himself is His hot house. His grace is sufficient when we are weak (II Cor. 12:9). And the power to thrive comes through our knowledge of him (II Peter 1:3).

I forget so often. My independent and prideful spirit makes me feel that I am doing just fine on my own. That takes all the glory for myself when it rightfully belongs to Him. And before long, my attitude starts to show in shriveled leaves and droopy flowers. It is clear to me that my faith is stunted when I totally lose it at the first sign of difficulty. But when I can respond with dependence on His grace and a recognition of His goodness and love, then I can not only survive, but thrive. It is the Lord that keeps me from being fragile and vulnerable.

Thank you Lord, for the growth that comes from You!

Philippians 4:19

And my God will meet all your needs according to the riches of his glory in Christ Jesus.

The Blue Jay

This clever scrub blue jay is carefully looking left and right before hiding away his treasured peanuts. His behavior is called "caching" rather than "hoarding," a term used for rodents. Caching is normally more short term and seasonal. And though he lives in a family group, he will not share. He selfishly hides the food and retrieves it in secret! If there is a shortage, there are no posted store signs to discourage this behavior and there is no one to see an overloaded shopping cart!

Today's verse reassures the believer that not only is the Lord aware of shortages, but He promises to meet our basic needs. There is never a question that God will not have enough. Riches in Christ Jesus are infinite and not subject to the variance of supply and demand. Paul says he is "amply supplied" and that he even has more than enough (verse 18), thanks to their gifts. He then assures them that because of their sharing, God will see to it that they do not lack for anything needed.

When I see shortages at the stores during this unusual time of pandemic, there is the temptation to "squirrel away" much more than I need. To some extent, stockpiling can be a reasonable response. But when it becomes hoarding or caching is when I have no intention of sharing with others. I know the Lord does not honor that kind of selfish spirit. Panic-induced hoarding can signal in me a lack of trust in my Heavenly Father. He does not ask me to put toilet paper first, but His Kingdom (Matthew 6:33). And when I do He takes care of all the rest.

Thank you, Lord, that You meet all my needs.

2 Thessalonians 2:16–17

May our Lord Jesus Christ himself and God our Father, who loved us and by his grace gave us eternal encouragement and good hope, encourage your hearts and strengthen you in every good deed and word.

Cape of Good Hope

This rocky promontory is one of the southernmost points of the African continent. It was discovered in 1488 by navigator Bartolomeu Dias. He originally named it Cape of Storms, as it is often pounded by high waves and stiff winds. But because of the excitement over finding a sea route from Europe to India, it was renamed Cape of Good Hope.

There is good hope in today's verse along with eternal encouragement. This is a hope that is good because of its source. Our hope is a good hope as it comes from a good God. The Lord declares Himself good to those whose hope is in Him (Lamentations 3:25). This hope is good as it does not shame or disappoint (Romans 5:5). Unlike flimsy hope, this is a sure conviction of what is to come based on His loving character and His Word. Hope in Him encourages our hearts and strengthens our resolve to continue serving Him.

No other hope is as sure as this one. Hoping in a change of circumstances is not a good hope. It may not happen as I envisioned. Hoping that somehow my problem could end today is not a good hope. It may not be realistic. I do not want my hopes to be disappointed or dashed. But that does not mean I do not hope at all! My unshakable sure hope is good when firmly anchored to Him! He will never let me down, as He is love. His Word is true and my future is secure in His loving hands.

Thank you, Lord, for this good hope.

Ezekiel 17:24

All the trees of the forest will know that I the Lord bring down the tall tree and make the low tree grow tall. I dry up the green tree and make the dry tree to flourish. I the Lord have spoken, and I will do it.

A Seeing Tree

The bark of this tree seems to have his eye on those passing through the forest! Behind our French house was a beautiful forest where I loved to stroll. On a hot day, I appreciated the drop in temperature and the stillness. The welcomed shade of the trees made it a bit dark, but I did not mind that. However, if I thought a tree were watching me, I don't think I would stick around!

Today's verse talks about trees in the forest knowing something that many humans fail to see. God has the ultimate say over what dies and what grows. He causes trees to dry up or to flourish, to grow tall, or to be brought down. This example in nature mirrors His control with men. God has the power to bring down the haughty, prideful man. He humbles the circumstances of those who ignore Him. He opposes the proud (James 4:6) and sends poverty to those He humbles (1 Samuel 2:7).

Thankfully, our God is also full of grace, and He promises to show favor to the humble. I show that humility by bending my knee in total submission to what He wants. His plan for my life may or may not involve recognition or praise from men. But it is His call how He may exalt me, whether on earth or in heaven with rewards. I want to be more concerned about giving Him the glory, honor, and praise that is due Him!

Lord, may my life be about You.

1 Samuel 2:2

There is no one holy like the Lord; there is no one beside you; there is no Rock like our God.

Moeraki Boulders

These strange spherical boulders on the Koekohe Beach in New Zealand have fired the imagination for years. The varied names given them include: eel pots, hooligan gallstones, giant gobstoppers, alien brains, bowling balls of the giants and dinosaur eggs! There are over fifty of them and the biggest one weighs seven tons! Their strange appearance makes for a unique landscape. They are made of mud, fine silt, and clay, cemented together by calcite, layered over many years.

Today's verse is part of Hannah's prayer as she dedicates her young son, Samuel, to full-time service in the temple. This is the child she had prayed for so ardently, being barren and snubbed. Although she was giving up Samuel, her heart rejoiced being vindicated before her enemies (verse 1). She felt delight at God's deliverance and praises Him for being her holy and unique Rock. Throughout Scripture our God is pictured as a Rock. What an image of His strength and permanence! Layers of faithfulness to His Word makes for a sure foundation.

I never need to worry whether my Rock will be there tomorrow or the day after. He is immoveable and unchanging. He is my strength, and my refuge. Being my Rock, He is a place of refreshment for my flagging spirit. The surface of this rock has a cool touch when I am too warm from stress and anxiety. But that same rock surface is warm from the sun and comforting when I am feeling cool and indifferent. I know He is faithful to meet my every need as I have "proved Him o'er and o'er."

Lord, be my Rock today.

Romans 8:31

What, then, shall we say in response to these things? If God is for us, who can be against us?

Tilting at Windmills

These windmills do not look much like the enemy, but try explaining that to Don Quixote! The English idiom "tilting at windmills" means to attack imaginary enemies. It comes from the story of this deluded but chivalrous knight in Miguel de Cervantes' classic story. Don Quixote sees a field of windmills, and thinking they are giants, he rides out to fight them. Unfortunately, he charges full speed at the closest one just as the sail descends, catching his lance and throwing him to the ground!

Today's verse reassures the believer that whoever we think might be our enemy, we can be confident that God is for us. The question in this verse can be answered in one word: "nothing." The list of "these things" includes: death, life, angels, demons, the present, the future, powers, height, depth, nor ANYTHING ELSE in all creation will separate us from the love of God in Christ Jesus (verses 37–39)! Whether our enemies are real or perceived, we are more than conquerors.

I do not know what my future holds, and I can imagine lots of unhappy scenarios. I can easily make a giant out of what is just an innocuous windmill. The future sometimes looms large in my thinking, taking on a power that it does not really have. But even in imagining the worst case scenario I can find comfort in the fact that God's love would carry me through. Because of His power and love there is no obstacle in my future that is insurmountable. Nothing is too hard for Him (Jeremiah 32:17). I belong to the Creator of giants and windmills!

Thank you, Lord, that You will always be there to fight my battles!

1 Peter 4:12

Dear friends, do not be surprised at the fiery ordeal that has come on you to test you, as though something strange were happening to you.

Whack-a-Mole

Our grandson practically trembles in anticipation as he stands ready to whack! The game "whack-a-mole" can use moles, sharks, or anything else that can pop up and defy being bonked. But in fact, there is little anyone can do to be really ready. That is because the sharks are ready as well with a sequence that is random and unpredictable. By the time the mallet comes down, the moment has passed, and up pops a new challenge!

Today's verse gives believers insight into the reason behind some of the hard times we go through. Sometimes as God's own, we feel as if we should be spared from life's difficulties. But Jesus promised a full and abundant life (John 10:10) not a life without problems. However, we can be confident that the Lord uses everything sudden and negative in our lives for His purpose. And His purpose is to strengthen our faith and dependence on Him.

The testing of my faith is never very comfortable. When am I ever ready for multiple troubles to arrive? But I can be sure that the hard times are never random, even in their timing. When I feel that I just can't anymore, that is when I learn dependence on the Lord. He does not ask me to face life in my own strength. Instead, He shows Himself strong through my weakness. Whatever threatens to defeat me, He has already conquered! I can share in His victory as I place my trust in His power.

Thank you, Lord, that You help me pass these tests of faith.

James 1:5–6

If any of you lacks wisdom, you should ask God, who gives generously to all without finding fault, and it will be given to you. But when you ask, you must believe and not doubt, because the one who doubts is like a wave of the sea, blown and tossed by the wind.

To Toss or Not to Toss

I t's a dilemma. If I toss my salad just before serving, all those tasty colorful additions get covered up and often end up at the bottom of the bowl. This means that the last one to serve himself gets the lion's share! But there is a similar problem if I keep everything visible on the top. The first few to serve themselves get most everything, leaving the latecomers with only lettuce. No more tossing for me! At my house, it's build your own salad and that solves the problem!

Today's verse describes a person who is tossed. This is the individual who doubts. He is like a wave of the sea driven and tossed by the wind. The one who doubts is hesitant, uncertain, and wavering. There is no stability as he first goes in one direction and then another. However, God promises wisdom to those who ask Him in faith. He never reproaches. He is generous and gives to everyone liberally. The condition is to ask in faith without any doubting.

His wisdom is something for which He wants me to ask. It is not part of the fruit of the Spirit. He waits for me to come to Him with humility, recognizing my need. And when I come believing, His gift of wisdom makes me stable and resolute. His wisdom makes me single-minded and focused. How much better it is to ask for His wisdom than to be tossed by doubts!

Thank you, Lord, for the wisdom You give.

Psalm 28:7

The Lord is my strength and my shield; my heart trusts in him, and he helps me. My heart leaps for joy and with my song I praise him.

Cholla Cactus

C an a cactus really jump? The cholla cactus is known as the "jumping cholla." Its barbed spines detach so easily that they seem to jump, hitching a ride on any passing human or animal! When they are finally shaken off, the cactus spine roots where it falls to the ground. What a great way to spread yourself! These cacti are some of the largest and most beautiful, but be careful not to be jumped on while stopping to admire them!

Today's verse describes a heart that trusts in God's strength, protection, and help. This is a heart that finds reasons for joy, so much so that the heart leaps with that joy! Because of our incredible salvation, we can be filled with inexpressible and glorious joy (1 Peter 1:8–9). And like the jumping cholla, this joy can spread! Even in an inhospitable desert soil where water is scarce, the joy of the believer can spread to others! This joy comes as we praise Him for His faithful care.

When I am not feeling this joy it is probably because I am focusing on the dry desert soil around me. I am not happy with my circumstances. The disappointments I am living with are clouding my vision of the eternal. I am not jumping up and down with joy. But that can and does change when I turn my heart toward Him in gratitude for His blessings. Praising Him changes everything! And when that deep-seated sense of well-being returns, I am in a good place to spread it!

Lord, keep me grateful.

2 Peter 1:3

His divine power has given us everything we need for a godly life through our knowledge of him who called us by his own glory and goodness.

The Capybara

Meet the largest rodent in the world! He looks to be a cross between a pig and a beaver but with no snout or tail. He can stay submerged like the hippo with eyes, ears, and nostrils near the top of his head. With his webbed feet, he can stay underwater five minutes at a time to hide from predators. Water is a source of life for the capybara. He uses it for his dry skin, for plant foods, and to escape danger.

Today's verse talks about God's divine power being the source of a godly life for the believer. Everything that is needed to live a godly life has already been given to us. Knowing Him is knowing the source of divine power. On our own, we are unable to do what He asks of us. But through knowing Him, we can participate in His divine nature. He is the source of goodness, knowledge, self-control, perseverance, godliness, affection, and love (verses 4–7).

What an amazing description of what is godly or like God! And when reading this list, I see how little they describe what I can come up with on my own! I so need His power to exhibit any of these characteristics. Thankfully, He has made His power available to me through His Spirit. Living a life that is godly is possible through Him. My problem comes when I think I can generate anything godly without Him (John 15:5). How good of Him to have already given me everything I need to live for Him!

Thank you, Lord, for being the source of anything godly in me.

Nehemiah 8:10

Nehemiah said, "Go and enjoy choice food and sweet drinks, and send some to those who have nothing prepared. This day is holy to our Lord. Do not grieve, for the joy of the Lord is your strength."

Strong or Weak?

I get a whole lot done in a day when I am happy. There is something about being joyful that energizes a person. Even when muscling through a long difficult task, I can be exhausted but it is a "happy tired." The reverse is also true. When I am feeling down and discouraged, I am also demotivated to do much of anything.

Today's verse is an encouragement to the Israelites not to grieve. This group of returned exiles from captivity should have been ecstatic, as their walls were now rebuilt and gates were in place. But instead of joy, they were weeping. The Book of the Law of Moses was being read to them from dawn to noon. Their response was intense grief as they understood how far they had strayed from God's laws. Sorrow over sin is necessary in asking forgiveness, but joy and celebration are to follow! New strength is found in that joy!

When I completely blow it, sadness over letting the Lord down dominates my thinking. But feeling that sorrow is not such a bad thing. It tells me my heart is still soft enough to be broken over my failures. What is so wonderful is that the Lord promises to be near those that are brokenhearted (Psalm 34:18). He is so good to restore that joy with the forgiveness He so freely gives! There is new energy in my step when rising from my knees! His joy gives me the motivation to persevere in living for Him!

Thank you, Lord, for giving me strength in joy.

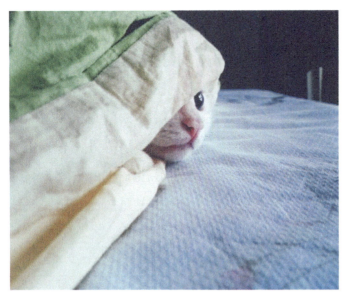

Matthew 16:25

For whoever wants to save their life will lose it, but whoever loses their life for me will find it.

Hiding Out

This is exactly the kind of behavior we would see from Tiger when thunder would clap over the house and he would run for cover! The instinct in animals for self-preservation is a strong one. And we as humans are not much different. It is normal to want to protect our lives from natural disasters, serious illness or accident. We do not look to put ourselves in harm's way. We take the necessary precautions. We take the safest route. We live our lives so as to avoid disaster.

The truth in today's verse seems contrary to human nature. Of course we are going to try to save our lives when we feel that they are threatened. But at what cost? Peter had just rebuked Jesus, trying to discourage Him from going to Jerusalem. Suffering and death awaited Jesus there and He knew it. Yet He turned toward what would be certain death. Unlike Peter, Jesus had in mind the concerns of God and not merely human concerns (verse 23). It was because Jesus walked in obedience to the Father that He could set aside the restraints of self-preservation.

Finding true rewarding and fulfilling life can only happen when I am willing to risk my own safety and comfort. Protecting my life at any cost makes me lose it! Christ bought my life at an incredible cost to Himself, not so that I can hide under the covers and wait for danger to pass. The goal of my life is not to preserve it but to spend it in service to Him. Following Him means picking up my cross daily in obedience (verse 24) despite personal risk.

Lord, may You find me faithful.

Isaiah 43:18–19

Forget the former things, do not dwell on the past. See, I am doing a new thing! Now, it springs up; do you not perceive it? I am making a way in the wilderness and streams in the wasteland.

Pulmonaria Spilled Milk

One can understand how this plant got its name! The leaves of this semi-evergreen perennial are splotched with white, looking like someone spilled milk on them. The phrase "don't cry over spilled milk" is attributed to James Howell, an Anglo-Welsh historian who used it in his writings in 1659. By it, we mean there is no use in being upset over what has already happened.

Today's verse tells us not to dwell on the past. Whether what is behind us is something negative or positive, we are not to keep our focus there but to be looking forward. We can miss the new thing He wants to create in our lives. To us it may not look like much. Our lives can even resemble a wilderness or wasteland. But He has a purpose in mind and His plans are always good. His way goes straight through the dry times to life-giving springs of water!

During uncertain and negative times, my thoughts turn to the past. It is easier to focus there than to look around and see less-than-perfect circumstances! But I do have a choice. I can either look at the wilderness and wasteland, OR I can look at the streams of water He has provided to meet my needs. I can bemoan the spilled milk all over the place representing some good things I have had to give up, OR I can look to my Lord for the new thing He wants to create in me and my world.

Lord, help me to trust You and the new thing You are doing!

Acts 13:39

Through him everyone who believes is set free from every sin, a justification you were not able to obtain under the law of Moses.

The Cooper Hawk

He looked almost as surprised to see me as I was to see him! This Cooper Hawk or Chicken Hawk watched me on my morning walk from the fence of my neighbor's yard. I recognized this hawk from a television story I had just seen about one that had inadvertently trapped himself in a huge skating rink in Canada. A team of wildlife rescuers were called in after two days. They spent hours with their nets trying to get the tired, hungry and frightened bird to fly into their nets. He was finally captured and released into the wild.

Today's verse comes from Paul's sermon explaining how Jesus was the promised Savior of the Old Testament. He explained the good news that Jesus was resurrected (verses 32–33) and that it is through Him that sins are forgiven (verse 38). It is this forgiveness that sets us free from the power of every sin to ensnare and imprison. What the law could not do, Jesus accomplished by fulfilling it and setting us free!

Just like that trapped hawk, I could easily live in the confines of rules, regulations and trappings of self-righteousness. But there is no set of rules that can make me righteous before God. The walls of my own prison are made up of unforgiven sin. Jesus is the only One who can free me. My own feeble attempts at fixing myself can be exhausting. Thankfully, His forgiveness offers true freedom from guilt and condemnation. He has captured me with His sacrificial love and has set me free in the wilds of His incredible grace!

Thank you, Lord, for setting me free!

Psalm 111:10

The fear of the Lord is the beginning of wisdom; all who follow his precepts have good understanding. To him belongs eternal praise.

Following Suit

The card game Uno is full of surprises. Normally, being able to "follow suit" quickly wins the game. It is almost a mindless exercise to just follow the color played ahead of you. But the smart player will look for other options if he is holding those special cards. Instead of just following suit, those cards allow for some strategy. And NOT following suit can pay off!

Following suit in life is a mindless exercise as well. Today's verse tells us that there is another option; following God's precepts. Rather than follow what everyone around us is doing, the believer has some special cards in his hand. They are God's ways and precepts. When one follows His Word, He develops wisdom and good understanding of life and how it should be played. Fear, awe, respect, and obedience to God are those special cards. The believer is under no obligation to follow what is played around him.

My problem is that following suit is just so much easier to do. I am holding those special cards but opt not to use them. The desire to fit in with the prevailing fad or thought is very strong. To follow what everyone else is doing requires no thought, less risk, and certainly no censure from others. But conforming to the world's system of thinking can be resisted when my thoughts are transformed through God's Word (Romans 12:1–2). I do not want to live mindlessly but with purpose, screening out the bad and holding on to the good (Romans 12:9). His Word and following His way makes me wise.

Lord, keep me from following suit today.

Made in the USA
Coppell, TX
07 July 2023

18825870R30203